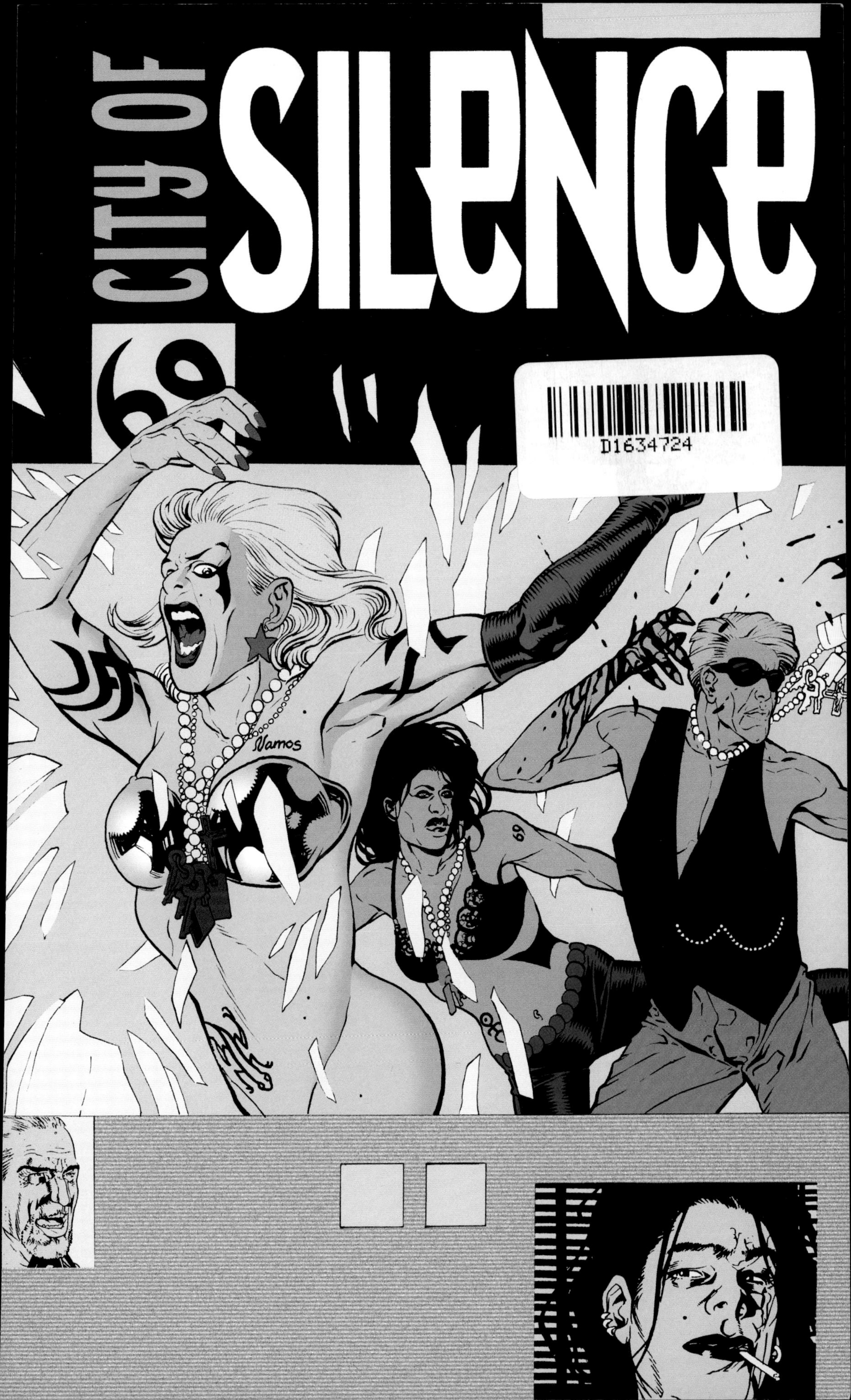
CITY OF
SILENCE
69
Vamos

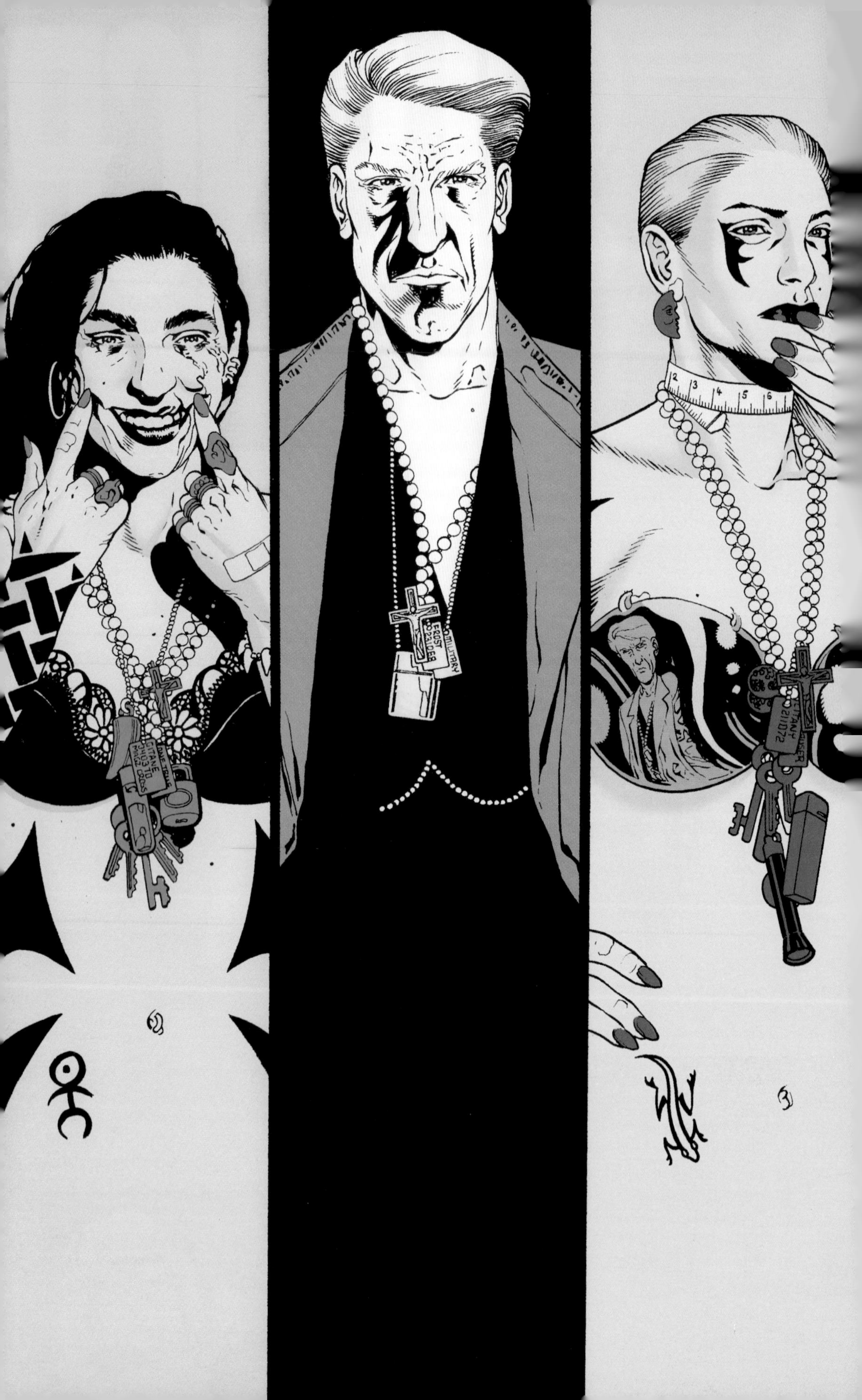
FROST
0231DE8
MILITARY

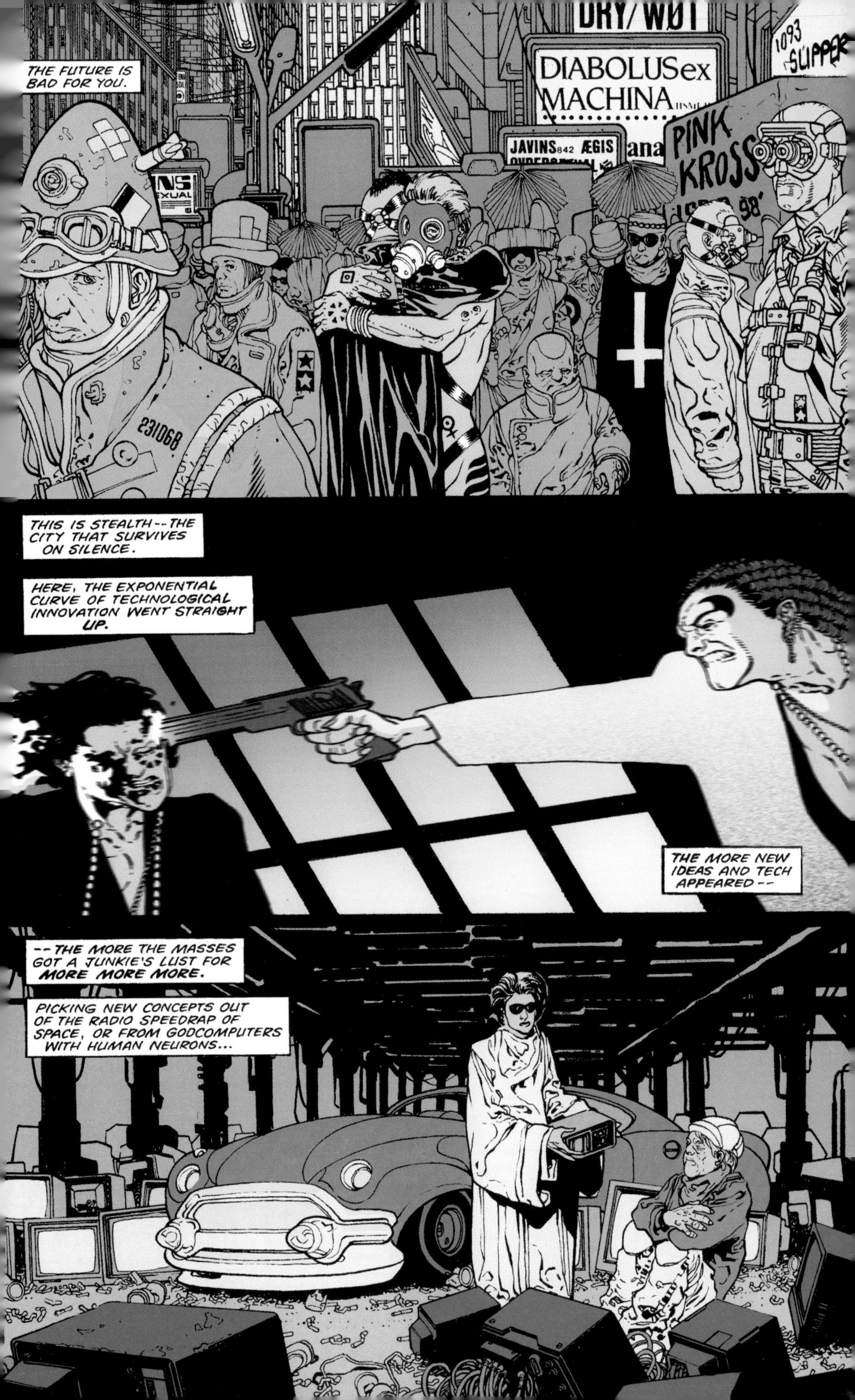
THE FUTURE IS BAD FOR YOU.
DRY/WØT
DIABOLUSex MACHINA
1093
SLIPPER
JAVINS842 ÆGIS
PINK KROSS
231068
THIS IS STEALTH--THE CITY THAT SURVIVES ON SILENCE.
HERE, THE EXPONENTIAL CURVE OF TECHNOLOGICAL INNOVATION WENT STRAIGHT UP.
THE MORE NEW IDEAS AND TECH APPEARED--
--THE MORE THE MASSES GOT A JUNKIE'S LUST FOR MORE MORE MORE.
PICKING NEW CONCEPTS OUT OF THE RADIO SPEEDRAP OF SPACE, OR FROM GODCOMPUTERS WITH HUMAN NEURONS...

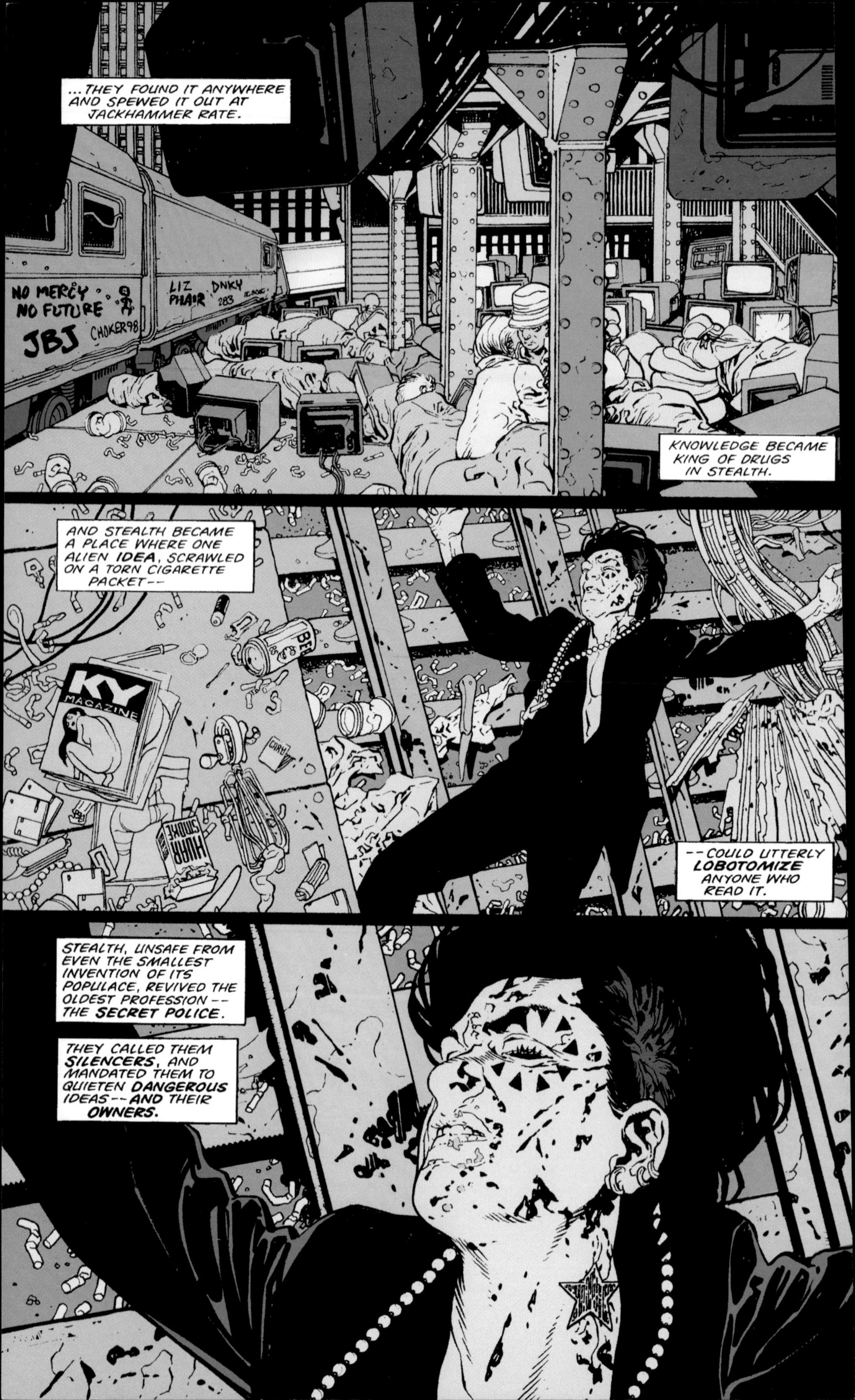
...THEY FOUND IT ANYWHERE AND SPEWED IT OUT AT JACKHAMMER RATE.
NO MERCY
NO FUTURE
JBJ
CHOKER98
LIZ PHAIR
DNKY
283
KNOWLEDGE BECAME KING OF DRUGS IN STEALTH.
AND STEALTH BECAME A PLACE WHERE ONE ALIEN IDEA, SCRAWLED ON A TORN CIGARETTE PACKET--
KY
MAGAZINE
--COULD UTTERLY LOBOTOMIZE ANYONE WHO READ IT.
STEALTH, UNSAFE FROM EVEN THE SMALLEST INVENTION OF ITS POPULACE, REVIVED THE OLDEST PROFESSION -- THE SECRET POLICE.
THEY CALLED THEM SILENCERS, AND MANDATED THEM TO QUIETEN DANGEROUS IDEAS--AND THEIR OWNERS.

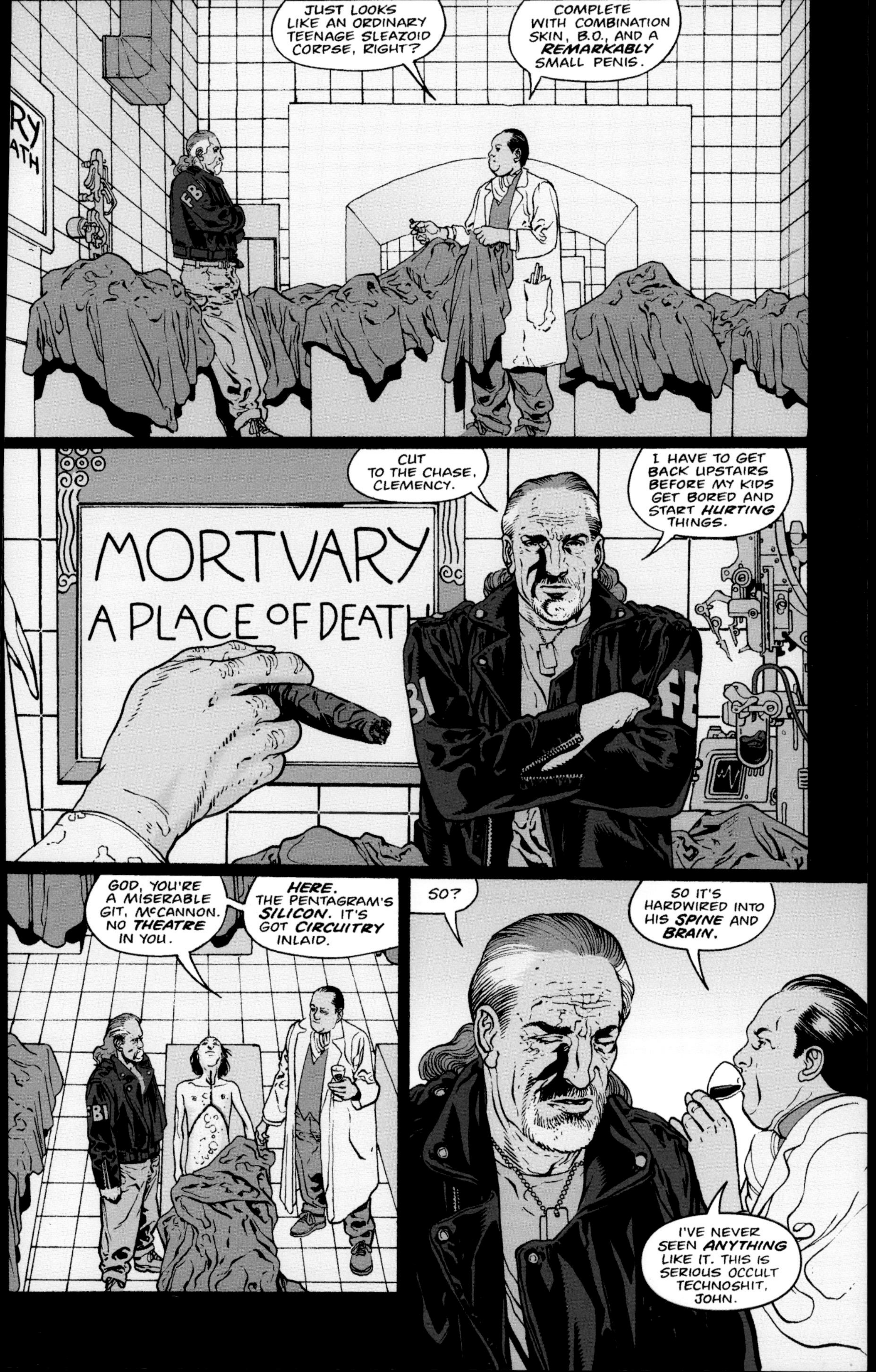
JUST LOOKS LIKE AN ORDINARY TEENAGE SLEAZOID CORPSE, RIGHT?
COMPLETE WITH COMBINATION SKIN, B.O., AND A *REMARKABLY* SMALL PENIS.
MORTVARY A PLACE OF DEATH
CUT TO THE CHASE, CLEMENCY.
I HAVE TO GET BACK UPSTAIRS BEFORE MY KIDS GET BORED AND START *HURTING* THINGS.
GOD, YOU'RE A MISERABLE GIT, McCANNON. NO *THEATRE* IN YOU.
HERE. THE PENTAGRAM'S *SILICON.* IT'S GOT *CIRCUITRY* INLAID.
SO?
SO IT'S HARDWIRED INTO HIS *SPINE* AND *BRAIN.*
I'VE NEVER SEEN *ANYTHING* LIKE IT. THIS IS SERIOUS OCCULT TECHNOSHIT, JOHN.

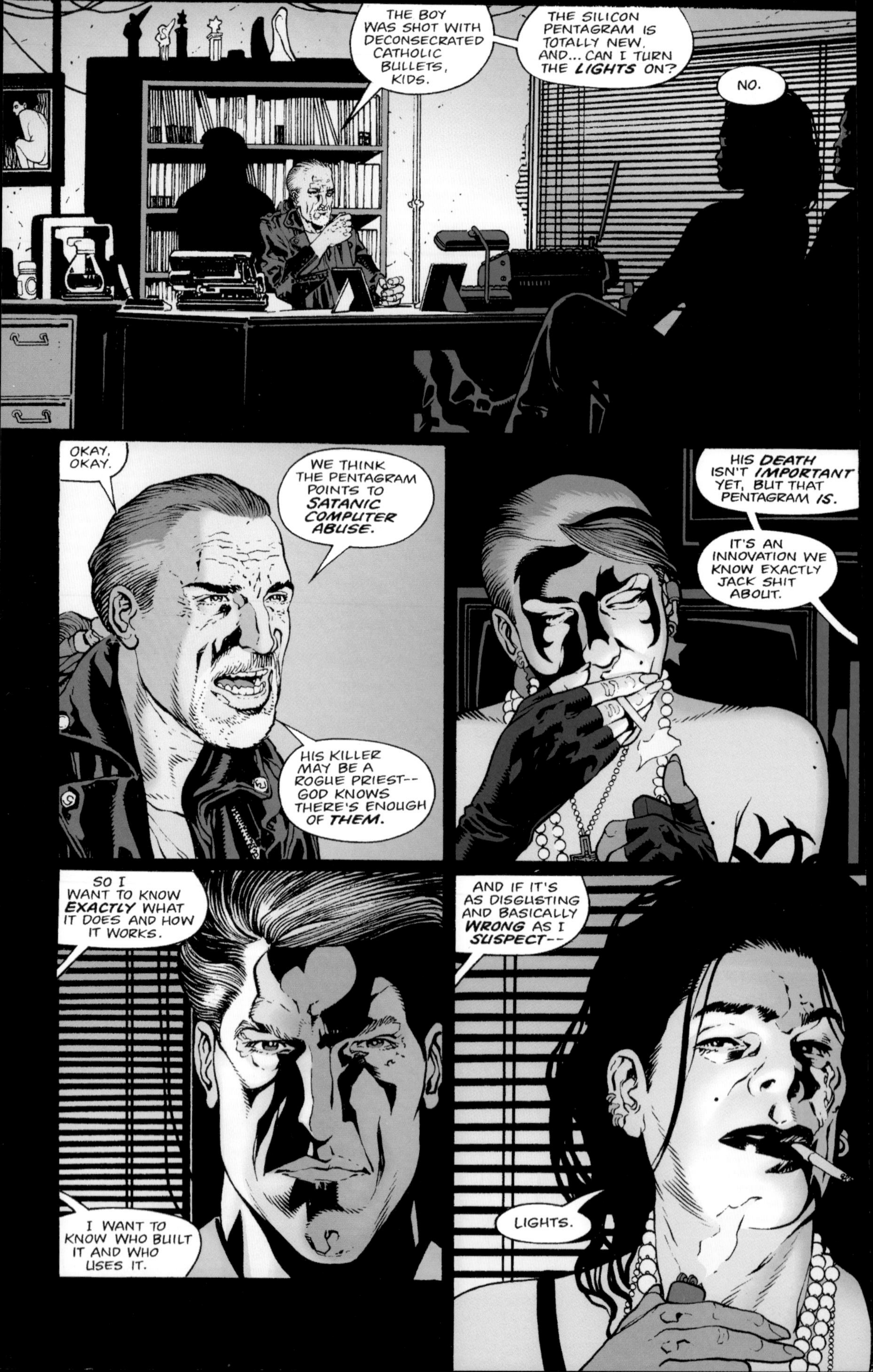
THE BOY WAS SHOT WITH DECONSECRATED CATHOLIC BULLETS, KIDS.
THE SILICON PENTAGRAM IS TOTALLY NEW. AND... CAN I TURN THE LIGHTS ON?
NO.
OKAY, OKAY.
WE THINK THE PENTAGRAM POINTS TO SATANIC COMPUTER ABUSE.
HIS KILLER MAY BE A ROGUE PRIEST-- GOD KNOWS THERE'S ENOUGH OF THEM.
HIS DEATH ISN'T IMPORTANT YET, BUT THAT PENTAGRAM IS.
IT'S AN INNOVATION WE KNOW EXACTLY JACK SHIT ABOUT.
SO I WANT TO KNOW EXACTLY WHAT IT DOES AND HOW IT WORKS.
I WANT TO KNOW WHO BUILT IT AND WHO USES IT.
AND IF IT'S AS DISGUSTING AND BASICALLY WRONG AS I SUSPECT--
LIGHTS.

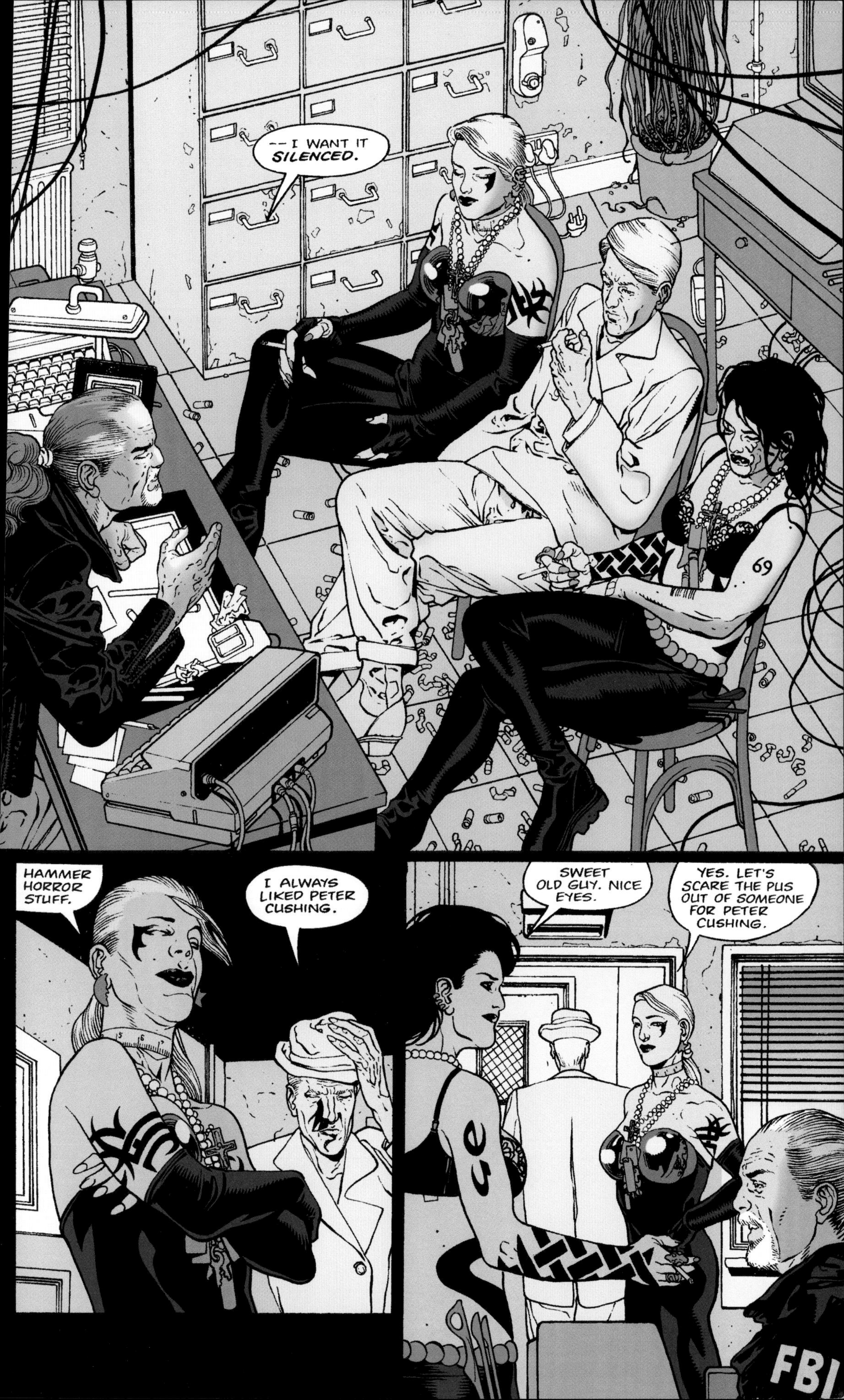
-- I WANT IT SILENCED.
HAMMER HORROR STUFF.
I ALWAYS LIKED PETER CUSHING.
SWEET OLD GUY. NICE EYES.
YES. LET'S SCARE THE PUS OUT OF SOMEONE FOR PETER CUSHING.
FBI

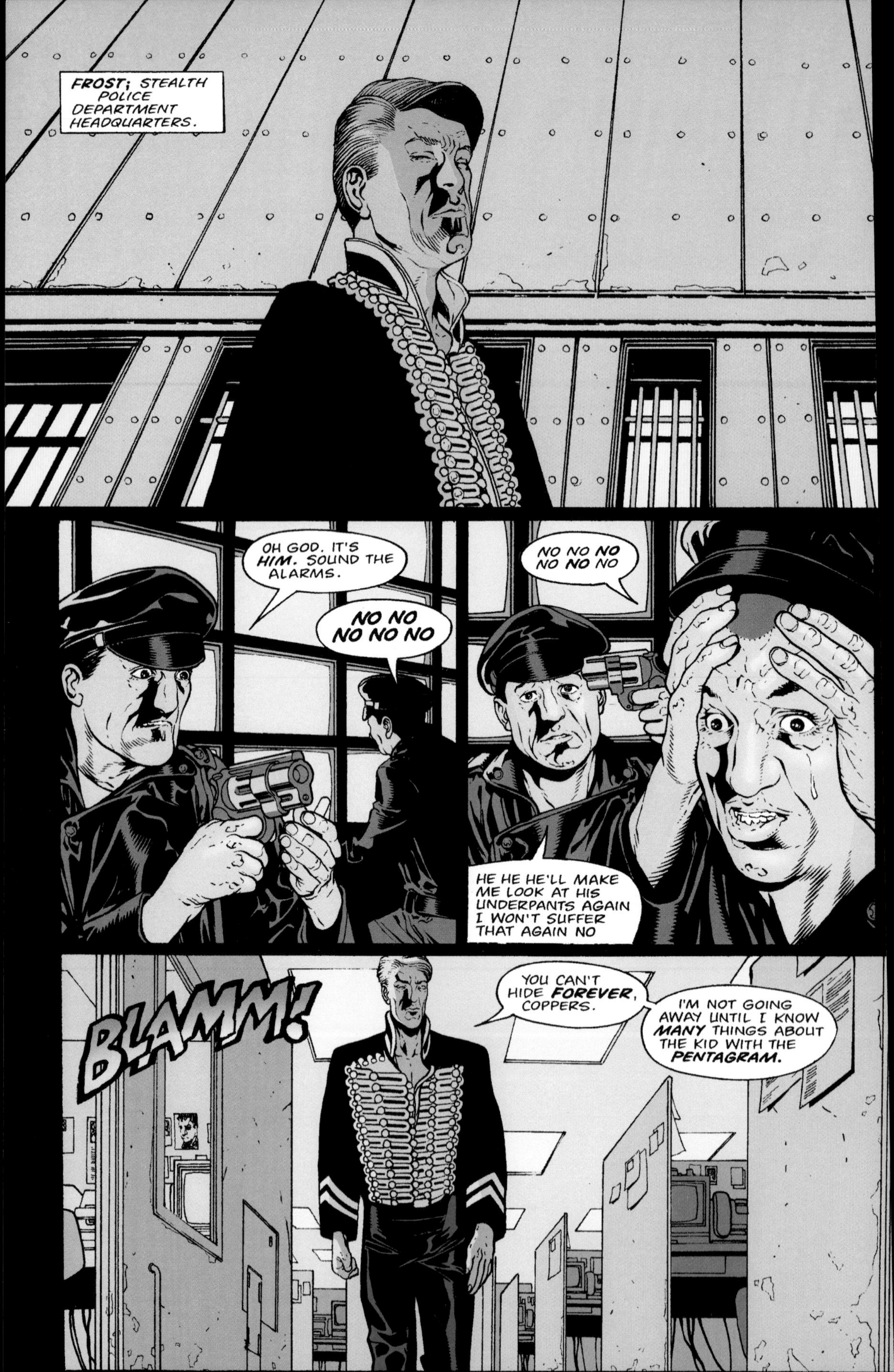
FROST; STEALTH POLICE DEPARTMENT HEADQUARTERS.
OH GOD. IT'S HIM. SOUND THE ALARMS.
NO NO NO NO NO
NO NO NO NO NO NO
HE HE HE'LL MAKE ME LOOK AT HIS UNDERPANTS AGAIN I WON'T SUFFER THAT AGAIN NO
BLAMM!
YOU CAN'T HIDE FOREVER, COPPERS.
I'M NOT GOING AWAY UNTIL I KNOW MANY THINGS ABOUT THE KID WITH THE PENTAGRAM.

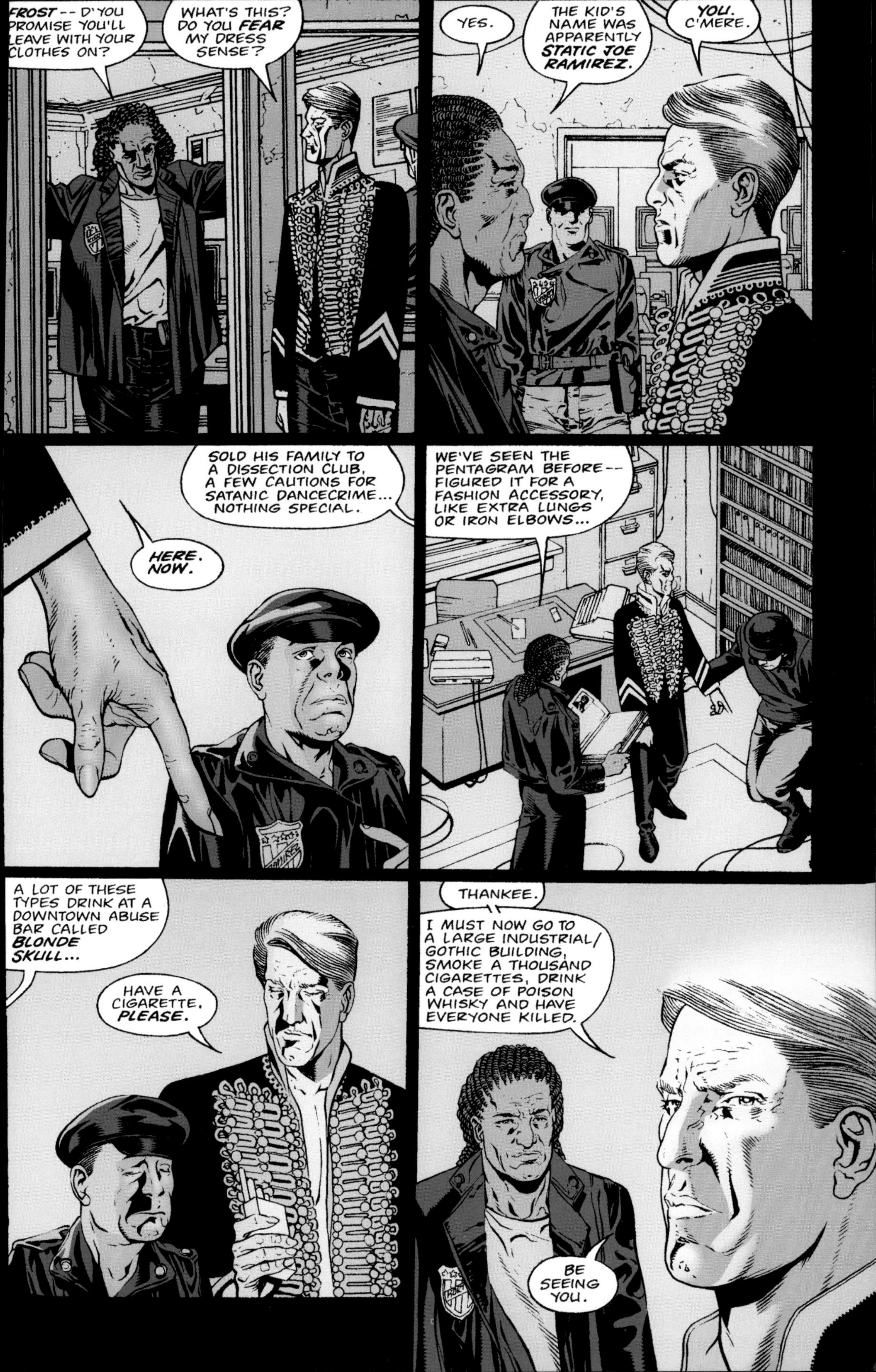
FROST -- D'YOU PROMISE YOU'LL LEAVE WITH YOUR CLOTHES ON?
WHAT'S THIS? DO YOU FEAR MY DRESS SENSE?
YES.
THE KID'S NAME WAS APPARENTLY STATIC JOE RAMIREZ.
YOU. C'MERE.
SOLD HIS FAMILY TO A DISSECTION CLUB, A FEW CAUTIONS FOR SATANIC DANCECRIME... NOTHING SPECIAL.
HERE. NOW.
WE'VE SEEN THE PENTAGRAM BEFORE-- FIGURED IT FOR A FASHION ACCESSORY, LIKE EXTRA LUNGS OR IRON ELBOWS...
A LOT OF THESE TYPES DRINK AT A DOWNTOWN ABUSE BAR CALLED BLONDE SKULL...
HAVE A CIGARETTE. PLEASE.
THANKEE.
I MUST NOW GO TO A LARGE INDUSTRIAL/ GOTHIC BUILDING, SMOKE A THOUSAND CIGARETTES, DRINK A CASE OF POISON WHISKY AND HAVE EVERYONE KILLED.
BE SEEING YOU.

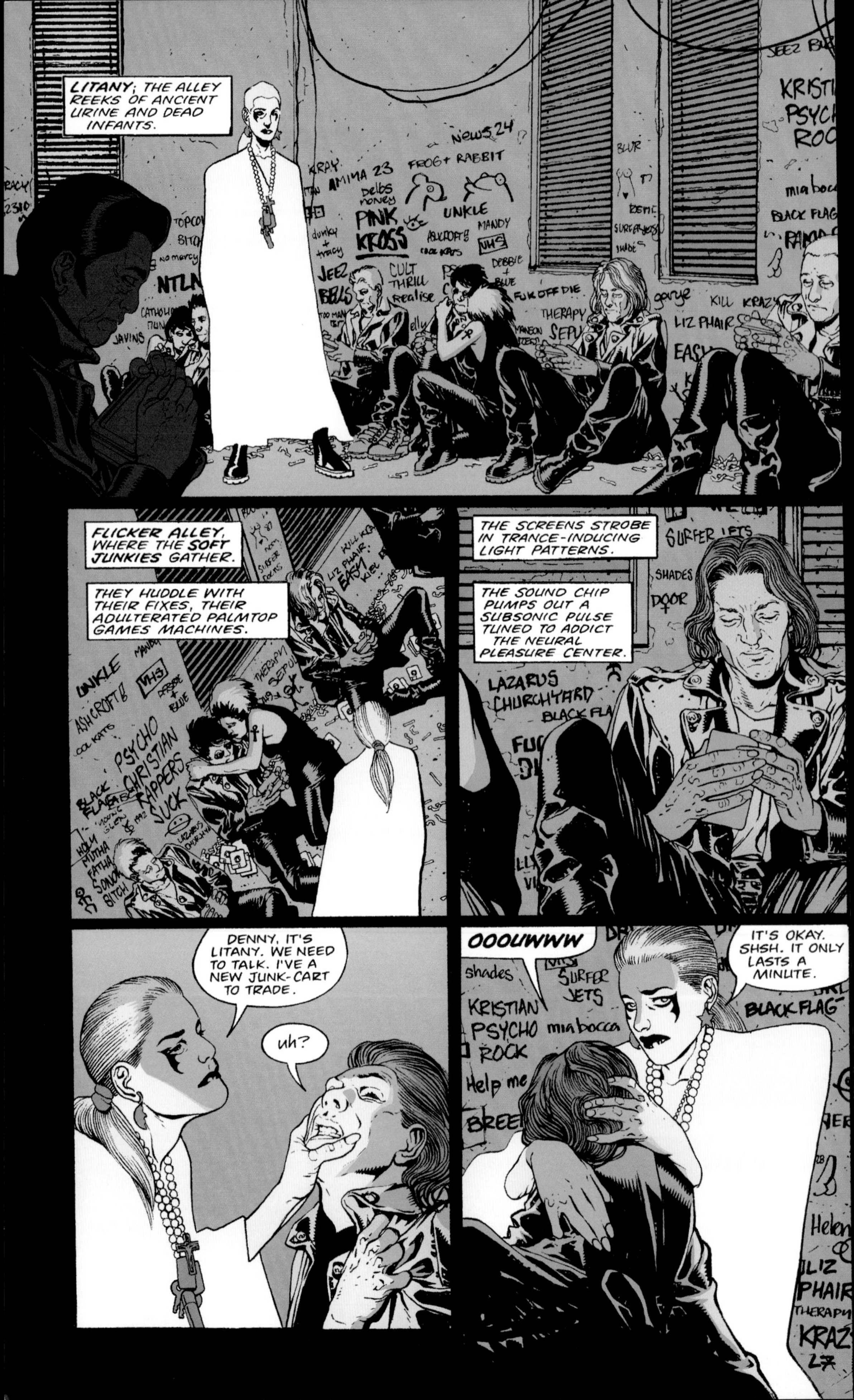
LITANY; THE ALLEY REEKS OF ANCIENT URINE AND DEAD INFANTS.
FLICKER ALLEY, WHERE THE SOFT JUNKIES GATHER.
THEY HUDDLE WITH THEIR FIXES, THEIR ADULTERATED PALMTOP GAMES MACHINES.
THE SCREENS STROBE IN TRANCE-INDUCING LIGHT PATTERNS.
THE SOUND CHIP PUMPS OUT A SUBSONIC PULSE TUNED TO ADDICT THE NEURAL PLEASURE CENTER.
DENNY, IT'S LITANY. WE NEED TO TALK. I'VE A NEW JUNK-CART TO TRADE.
uh?
OOOUWWW
IT'S OKAY. SHSH. IT ONLY LASTS A MINUTE.
27

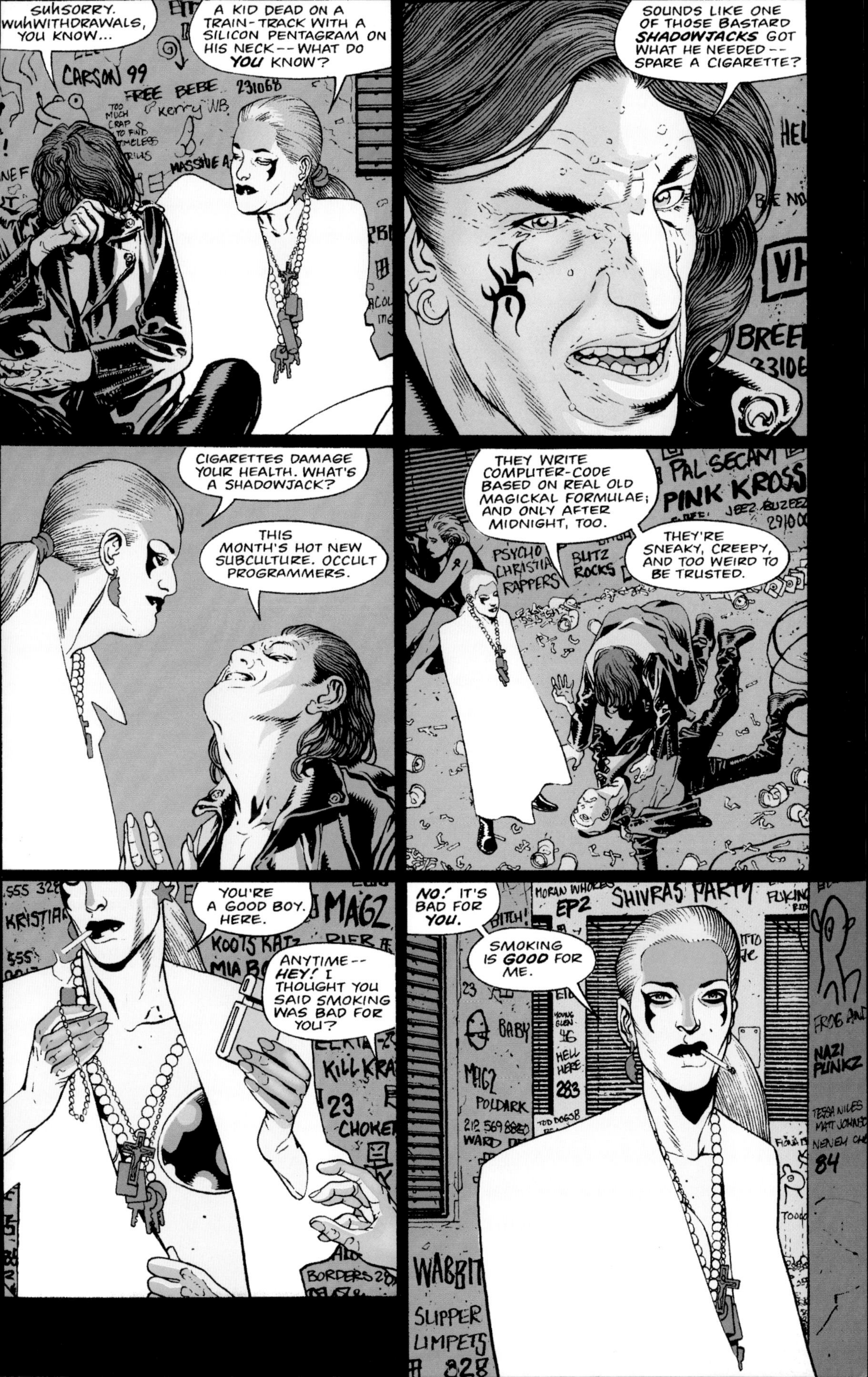
SUHSORRY. WUHWITHDRAWALS, YOU KNOW...
A KID DEAD ON A TRAIN-TRACK WITH A SILICON PENTAGRAM ON HIS NECK--WHAT DO YOU KNOW?
SOUNDS LIKE ONE OF THOSE BASTARD SHADOWJACKS GOT WHAT HE NEEDED--SPARE A CIGARETTE?
CIGARETTES DAMAGE YOUR HEALTH. WHAT'S A SHADOWJACK?
THIS MONTH'S HOT NEW SUBCULTURE. OCCULT PROGRAMMERS.
THEY WRITE COMPUTER-CODE BASED ON REAL OLD MAGICKAL FORMULAE; AND ONLY AFTER MIDNIGHT, TOO.
THEY'RE SNEAKY, CREEPY, AND TOO WEIRD TO BE TRUSTED.
YOU'RE A GOOD BOY. HERE.
ANYTIME--HEY! I THOUGHT YOU SAID SMOKING WAS BAD FOR YOU?
NO! IT'S BAD FOR YOU.
SMOKING IS GOOD FOR ME.

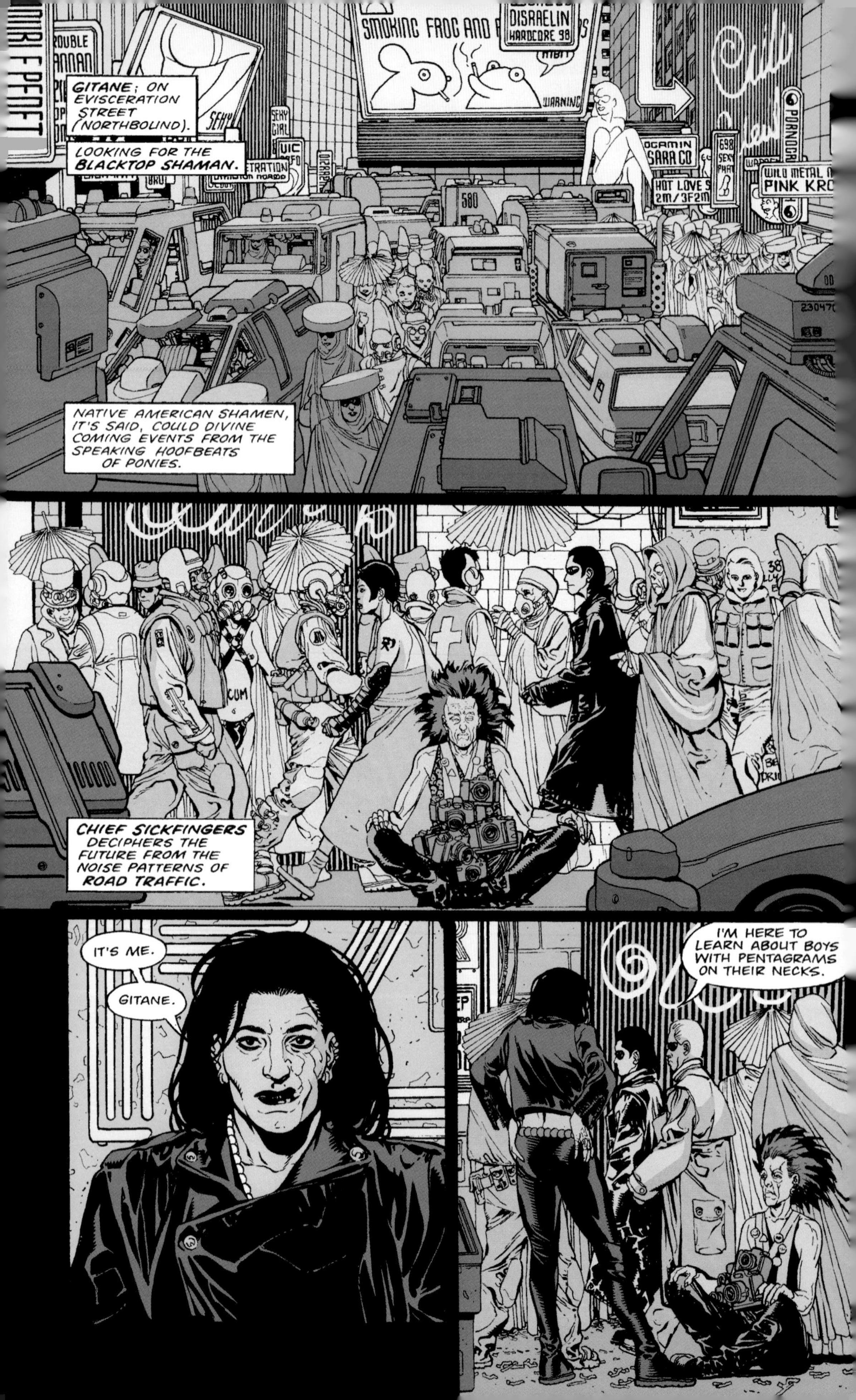
SMOKING FROG AND
DISRAELIN
HARDCORE 98
WARNING
GITANE; ON EVISCERATION STREET (NORTHBOUND).
LOOKING FOR THE BLACKTOP SHAMAN.
OGAMIN SARA CO
HOT LOVE S
2M/3F2M
WILD METAL
PINK KRO
580
NATIVE AMERICAN SHAMEN, IT'S SAID, COULD DIVINE COMING EVENTS FROM THE SPEAKING HOOFBEATS OF PONIES.
CHIEF SICKFINGERS DECIPHERS THE FUTURE FROM THE NOISE PATTERNS OF ROAD TRAFFIC.
IT'S ME.
GITANE.
I'M HERE TO LEARN ABOUT BOYS WITH PENTAGRAMS ON THEIR NECKS.

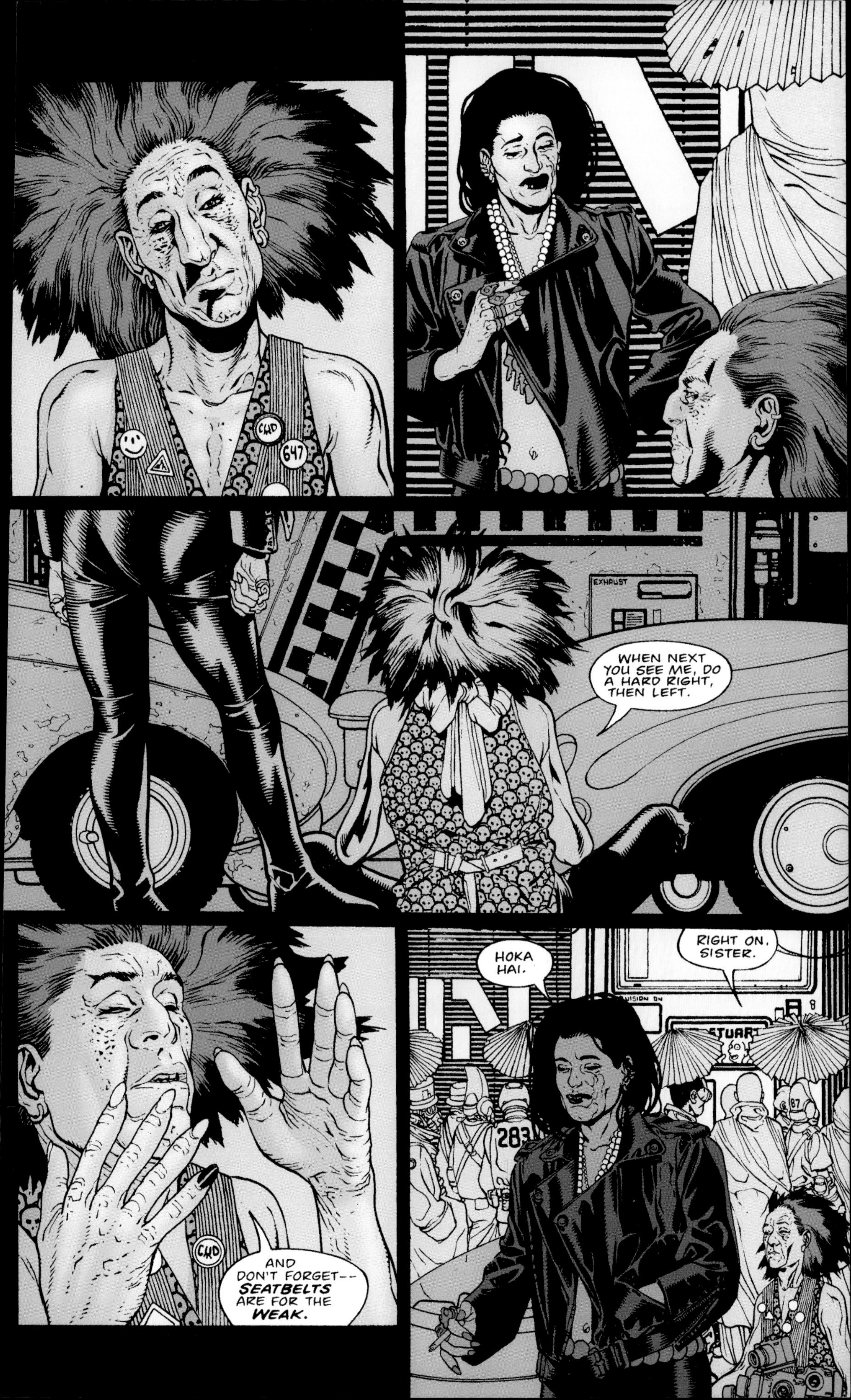
CHD
647
EXHAUST
WHEN NEXT YOU SEE ME, DO A HARD RIGHT, THEN LEFT.
CHD
AND DON'T FORGET-- SEATBELTS ARE FOR THE WEAK.
HOKA HAI.
RIGHT ON, SISTER.
283

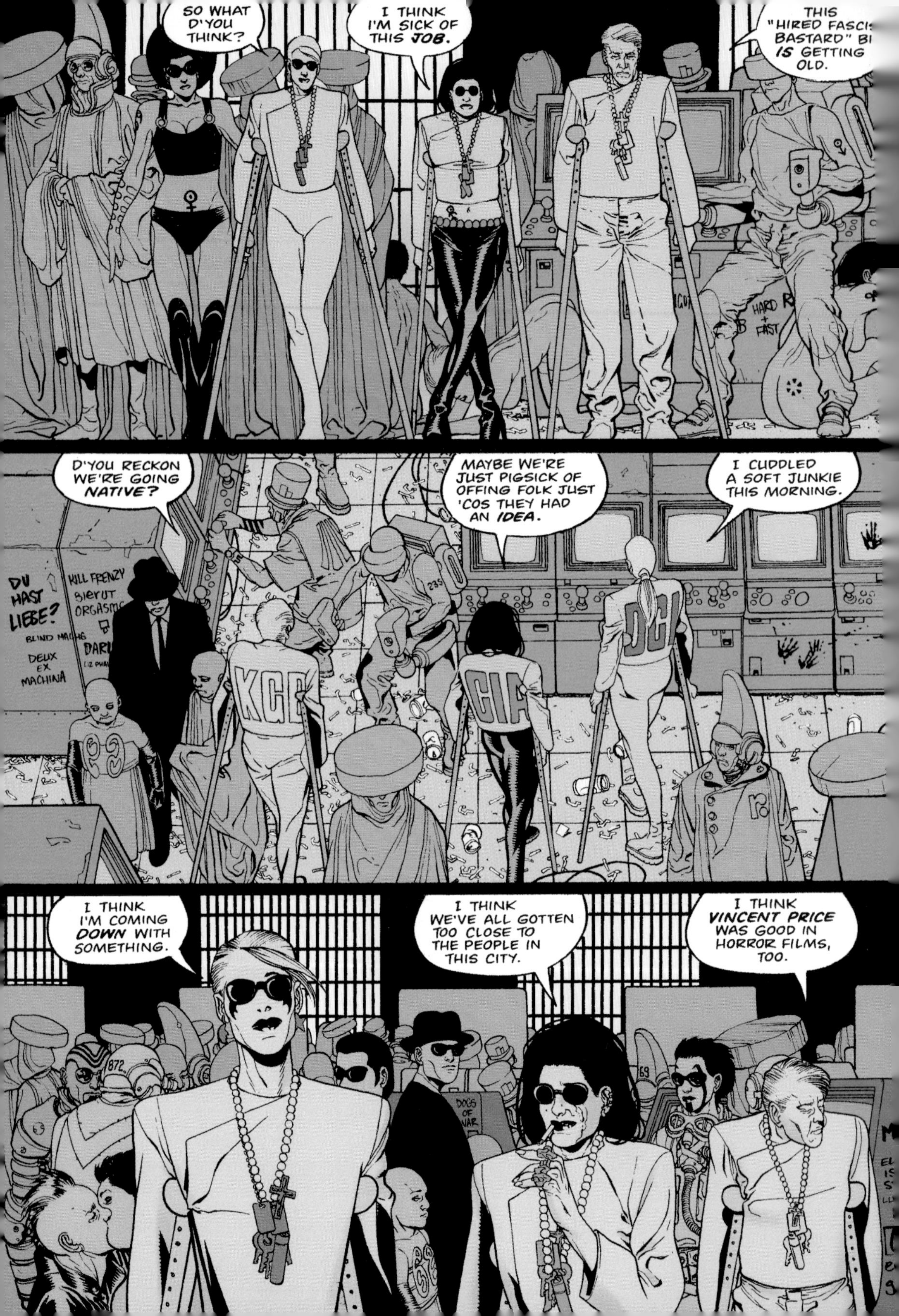
SO WHAT D'YOU THINK?
I THINK I'M SICK OF THIS *JOB.*
THIS "HIRED FASCIS BASTARD" BI *IS* GETTING OLD.
HARD + FAST
D'YOU RECKON WE'RE GOING *NATIVE?*
MAYBE WE'RE JUST PIGSICK OF OFFING FOLK JUST 'COS THEY HAD AN *IDEA.*
I CUDDLED A SOFT JUNKIE THIS MORNING.
DU HAST LIEBE?
KILL FRENZY
DEUX EX MACHINA
KGB
CIA
DCI
I THINK I'M COMING *DOWN* WITH SOMETHING.
I THINK WE'VE ALL GOTTEN TOO CLOSE TO THE PEOPLE IN THIS CITY.
I THINK *VINCENT PRICE* WAS GOOD IN HORROR FILMS, TOO.
DOGS OF WAR

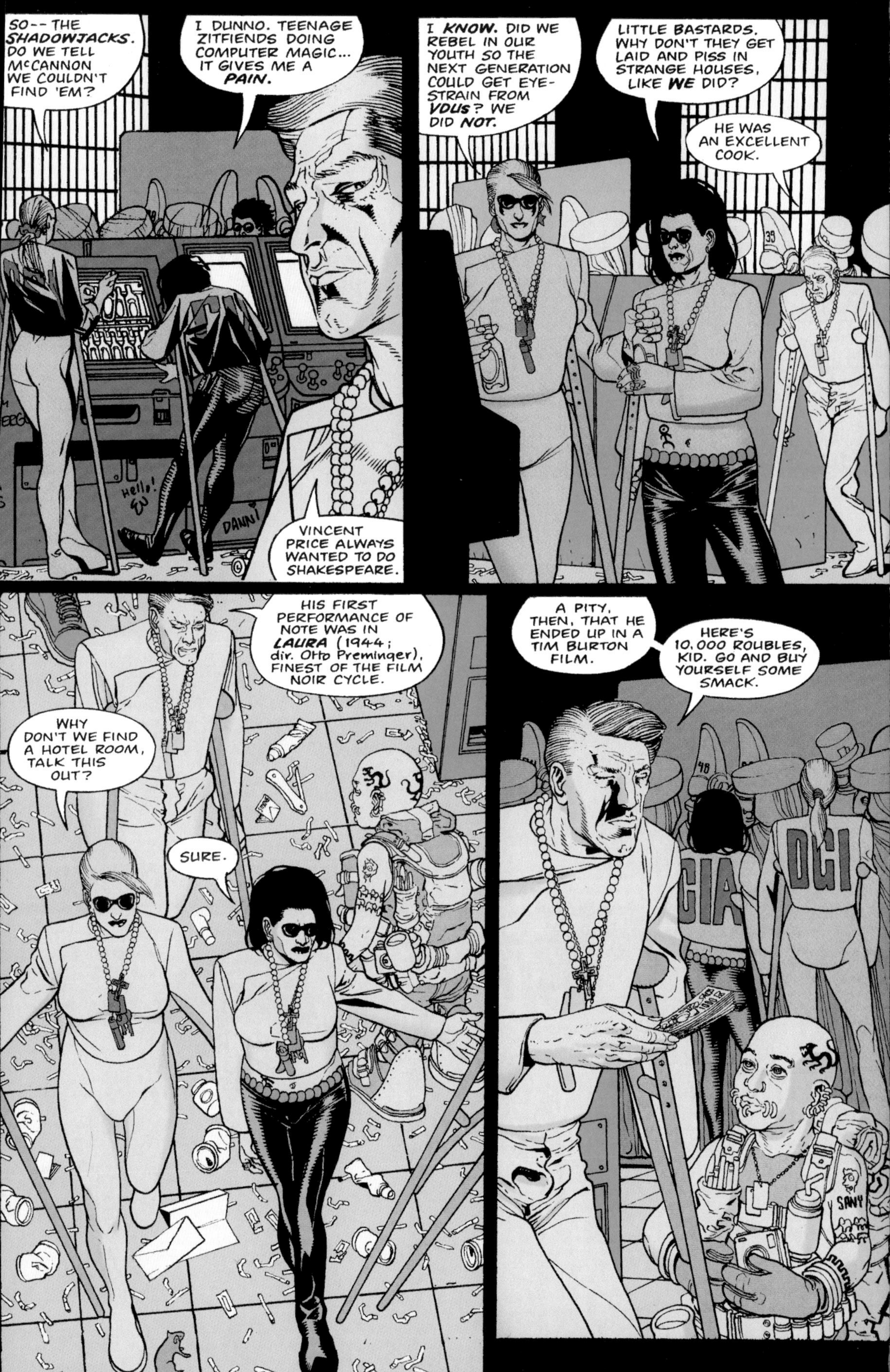
SO-- THE SHADOWJACKS. DO WE TELL McCANNON WE COULDN'T FIND 'EM?
I DUNNO. TEENAGE ZITFIENDS DOING COMPUTER MAGIC... IT GIVES ME A PAIN.
Hello! EV
DANNI
VINCENT PRICE ALWAYS WANTED TO DO SHAKESPEARE.
I KNOW. DID WE REBEL IN OUR YOUTH SO THE NEXT GENERATION COULD GET EYE-STRAIN FROM VDUS? WE DID NOT.
LITTLE BASTARDS. WHY DON'T THEY GET LAID AND PISS IN STRANGE HOUSES, LIKE WE DID?
HE WAS AN EXCELLENT COOK.
HIS FIRST PERFORMANCE OF NOTE WAS IN LAURA (1944; dir. Otto Preminger), FINEST OF THE FILM NOIR CYCLE.
WHY DON'T WE FIND A HOTEL ROOM, TALK THIS OUT?
SURE.
A PITY, THEN, THAT HE ENDED UP IN A TIM BURTON FILM.
HERE'S 10,000 ROUBLES, KID. GO AND BUY YOURSELF SOME SMACK.
CIA
DGI

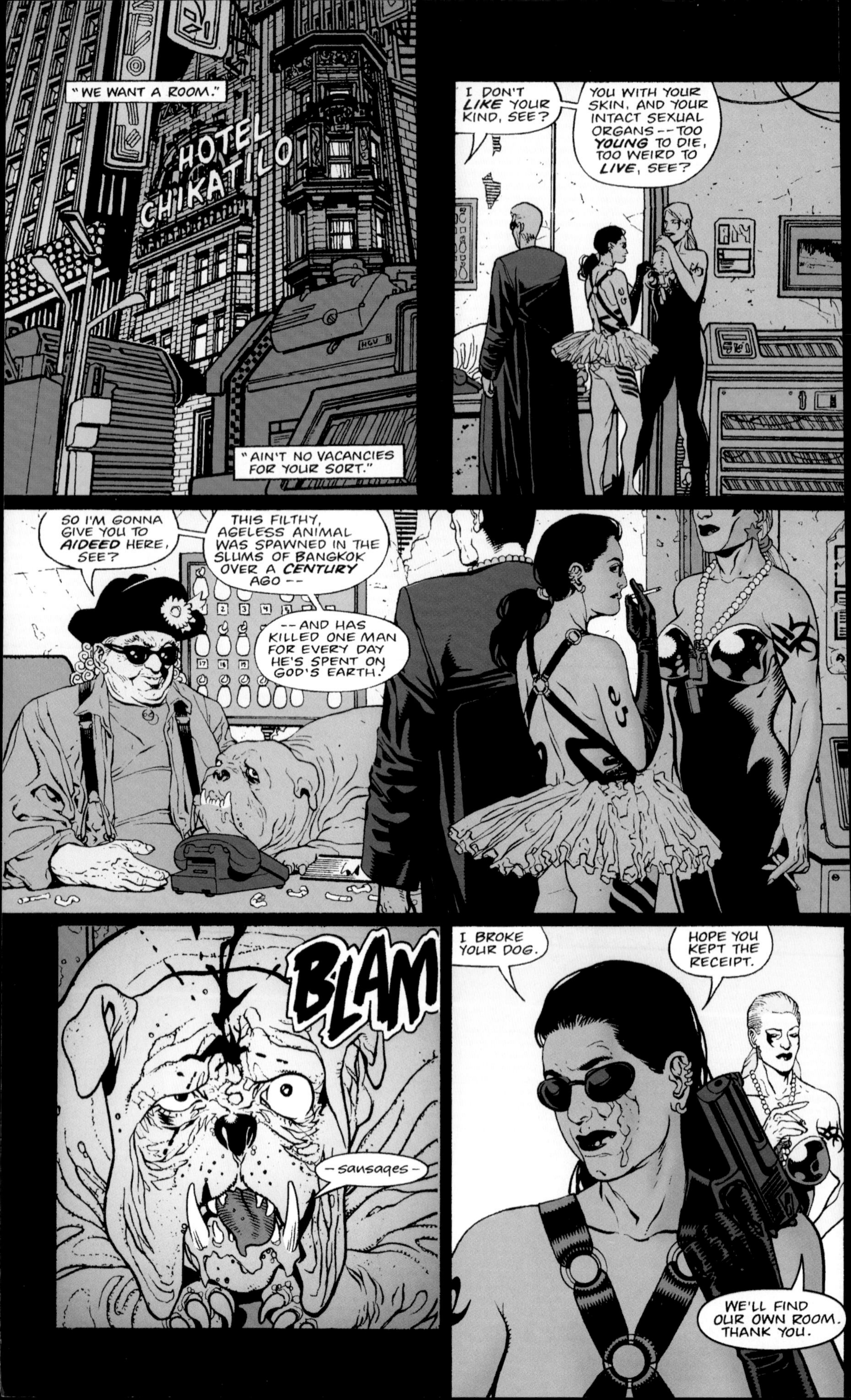
"WE WANT A ROOM."
HOTEL CHIKATILO
"AIN'T NO VACANCIES FOR YOUR SORT."
I DON'T *LIKE* YOUR KIND, SEE?
YOU WITH YOUR SKIN, AND YOUR INTACT SEXUAL ORGANS--TOO *YOUNG* TO DIE, TOO WEIRD TO *LIVE*, SEE?
SO I'M GONNA GIVE YOU TO *AIDEED* HERE, SEE?
THIS FILTHY, AGELESS ANIMAL WAS SPAWNED IN THE SLUMS OF BANGKOK OVER A *CENTURY* AGO--
--AND HAS KILLED ONE MAN FOR EVERY DAY HE'S SPENT ON GOD'S EARTH!
BLAM
-sausages-
I BROKE YOUR DOG.
HOPE YOU KEPT THE RECEIPT.
WE'LL FIND OUR OWN ROOM. THANK YOU.

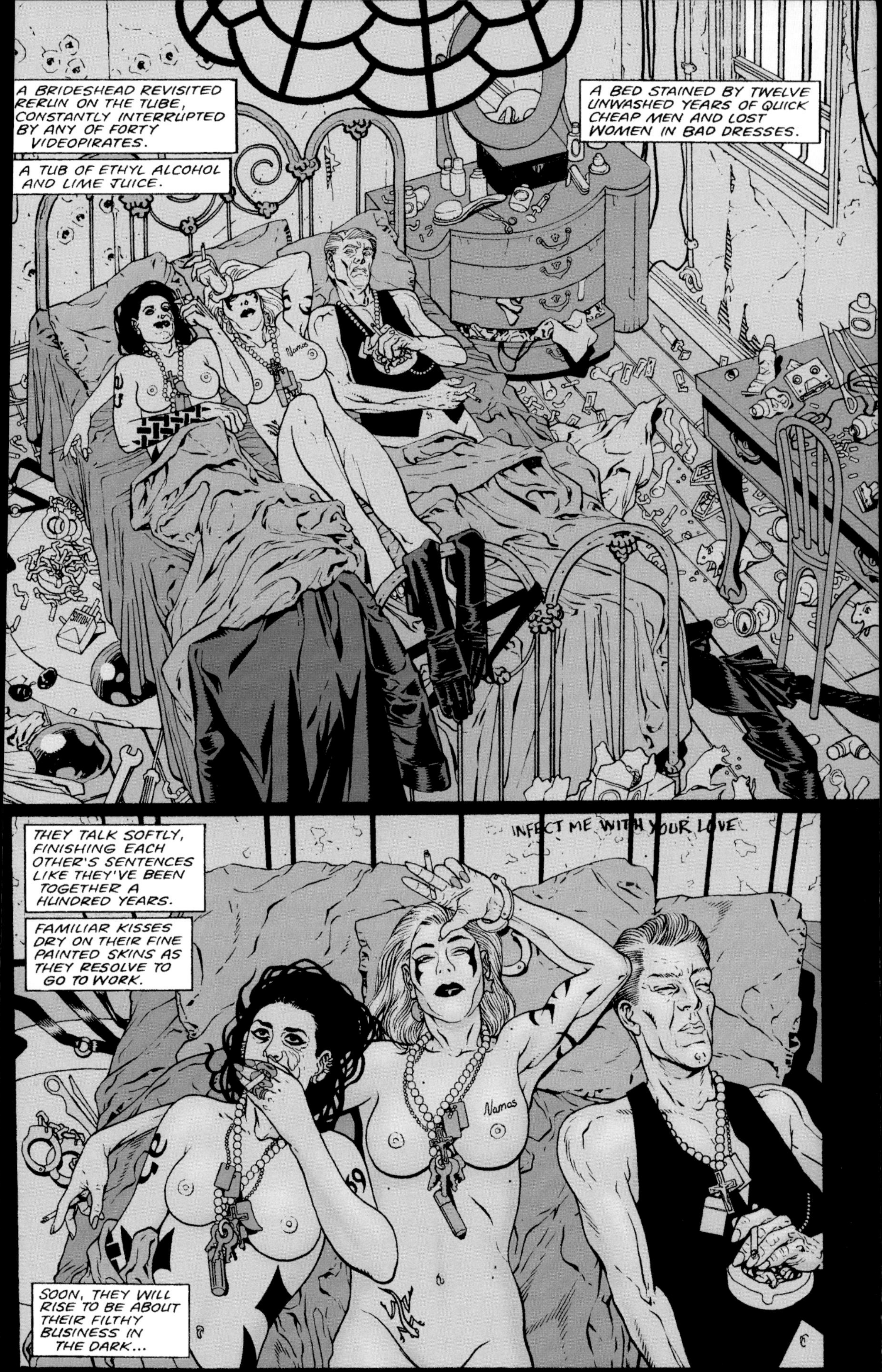
A BRIDESHEAD REVISITED RERUN ON THE TUBE, CONSTANTLY INTERRUPTED BY ANY OF FORTY VIDEOPIRATES.
A TUB OF ETHYL ALCOHOL AND LIME JUICE.
A BED STAINED BY TWELVE UNWASHED YEARS OF QUICK CHEAP MEN AND LOST WOMEN IN BAD DRESSES.
THEY TALK SOFTLY, FINISHING EACH OTHER'S SENTENCES LIKE THEY'VE BEEN TOGETHER A HUNDRED YEARS.
INFECT ME WITH YOUR LOVE
FAMILIAR KISSES DRY ON THEIR FINE PAINTED SKINS AS THEY RESOLVE TO GO TO WORK.
SOON, THEY WILL RISE TO BE ABOUT THEIR FILTHY BUSINESS IN THE DARK...

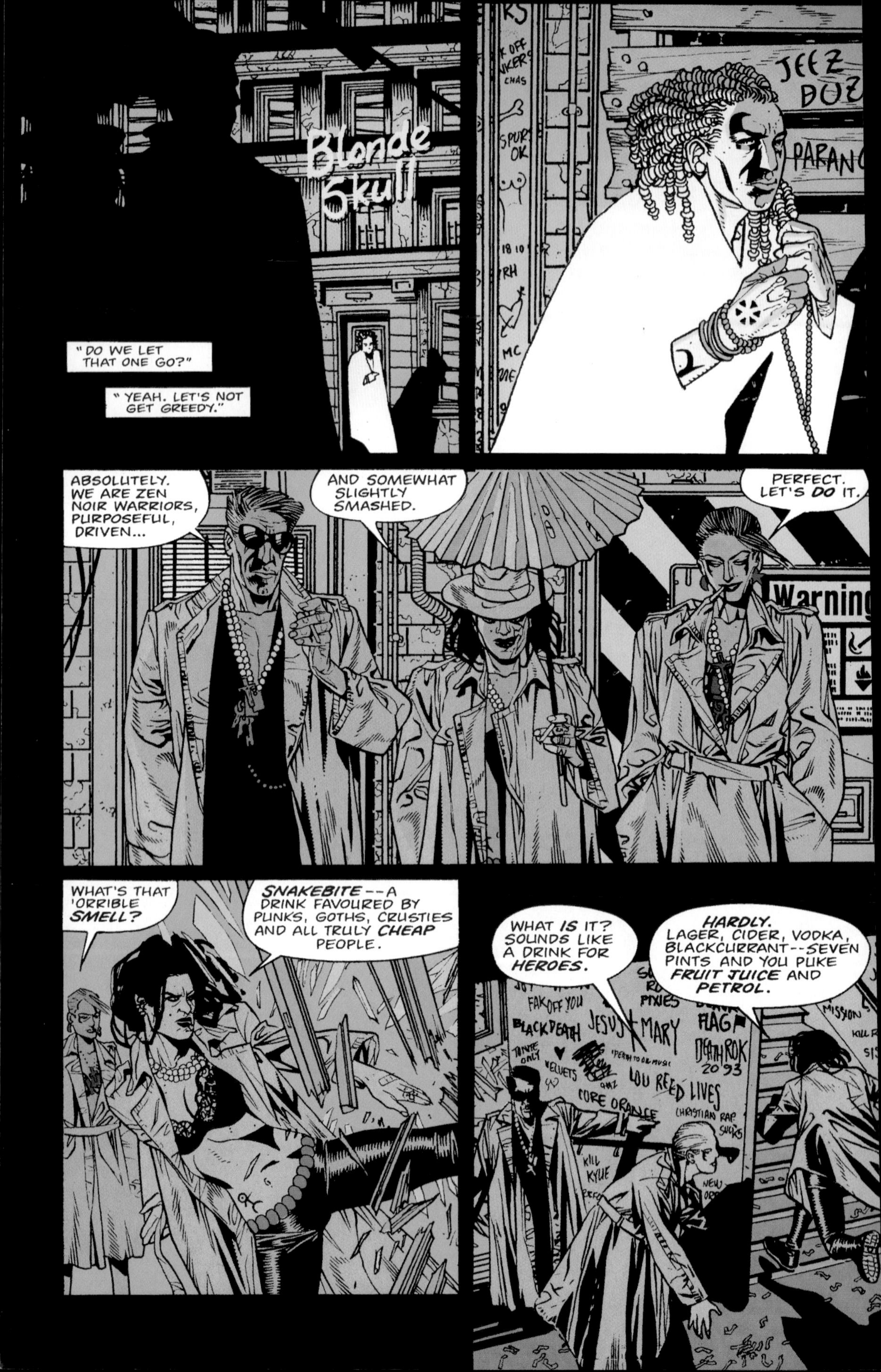
Blonde Skull
"DO WE LET THAT ONE GO?"
"YEAH. LET'S NOT GET GREEDY."
JEEZ
ABSOLUTELY. WE ARE ZEN NOIR WARRIORS, PURPOSEFUL, DRIVEN...
AND SOMEWHAT SLIGHTLY SMASHED.
PERFECT. LET'S DO IT.
Warning
WHAT'S THAT 'ORRIBLE SMELL?
SNAKEBITE--A DRINK FAVOURED BY PUNKS, GOTHS, CRUSTIES AND ALL TRULY CHEAP PEOPLE.
WHAT IS IT? SOUNDS LIKE A DRINK FOR HEROES.
HARDLY. LAGER, CIDER, VODKA, BLACKCURRANT--SEVEN PINTS AND YOU PUKE FRUIT JUICE AND PETROL.
BLACKDEATH
JESUS + MARY
DEATH ROK 2093
LOU REED LIVES
CHRISTIAN RAP SUCKS
KILL KYLIE

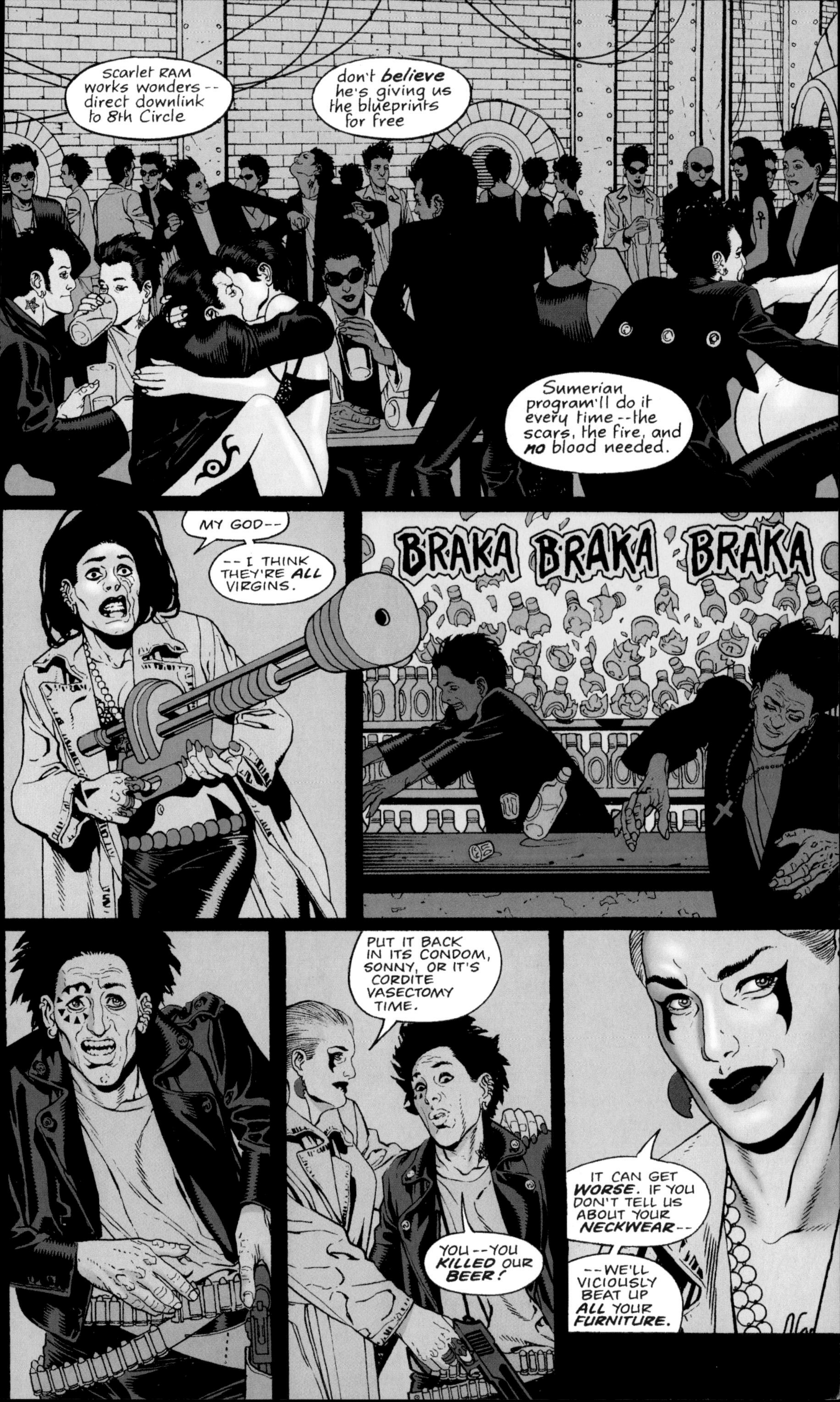
scarlet RAM works wonders -- direct downlink to 8th Circle
don't **believe** he's giving us the blueprints for free
Sumerian program'll do it every time -- the scars, the fire, and **NO** blood needed.
MY GOD--
-- I THINK THEY'RE **ALL** VIRGINS.
BRAKA BRAKA BRAKA
PUT IT BACK IN ITS CONDOM, SONNY, OR IT'S CORDITE VASECTOMY TIME.
YOU -- YOU **KILLED** OUR **BEER!**
IT CAN GET **WORSE**. IF YOU DON'T TELL US ABOUT YOUR **NECKWEAR**--
--WE'LL VICIOUSLY BEAT UP **ALL** YOUR **FURNITURE**.

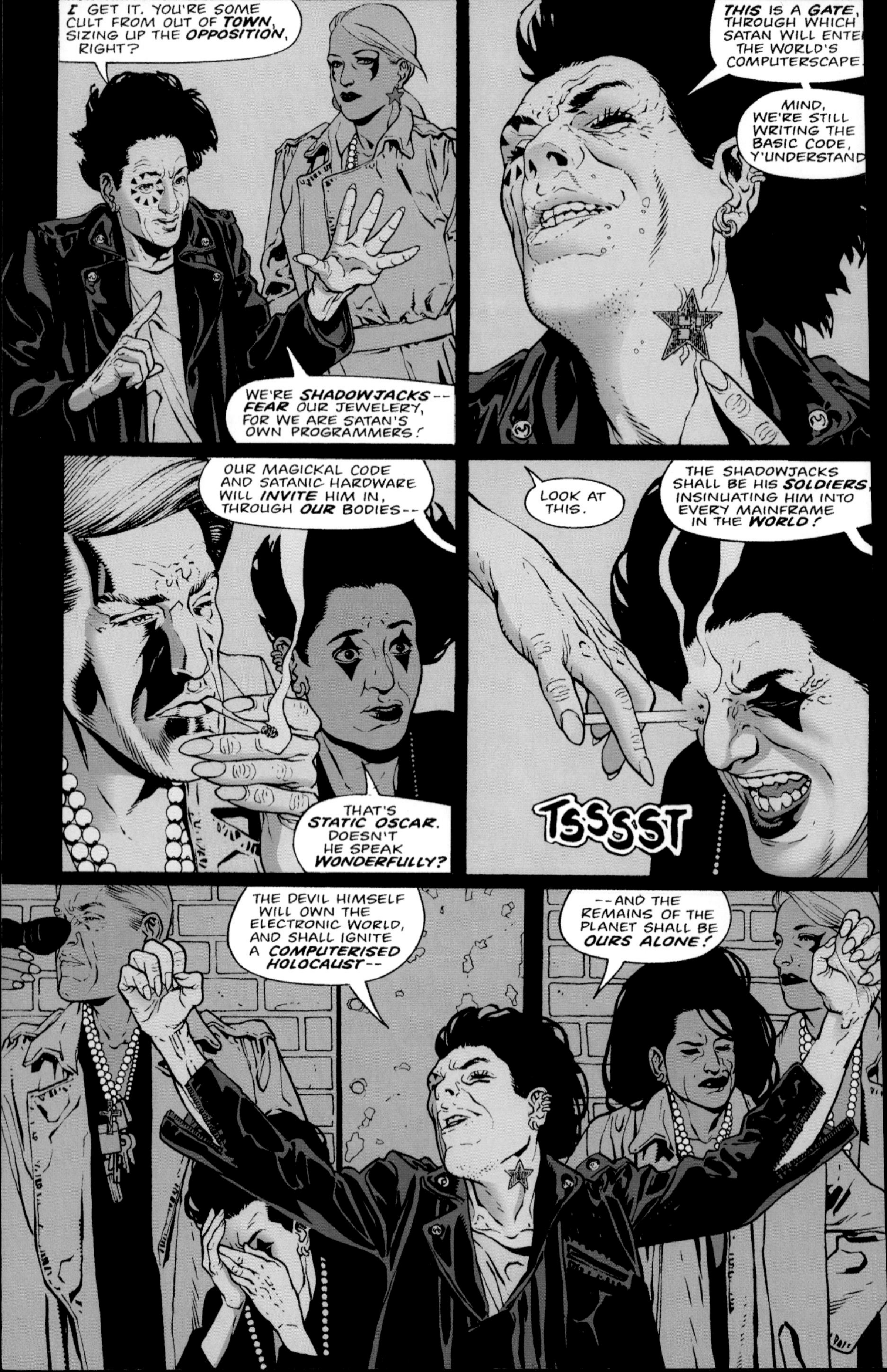
I GET IT. YOU'RE SOME CULT FROM OUT OF TOWN, SIZING UP THE OPPOSITION, RIGHT?
WE'RE SHADOWJACKS -- FEAR OUR JEWELERY, FOR WE ARE SATAN'S OWN PROGRAMMERS!
THIS IS A GATE, THROUGH WHICH SATAN WILL ENTE THE WORLD'S COMPUTERSCAPE.
MIND, WE'RE STILL WRITING THE BASIC CODE, Y'UNDERSTAND
OUR MAGICKAL CODE AND SATANIC HARDWARE WILL INVITE HIM IN, THROUGH OUR BODIES--
THAT'S STATIC OSCAR. DOESN'T HE SPEAK WONDERFULLY?
LOOK AT THIS.
THE SHADOWJACKS SHALL BE HIS SOLDIERS, INSINUATING HIM INTO EVERY MAINFRAME IN THE WORLD!
TSSSST
THE DEVIL HIMSELF WILL OWN THE ELECTRONIC WORLD, AND SHALL IGNITE A COMPUTERISED HOLOCAUST--
--AND THE REMAINS OF THE PLANET SHALL BE OURS ALONE!

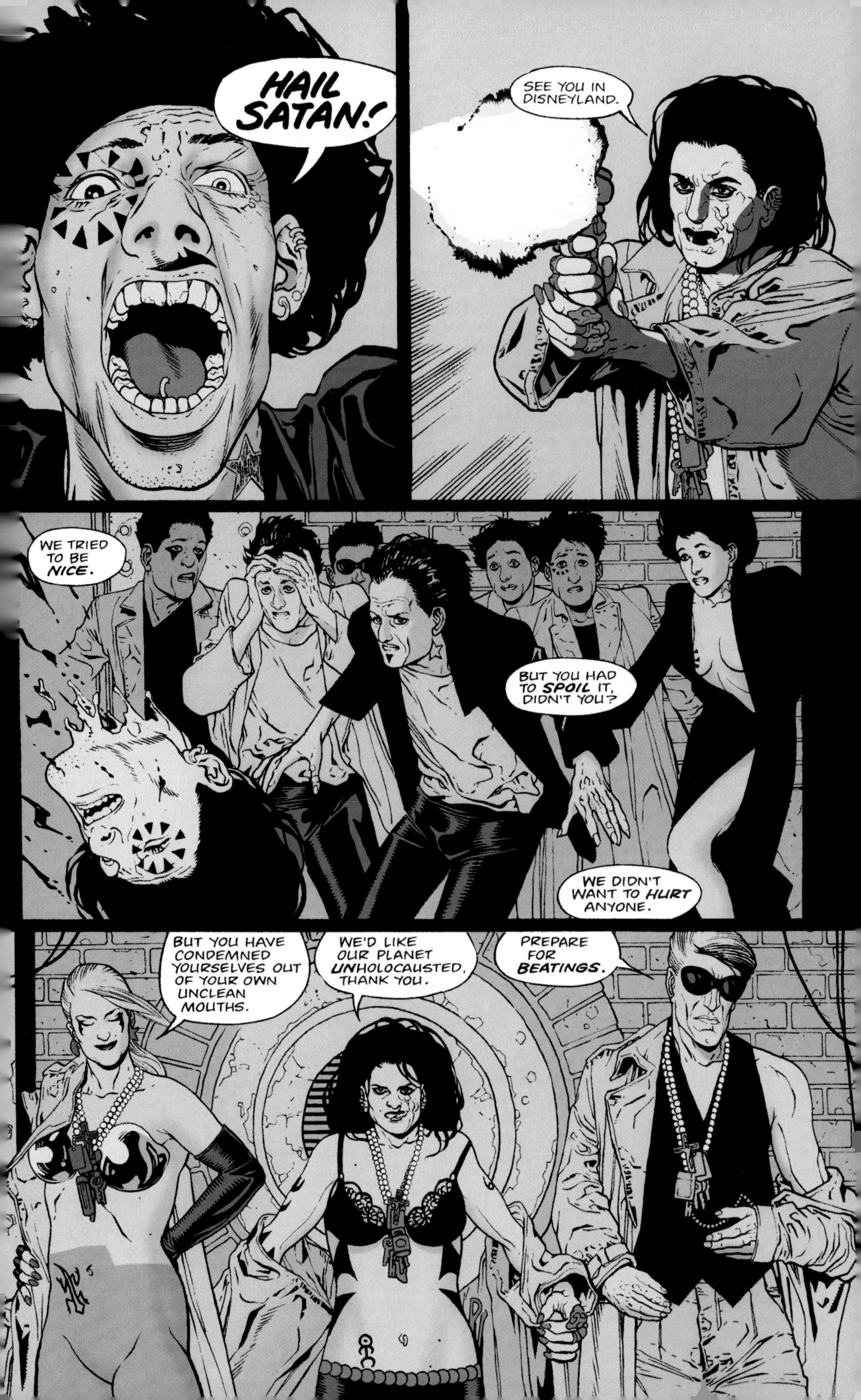
HAIL SATAN!
SEE YOU IN DISNEYLAND.
WE TRIED TO BE NICE.
BUT YOU HAD TO SPOIL IT, DIDN'T YOU?
WE DIDN'T WANT TO HURT ANYONE.
BUT YOU HAVE CONDEMNED YOURSELVES OUT OF YOUR OWN UNCLEAN MOUTHS.
WE'D LIKE OUR PLANET UNHOLOCAUSTED, THANK YOU.
PREPARE FOR BEATINGS.

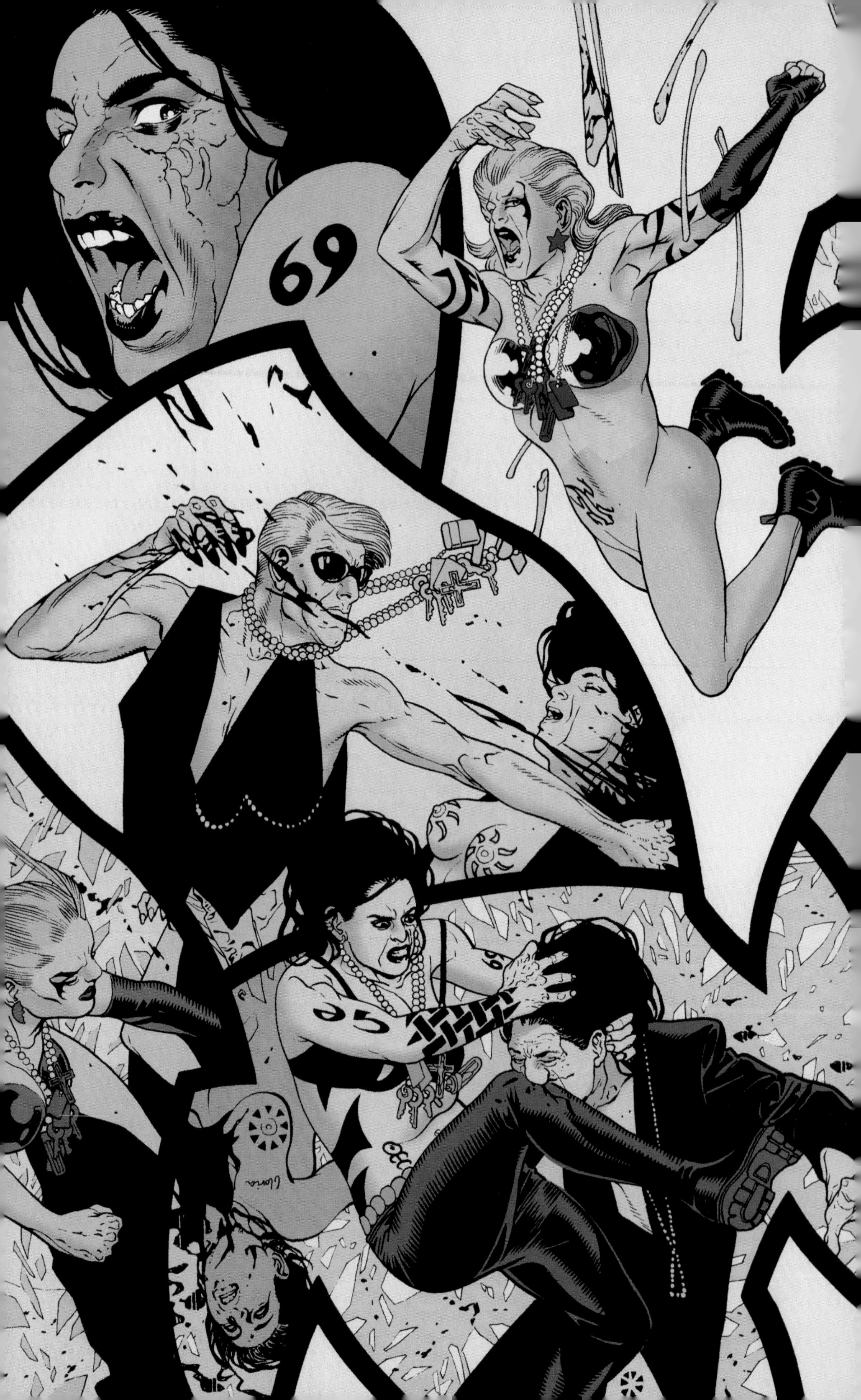
69

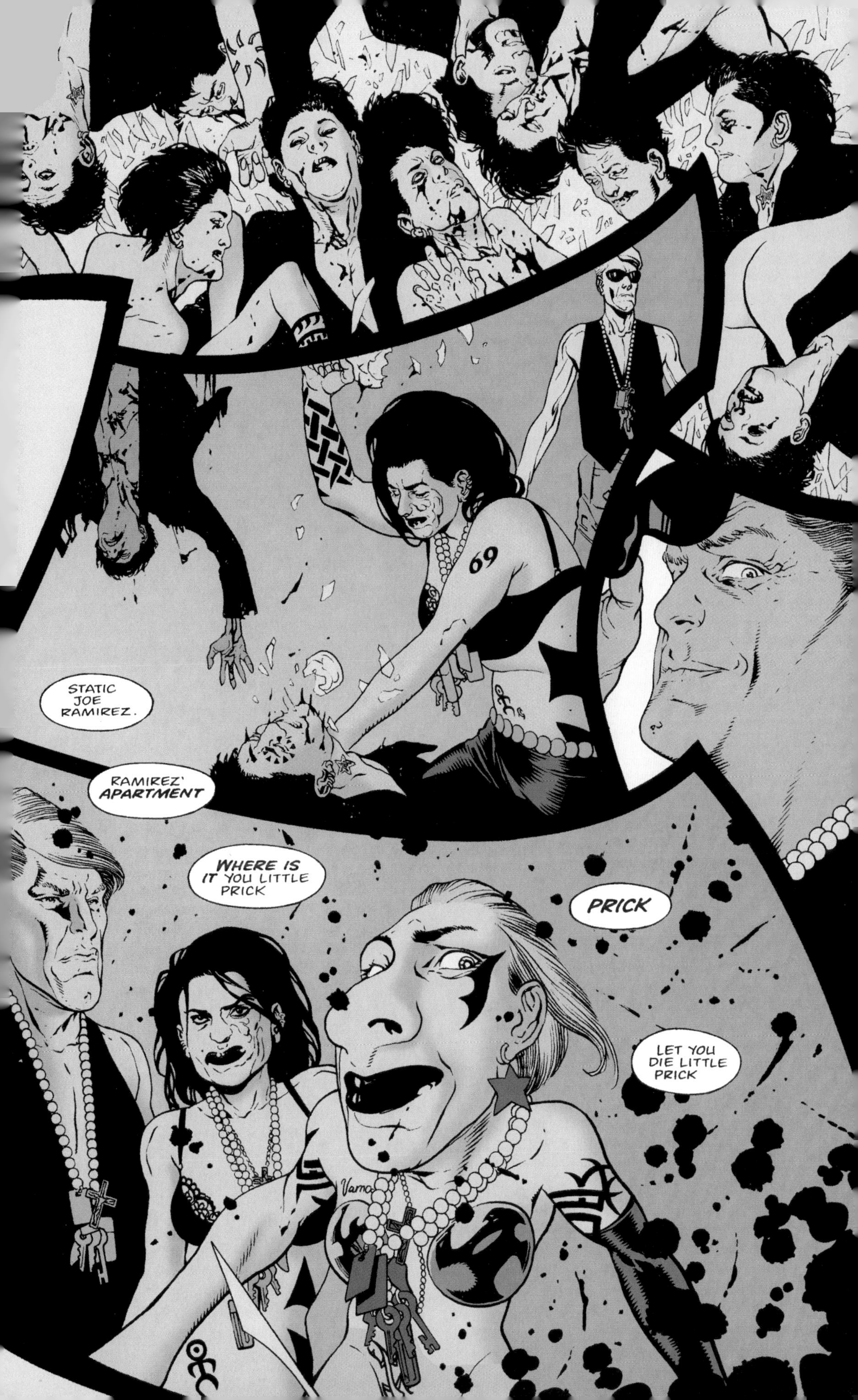
STATIC JOE RAMIREZ.
RAMIREZ' APARTMENT
WHERE IS IT YOU LITTLE PRICK
PRICK
LET YOU DIE LITTLE PRICK

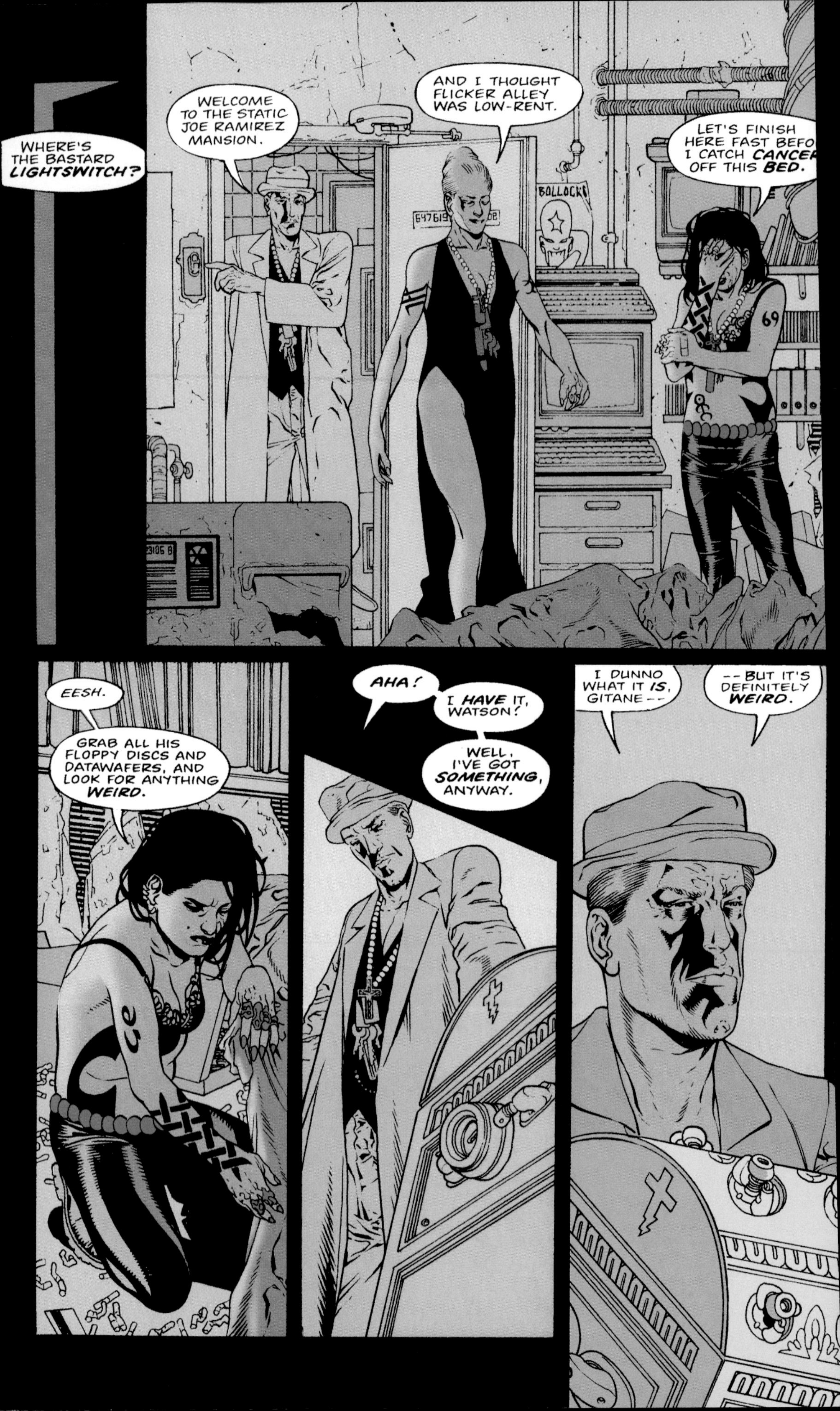

WHERE'S THE BASTARD LIGHTSWITCH?
WELCOME TO THE STATIC JOE RAMIREZ MANSION.
AND I THOUGHT FLICKER ALLEY WAS LOW-RENT.
LET'S FINISH HERE FAST BEFO I CATCH CANCER OFF THIS BED.
BOLLOCK
EESH.
GRAB ALL HIS FLOPPY DISCS AND DATAWAFERS, AND LOOK FOR ANYTHING WEIRD.
AHA!
I HAVE IT, WATSON!
WELL, I'VE GOT SOMETHING, ANYWAY.
I DUNNO WHAT IT IS, GITANE --
-- BUT IT'S DEFINITELY WEIRD.

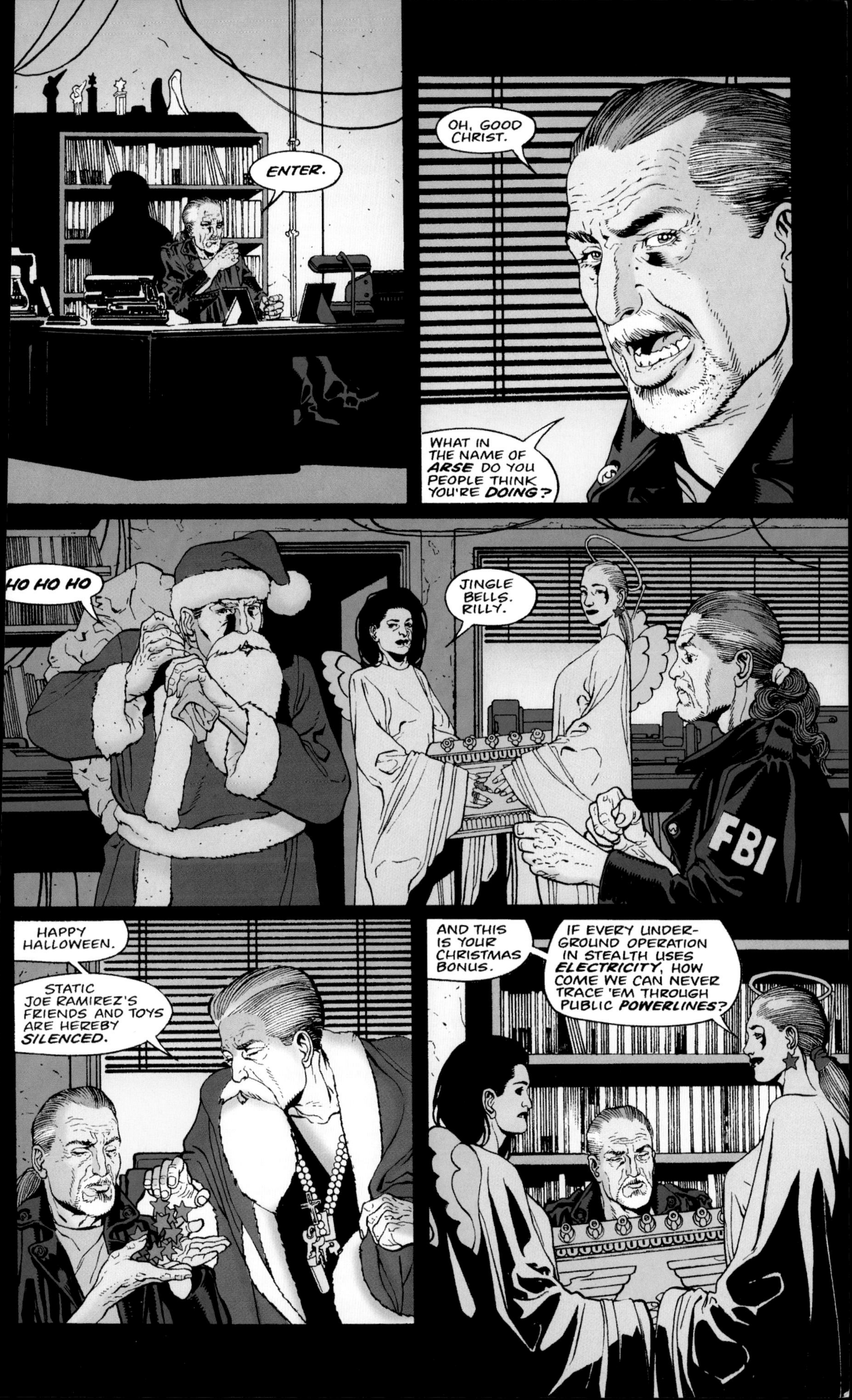
ENTER.
OH, GOOD CHRIST.
WHAT IN THE NAME OF ARSE DO YOU PEOPLE THINK YOU'RE DOING?
HO HO HO
JINGLE BELLS. RILLY.
HAPPY HALLOWEEN.
STATIC JOE RAMIREZ'S FRIENDS AND TOYS ARE HEREBY SILENCED.
AND THIS IS YOUR CHRISTMAS BONUS.
IF EVERY UNDER-GROUND OPERATION IN STEALTH USES ELECTRICITY, HOW COME WE CAN NEVER TRACE 'EM THROUGH PUBLIC POWERLINES?

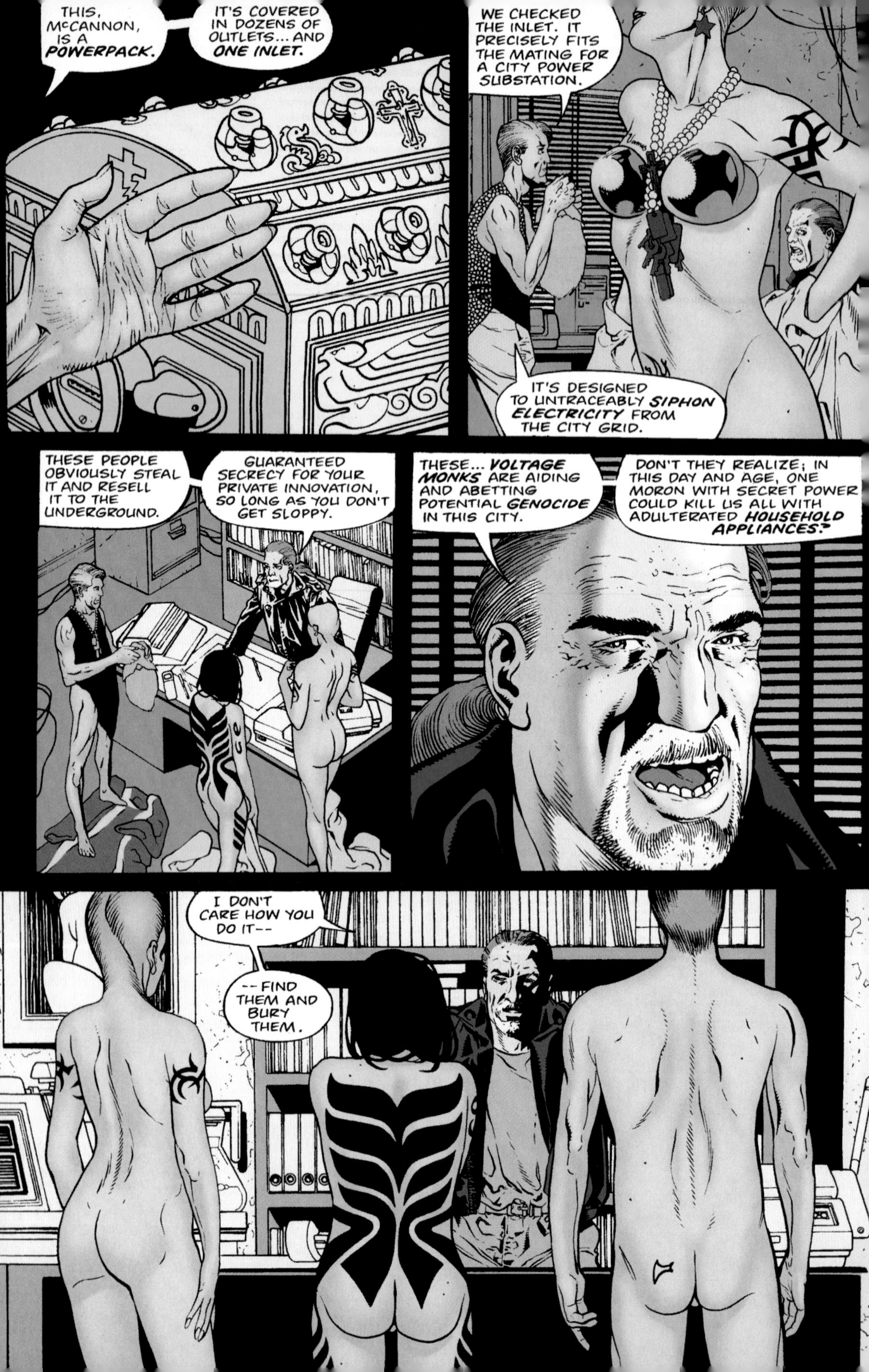
THIS, McCANNON, IS A POWERPACK.
IT'S COVERED IN DOZENS OF OUTLETS... AND ONE INLET.
WE CHECKED THE INLET. IT PRECISELY FITS THE MATING FOR A CITY POWER SUBSTATION.
IT'S DESIGNED TO UNTRACEABLY SIPHON ELECTRICITY FROM THE CITY GRID.
THESE PEOPLE OBVIOUSLY STEAL IT AND RESELL IT TO THE UNDERGROUND.
GUARANTEED SECRECY FOR YOUR PRIVATE INNOVATION, SO LONG AS YOU DON'T GET SLOPPY.
THESE... VOLTAGE MONKS ARE AIDING AND ABETTING POTENTIAL GENOCIDE IN THIS CITY.
DON'T THEY REALIZE; IN THIS DAY AND AGE, ONE MORON WITH SECRET POWER COULD KILL US ALL WITH ADULTERATED HOUSEHOLD APPLIANCES?
I DON'T CARE HOW YOU DO IT--
--FIND THEM AND BURY THEM.

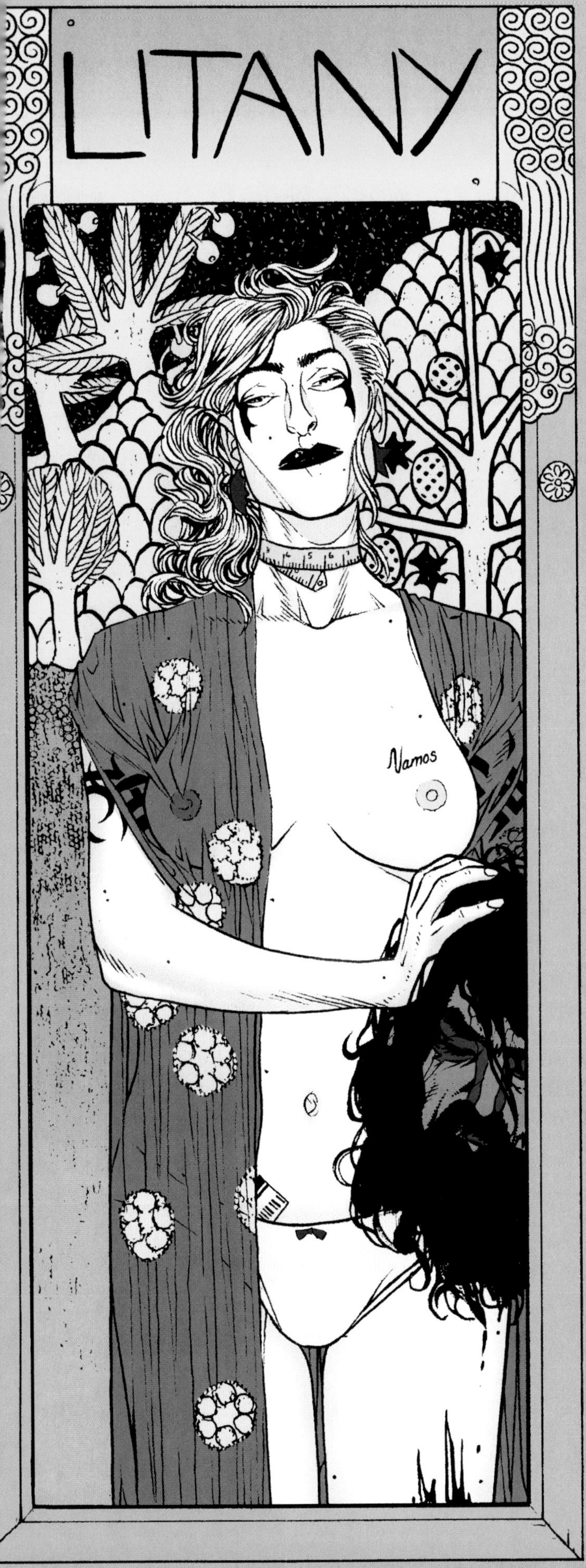
LITANY
Vamos

LITANY

REAL NAME: Litany

OCCUPATION: Silencer

FORMER OCCUPATION: Cabaret singer, escapologist, police sniper, street sweeper

PLACE OF BIRTH: Unlisted, possibly the rear of a taxi in Chicago

MARITAL STATUS: Confused and probably illegal

CITIZENSHIP: Separated States of America, Cyprus, Holland, Scunthorpe

ORIGIN: Real people don't have origins, just births and lives, asshole

TAPE IN PERSONAL SONY DATman: Compilation, including -- early Pixies, but not that crappy last album; bootlegged tracks by Bratmobile; Marianne Faithfull; Fur Bible; Diamanda Galas, with "Wild Women With Steak Knives" recorded twice

HISTORY: Listen, it's rough enough for a girl just to get her ass *born,* let alone having to remember what happened *afterwards*. Why should I strain my brain just to keep a bunch of fact-crazy anal retentive pubeless voidoids happy? Bang goes the speculative value on *this* comic book.

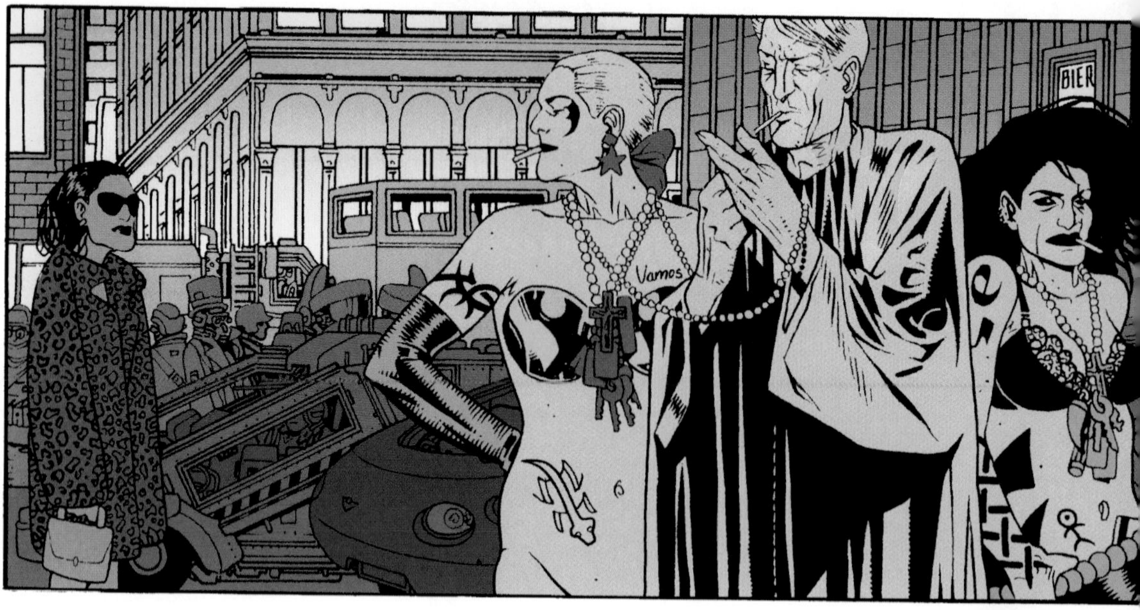
BIER
Vamos

CERTAIN areas of the City cannot be visited, due to their complete absence. The Police Sector house for the province of **Necrolux** is one such. Captain of Detectives Eli Kiltende, a secret quantum magician, staged a takeover of the Sector House, and, once commanding the House's entire complement of of officers, committed an illegal act of magic. He rotated the entire building one quarter turn out of reality. The original site of the Necrolux Sector House, despite having eighteen physical miracles attributed to it, is out of bounds. Illegal visitors can by law be incinerated without trial. Watch for **arrest portals** -- smoking doorways in the air. These are the entrance points into reality for Necrolux police. Mutated by extradimensional radiations, they are hideous to behold, and will arrest you for possession of offensive relatives at their whim.

You should, however, visit the missing half mile of the river **Miroslava.** The absent half-mile tract of water flows into an unexplained spacefold, passes through George Square, Glasgow (Scotland) and the main road of Zealotry, Iowa before returning to Stealth. Swimming in the Miroslava is not allowed. Drinking the water is not advised either, as it's been established that the citizenry of Zealotry deliberately defecate into their portion of the river.

Halflife Square, on the East Side, was recently infected by chronal leprosy. Police cordons have been established outside the infected area. Stand behind the tetrapoided liveglass there, and you will see the misty emerald ghosts of people who are having their history eaten away by the disease. The infection has already spread to two years ago, and is expected to reach into the decade before last by the time the medication takes effect (antibiotic bombings take place on the 3rd and 17th of each month).

WARREN ELLIS

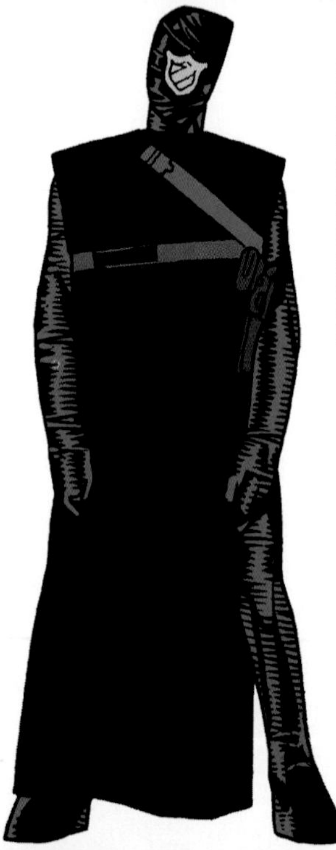
NECROLUX POLICEMAN

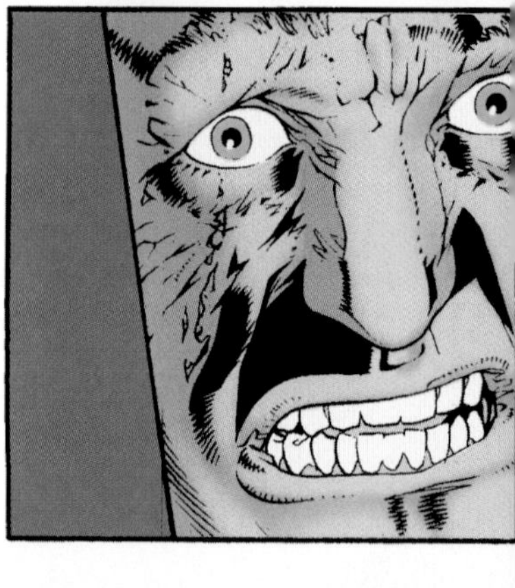

I was thirteen. She was thirty one. I was a fake street tough, scared shitless of my own shadow but ready to start an idiot fight with any poor fool in punching distance. I figured I'd keep hitting people until I was no longer frightened of them.

She was a surgeon. And I mean _was_ — she was dis- barred from practice before I met her. She had big strange ideas. She injected untested nanotech and blank DNA into a foetus, having drugged the mother first. What came out was a cloud of live steel and fleshy dust, with radio parts instead of vocal chords. She liked to tinker.

We met on the street. A bunch of Tarmac Lizards tried to roll her for her kidneys, and I beat them off... used electrified dacoit cords, as I recall. I didn't need to start trouble with the Lizards, but those legs gave my 13-year-old hormones all the excuse they needed, I guess...

She had big ideas, all right. We'd been lovers three months when she showed me the prints. She had a lot of magic books, a lot of technical knowledge, and, in retrospect, absolutely no marbles whatsoever. She led me by my penis into her rigged-up operating theatre, red fingernails working my glans encouragingly.

She called the operation The Import. She wanted to create a posthuman for the world of electronic media, as well as magic. In the Quabala system of magic, there is something called Sephiroth Dex -- the Tenth Key, that releases the secrets of the world. The ports and jacks and inlets that she hammer- ed, burned and smashed into my body would connect me into any computer, transmission or reception apparatus that existed. My own poor body became Sephiroth Dex.

So when I woke up, I grabbed a scalpel and a claw hammer, and I cut and slammed her to death. I burst her perfect flat stomach and slit those deep dark eyes and _and_

She spoke. Once. Made me promise to use her gift to release the secrets of the world. I didn't know what she meant, then. So I flexed my rough, ruined holed body and tore out her tongue with the claw hammer.

I still have it. The tongue, I mean.

I was t
scared
fight w
keep hi
Sh
barred
ideas.
into a
out wa
parts i
We
tried to
used e
to star
13-yea
guess.
Sh
months
magic
retrosp
by my
fingerr
Sh
a posth
In the
Sephir
the wo
ed, b
into a
that e
S
hamm
perfect
S
release
meant,
tore ou

FAXPRINT 09/10/93 00.10am ROB COUR; McCANNON 0101-212-0702-460073 PAGE 02

Religious Information Repository

REQUESTED DATA ON RELIGIOUS ORDERS (STEALTH LOCALITY) WITH HOMICIDAL DOGMA OR ROGUE PRELATURE W/HOMICIDAL TENDENCIES

CHURCH OF THE SPAM-EATING GOAT WITH AN AQUALUNG WHO SPITS ON THE SHOELACES OF EVIL, The

-- entire cult recently underwent extensive plastic surgery to resemble their idol. The now entirely mad membership mostly indulges in animal mutation of a sexual nature; though murders of amorous, if dim, farmhands have been recorded

CHURCH OF THE FASCINATING MEDICIDE BORN OF WASHINGTON POPPIES, The

-- Sect of ex-political aides deeply sunk in the abuse and worship of the opium poppy. Five of them were sentenced last year for the murder of a DEA agent, committed solely with antique NIXON/HAIG '96 bumper stickers. These subhuman flowersuckers are dangerous when cornered, but not homicidal in the first instance

CHURCH OF ROBERTO CALVI'S LEFT HAND, WHICH DOESN'T KNOW WHAT THE RIGHT ONE IS DOING, The

-- Splinter Roman Catholic group of accountants and finance brokers apparently visited by the, quote, Divine Apparition, unquote, of the mythical patron saint of crooked bankers. Their form of worship is in the zealous gathering of monies, legal and otherwise, and blowing it on increasingly ornate statues depicting Calvi in his martyrdom (hanging from Tower Bridge with a noose around his chops). The cultists are frequently armed, many claiming a spiritual descendancy from Sicilian patron saints of unnecessary violence, and generally seem like your best bet.

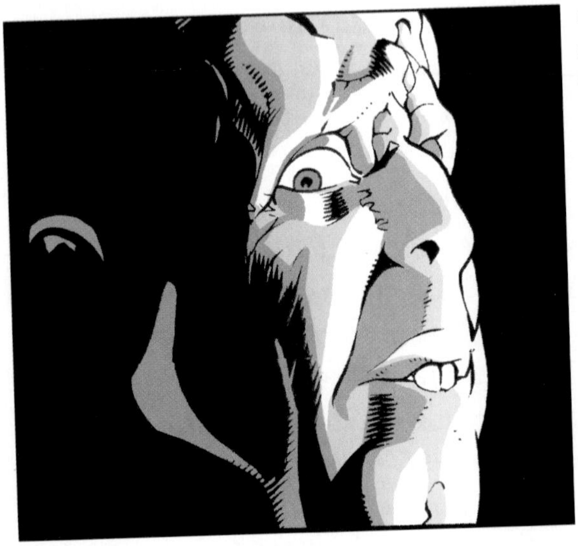

GRAND BEARDED WIZARD of the Church Of The Spam-Eating Goat etc.,

Seargent-Doctor Eamonn Mucilage of Dogshit, Nebraska

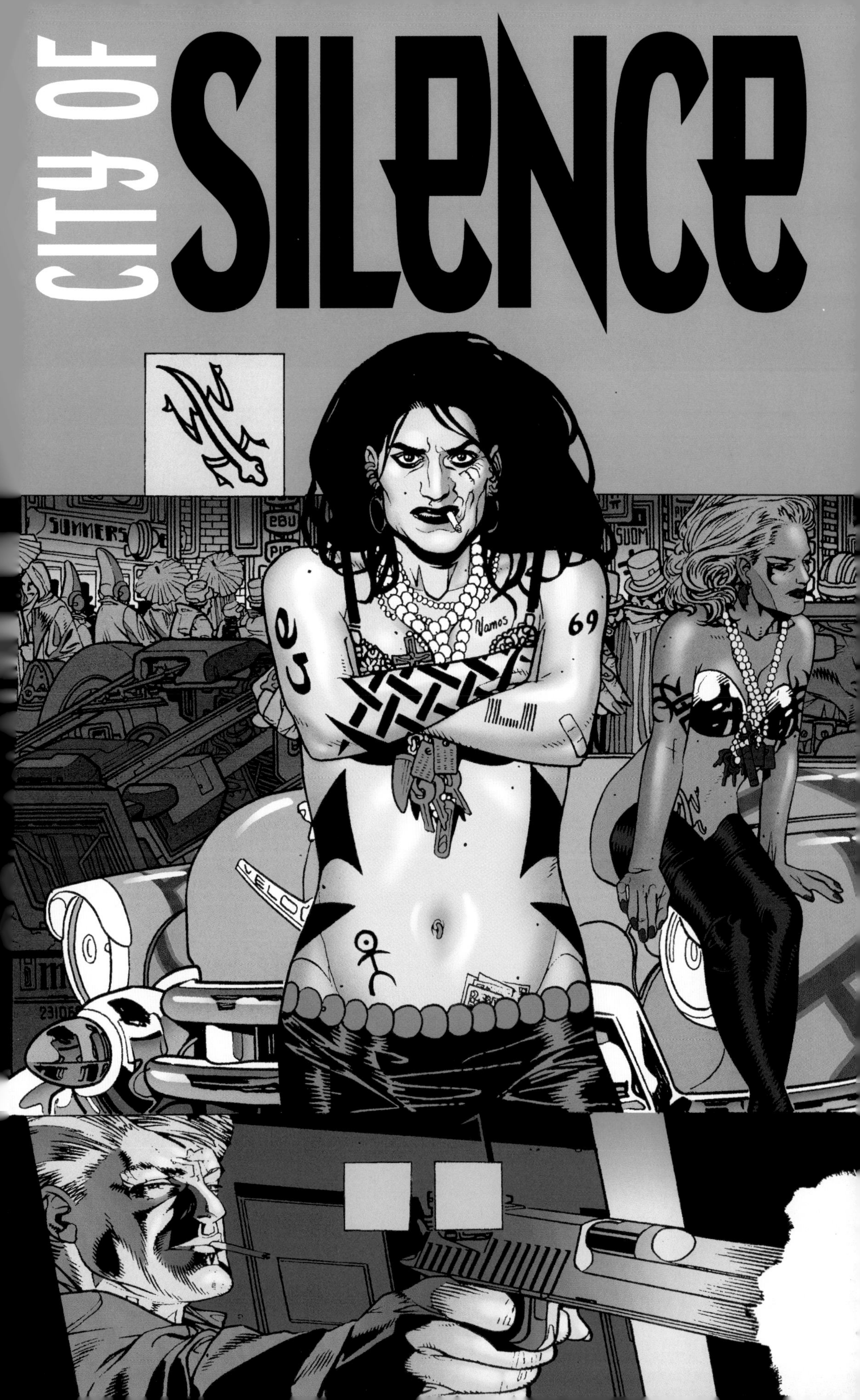
CITY OF
SILENCE
SUMMERS
Vamos
69

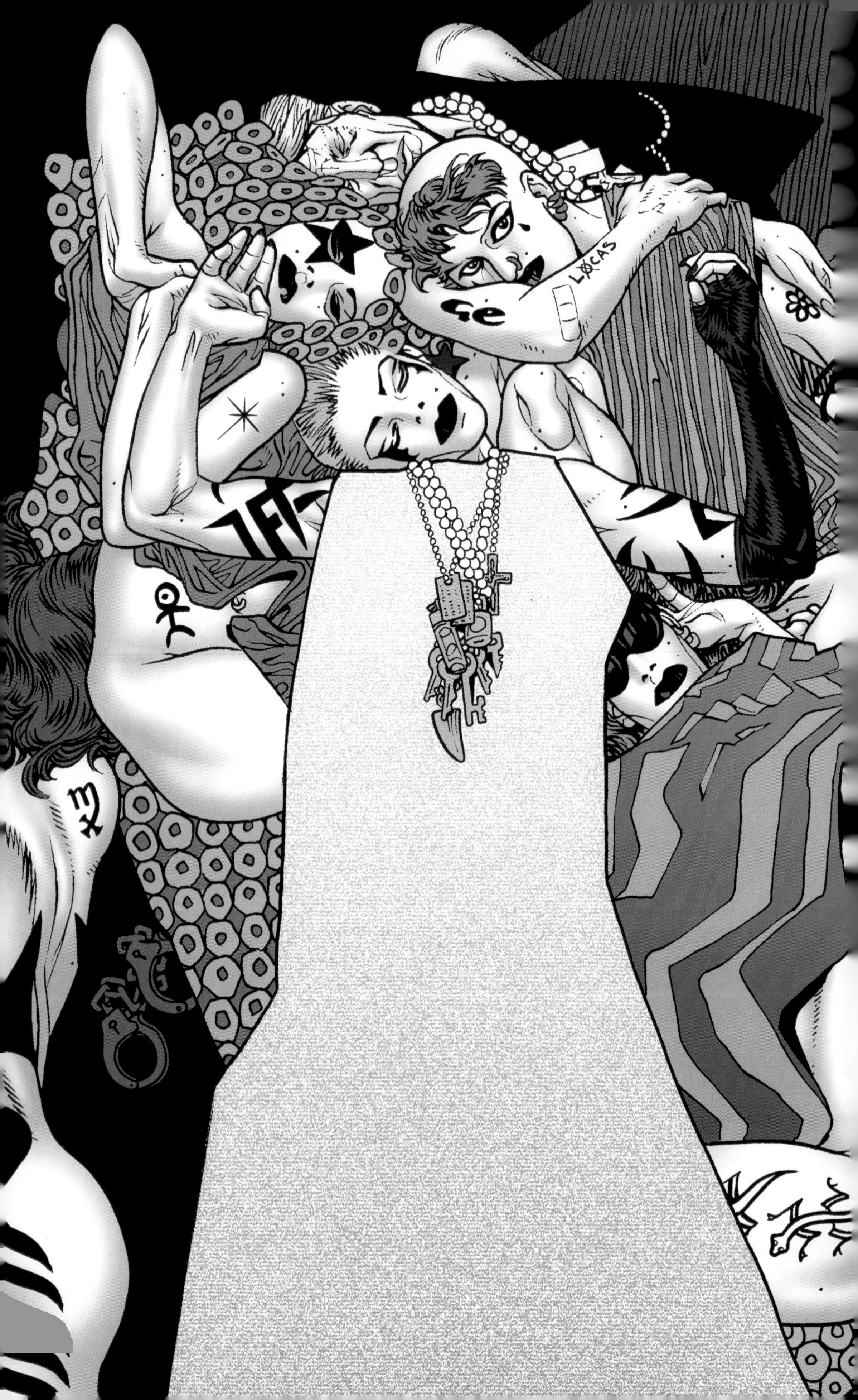
LØCAS

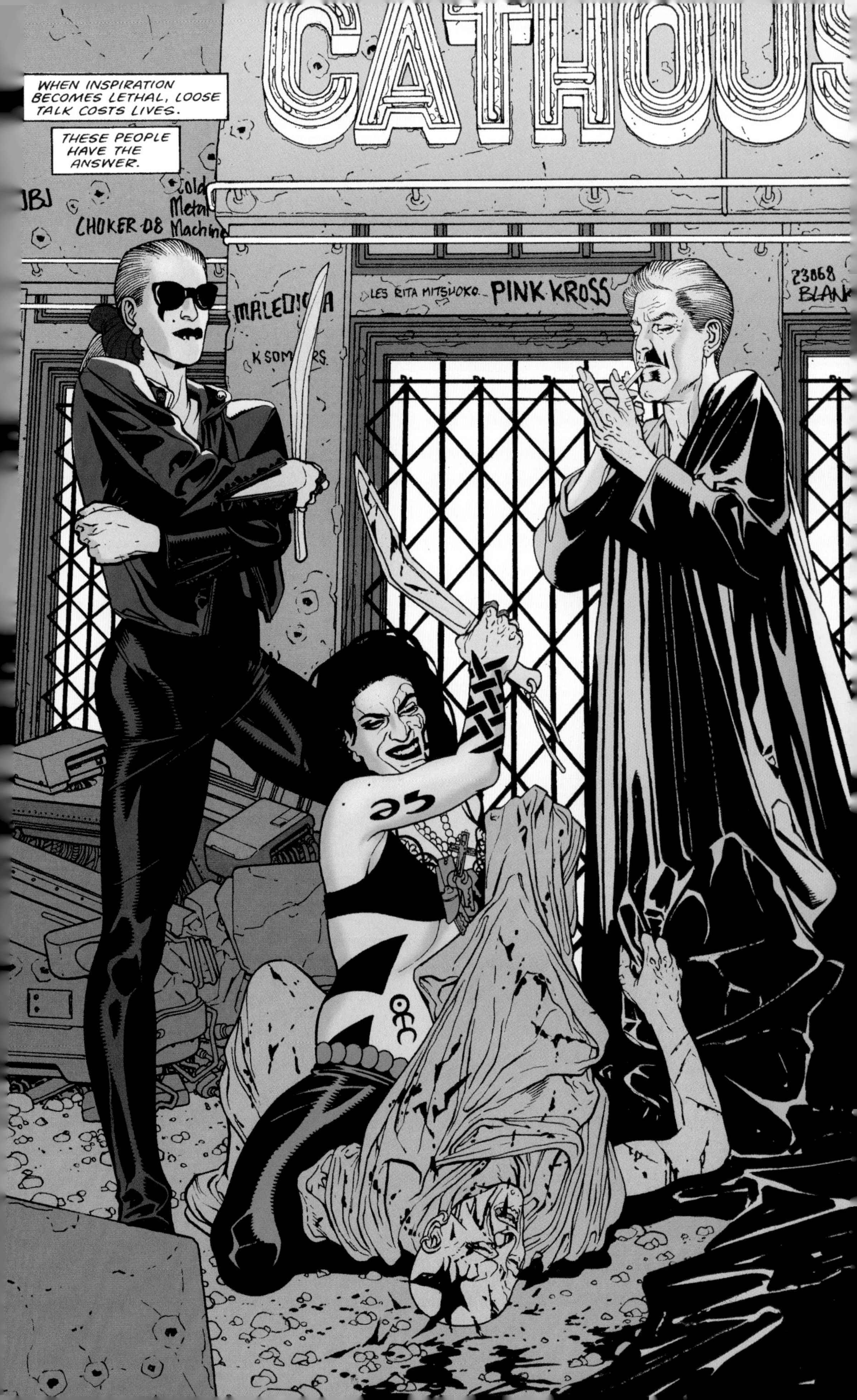
WHEN INSPIRATION BECOMES LETHAL, LOOSE TALK COSTS LIVES.
THESE PEOPLE HAVE THE ANSWER.
CATHOUS
JBJ
Cold Metal Machine
CHOKER D8
LES RITA MITSUOKO
PINK KROSS
23868

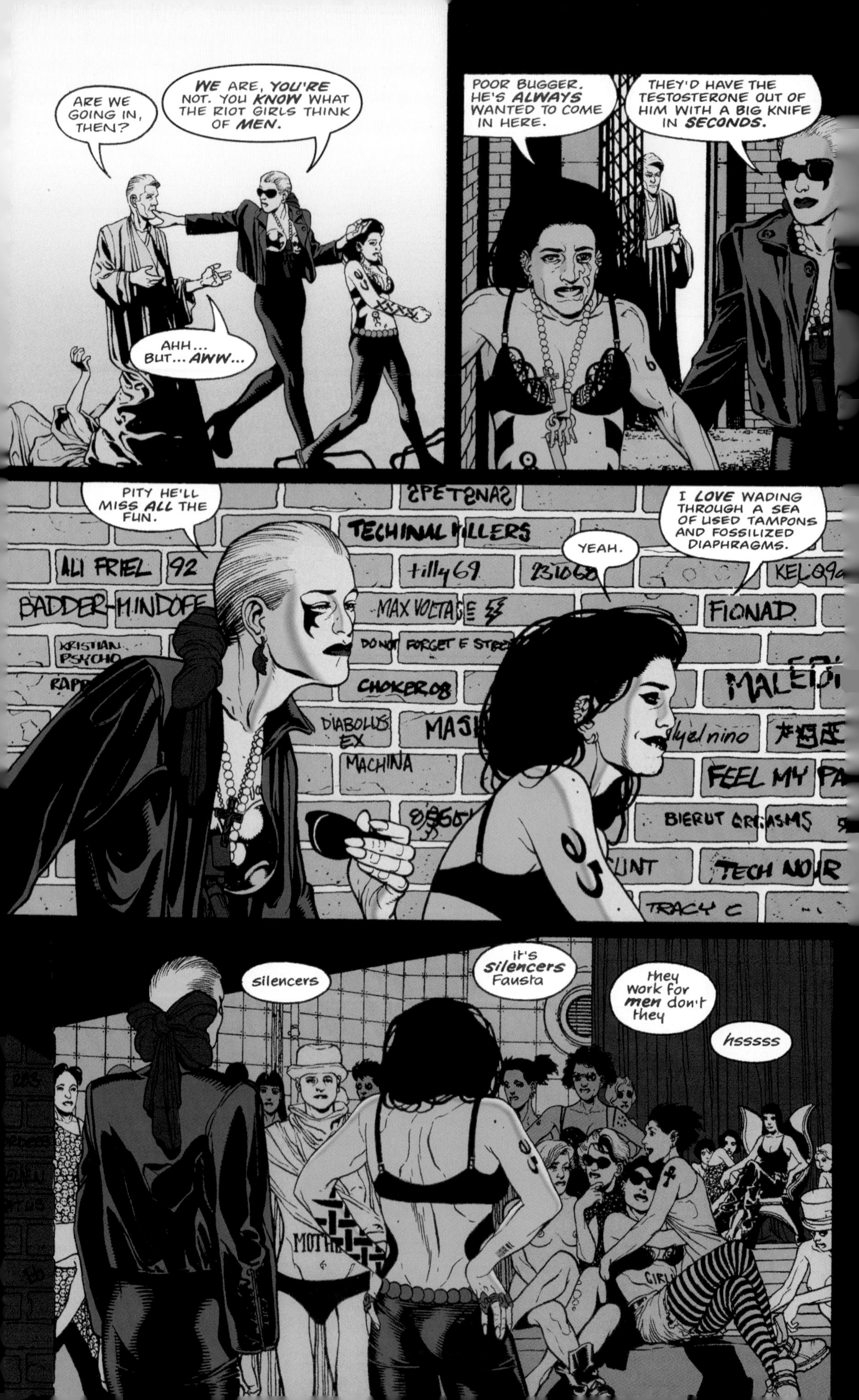
ARE WE GOING IN, THEN?
WE ARE, YOU'RE NOT. YOU KNOW WHAT THE RIOT GIRLS THINK OF MEN.
AHH... BUT... AWW...
POOR BUGGER. HE'S ALWAYS WANTED TO COME IN HERE.
THEY'D HAVE THE TESTOSTERONE OUT OF HIM WITH A BIG KNIFE IN SECONDS.
PITY HE'LL MISS ALL THE FUN.
YEAH.
I LOVE WADING THROUGH A SEA OF USED TAMPONS AND FOSSILIZED DIAPHRAGMS.
silencers
it's silencers Fausta
they work for men don't they
hsssss

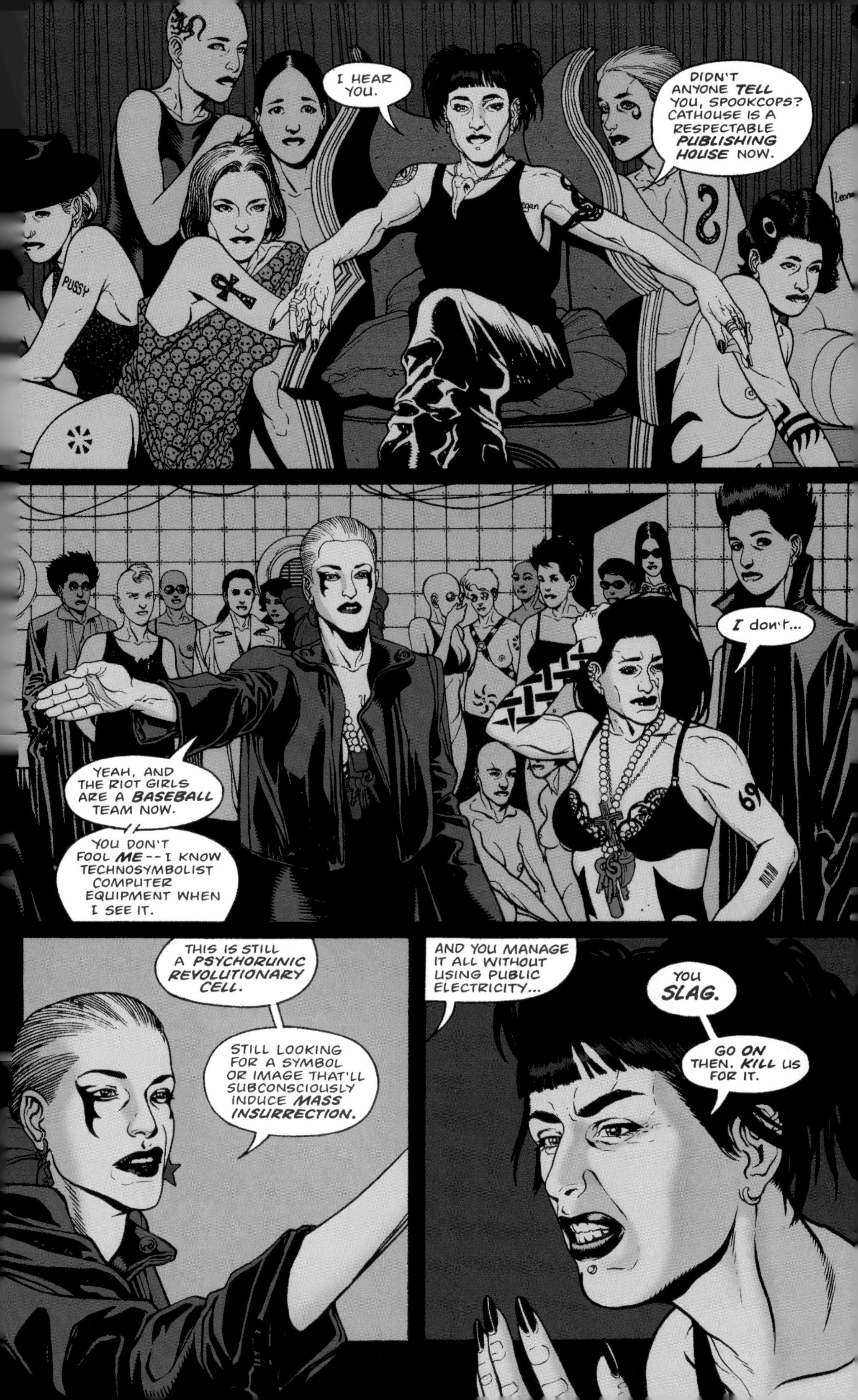
I HEAR YOU.
DIDN'T ANYONE TELL YOU, SPOOKCOPS? CATHOUSE IS A RESPECTABLE PUBLISHING HOUSE NOW.
PUSSY
YEAH, AND THE RIOT GIRLS ARE A BASEBALL TEAM NOW.
YOU DON'T FOOL ME -- I KNOW TECHNOSYMBOLIST COMPUTER EQUIPMENT WHEN I SEE IT.
I don't...
THIS IS STILL A PSYCHORUNIC REVOLUTIONARY CELL.
STILL LOOKING FOR A SYMBOL OR IMAGE THAT'LL SUBCONSCIOUSLY INDUCE MASS INSURRECTION.
AND YOU MANAGE IT ALL WITHOUT USING PUBLIC ELECTRICITY...
YOU SLAG.
GO ON THEN. KILL US FOR IT.

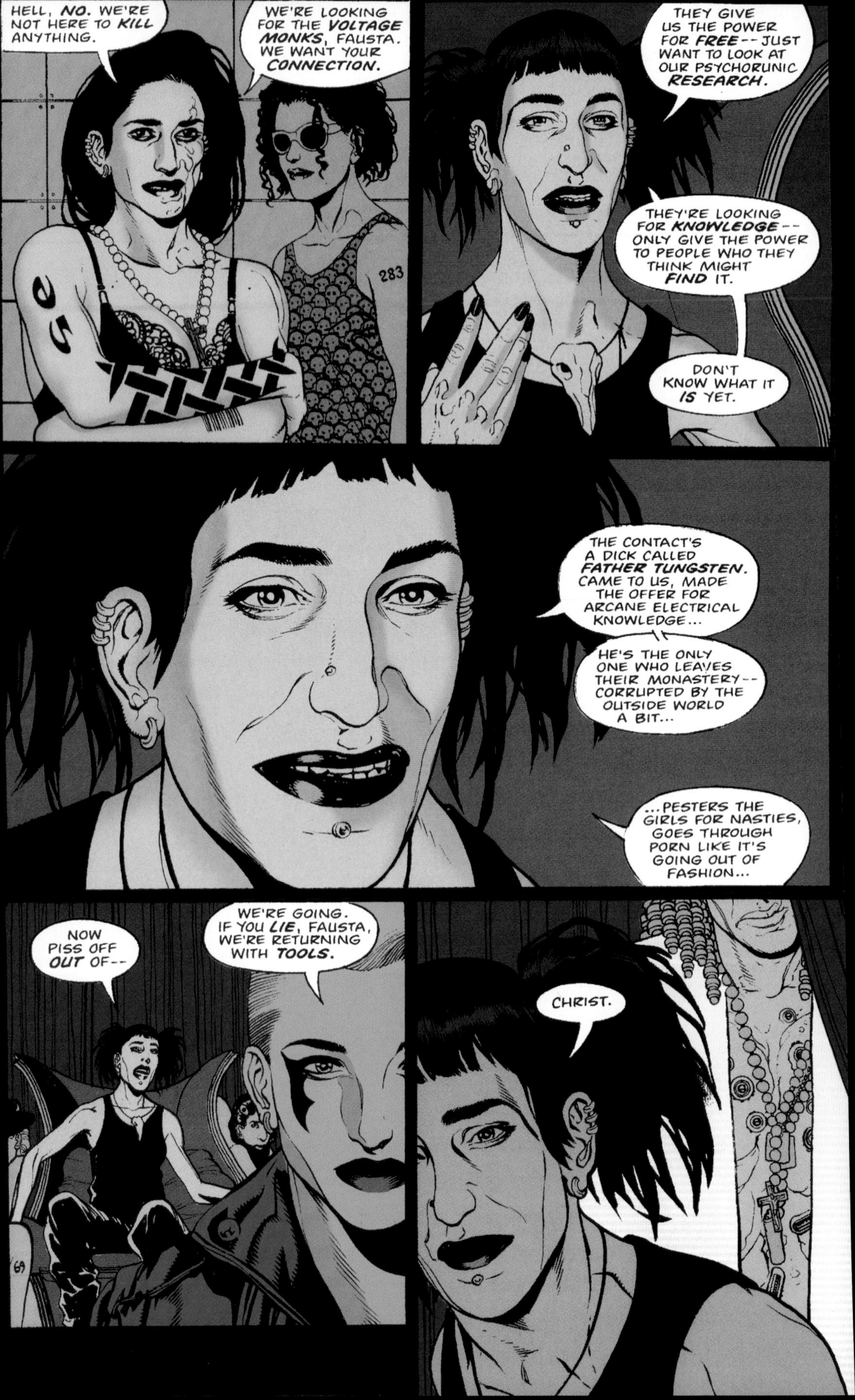
HELL, NO. WE'RE NOT HERE TO KILL ANYTHING.
WE'RE LOOKING FOR THE VOLTAGE MONKS, FAUSTA. WE WANT YOUR CONNECTION.
283
THEY GIVE US THE POWER FOR FREE--JUST WANT TO LOOK AT OUR PSYCHORUNIC RESEARCH.
THEY'RE LOOKING FOR KNOWLEDGE--ONLY GIVE THE POWER TO PEOPLE WHO THEY THINK MIGHT FIND IT.
DON'T KNOW WHAT IT IS YET.
THE CONTACT'S A DICK CALLED FATHER TUNGSTEN. CAME TO US, MADE THE OFFER FOR ARCANE ELECTRICAL KNOWLEDGE...
HE'S THE ONLY ONE WHO LEAVES THEIR MONASTERY--CORRUPTED BY THE OUTSIDE WORLD A BIT...
...PESTERS THE GIRLS FOR NASTIES, GOES THROUGH PORN LIKE IT'S GOING OUT OF FASHION...
NOW PISS OFF OUT OF--
WE'RE GOING. IF YOU LIE, FAUSTA, WE'RE RETURNING WITH TOOLS.
CHRIST.

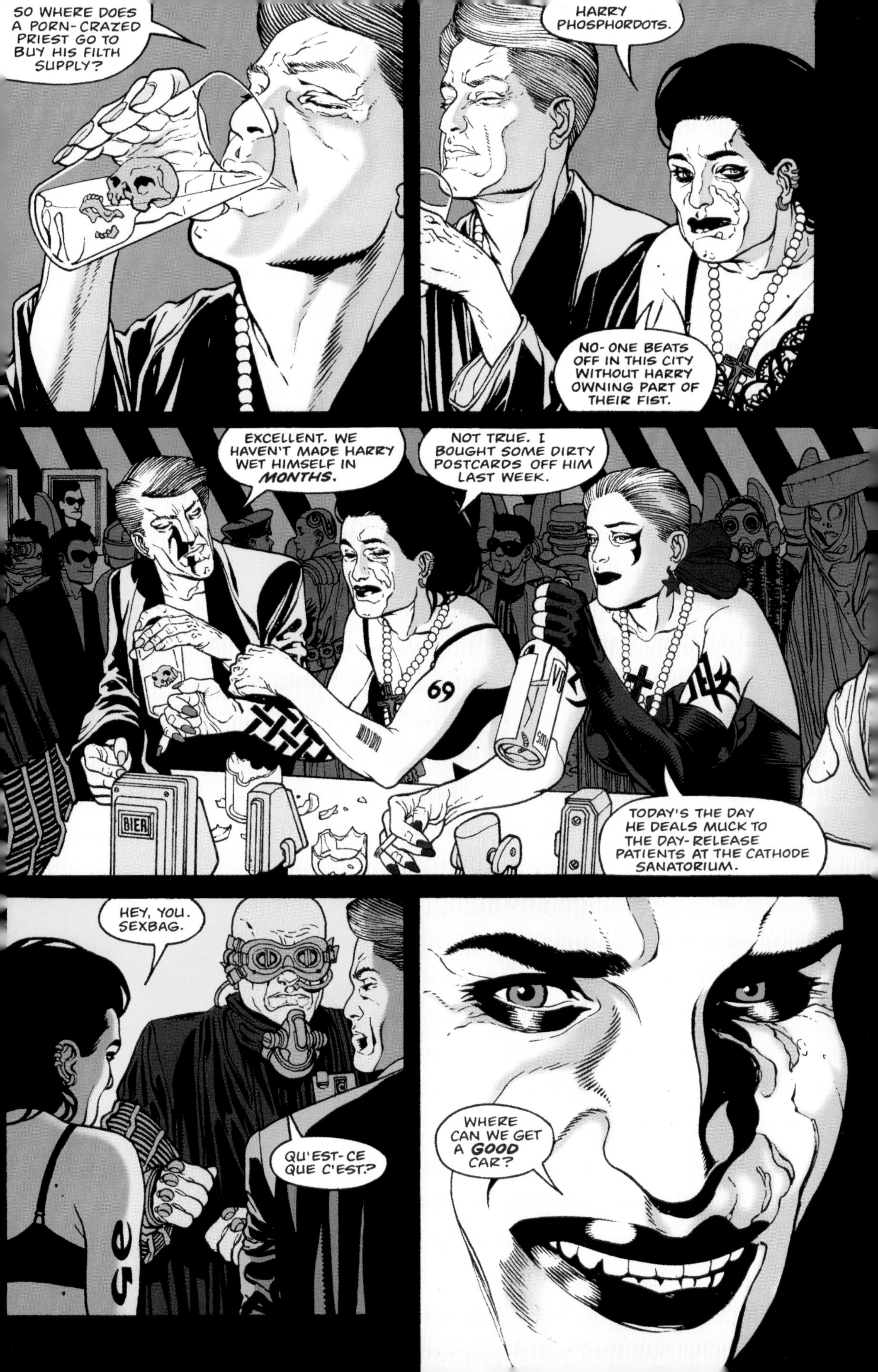
SO WHERE DOES A PORN-CRAZED PRIEST GO TO BUY HIS FILTH SUPPLY?
HARRY PHOSPHORDOTS.
NO-ONE BEATS OFF IN THIS CITY WITHOUT HARRY OWNING PART OF THEIR FIST.
EXCELLENT. WE HAVEN'T MADE HARRY WET HIMSELF IN MONTHS.
NOT TRUE. I BOUGHT SOME DIRTY POSTCARDS OFF HIM LAST WEEK.
TODAY'S THE DAY HE DEALS MUCK TO THE DAY-RELEASE PATIENTS AT THE CATHODE SANATORIUM.
BIER
HEY, YOU. SEXBAG.
QU'EST-CE QUE C'EST?
WHERE CAN WE GET A GOOD CAR?

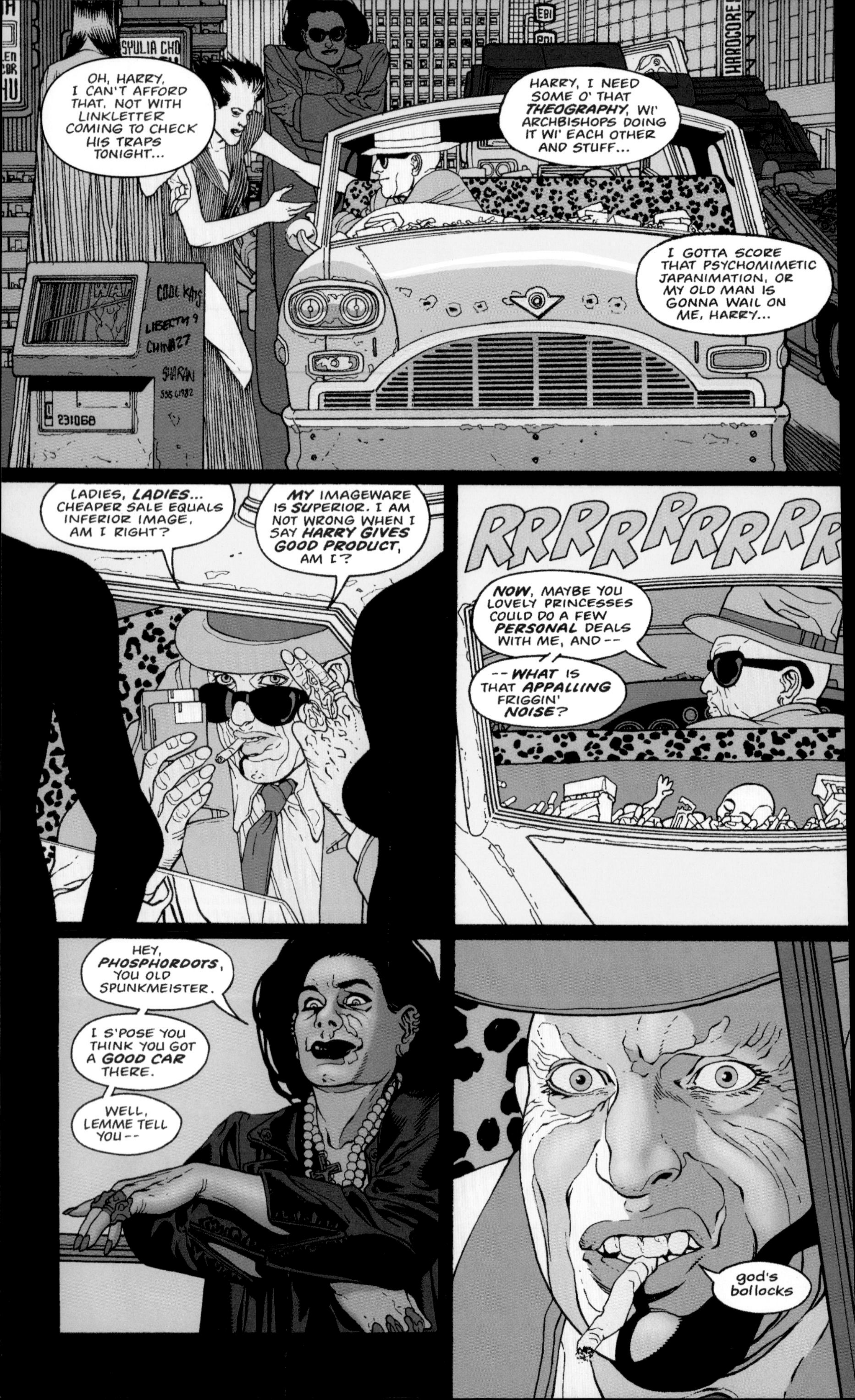
OH, HARRY, I CAN'T AFFORD THAT, NOT WITH LINKLETTER COMING TO CHECK HIS TRAPS TONIGHT...
HARRY, I NEED SOME O' THAT THEOGRAPHY, WI' ARCHBISHOPS DOING IT WI' EACH OTHER AND STUFF...
I GOTTA SCORE THAT PSYCHOMIMETIC JAPANIMATION, OR MY OLD MAN IS GONNA WAIL ON ME, HARRY...
LADIES, LADIES... CHEAPER SALE EQUALS INFERIOR IMAGE, AM I RIGHT?
MY IMAGEWARE IS SUPERIOR. I AM NOT WRONG WHEN I SAY HARRY GIVES GOOD PRODUCT, AM I?
RRRRRRRRRR
NOW, MAYBE YOU LOVELY PRINCESSES COULD DO A FEW PERSONAL DEALS WITH ME, AND --
-- WHAT IS THAT APPALLING FRIGGIN' NOISE?
HEY, PHOSPHORDOTS, YOU OLD SPUNKMEISTER.
I S'POSE YOU THINK YOU GOT A GOOD CAR THERE.
WELL, LEMME TELL YOU --
god's bollocks

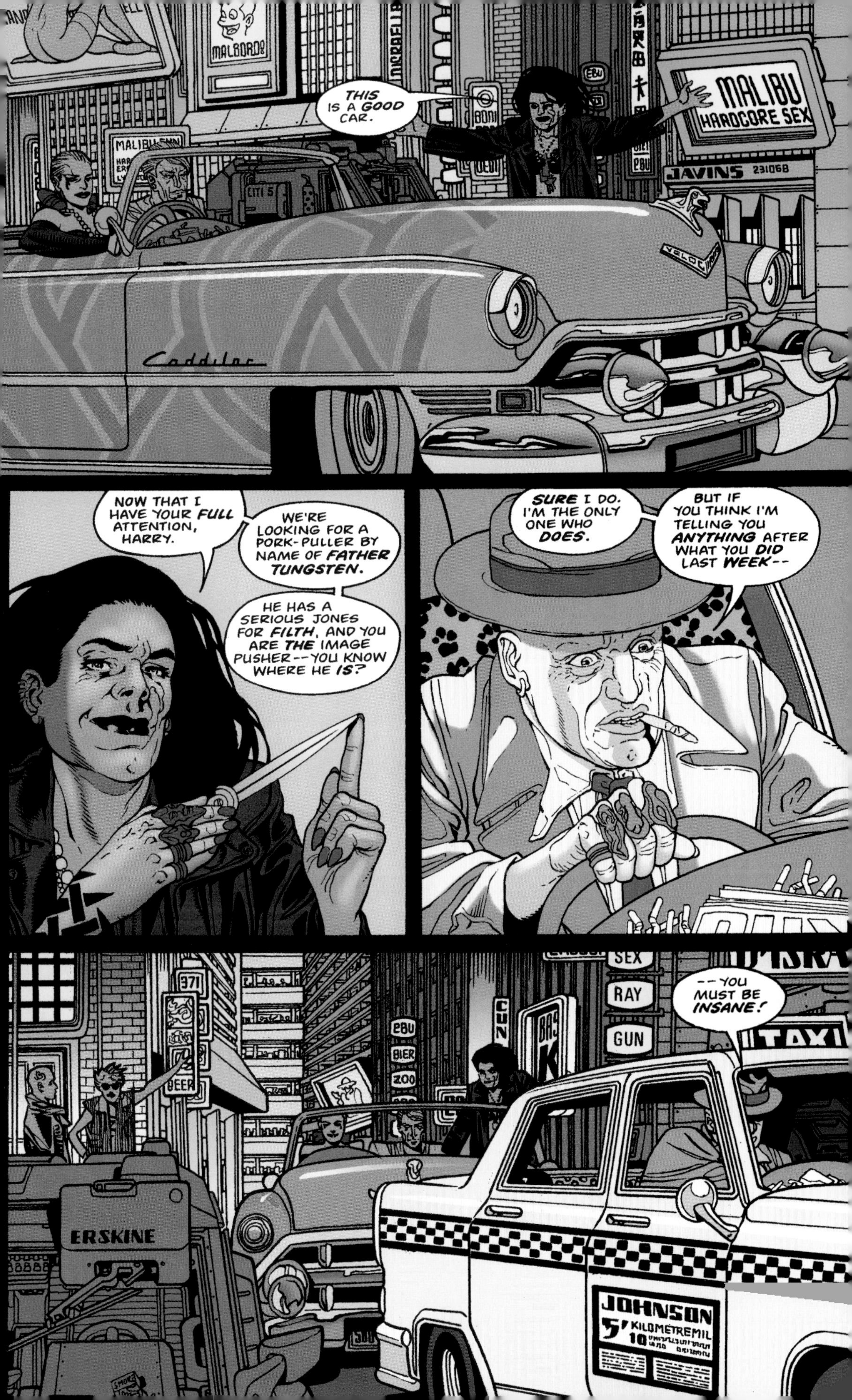
MALBORO
MALIBU
HARDCORE SEX
JAVINS 231068
THIS IS A GOOD CAR.
NOW THAT I HAVE YOUR FULL ATTENTION, HARRY.
WE'RE LOOKING FOR A PORK-PULLER BY NAME OF FATHER TUNGSTEN.
HE HAS A SERIOUS JONES FOR FILTH, AND YOU ARE THE IMAGE PUSHER--YOU KNOW WHERE HE IS?
SURE I DO. I'M THE ONLY ONE WHO DOES.
BUT IF YOU THINK I'M TELLING YOU ANYTHING AFTER WHAT YOU DID LAST WEEK--
SEX
RAY
GUN
BEER
ERSKINE
--YOU MUST BE INSANE!
TAXI
JOHNSON
KILOMETREMIL

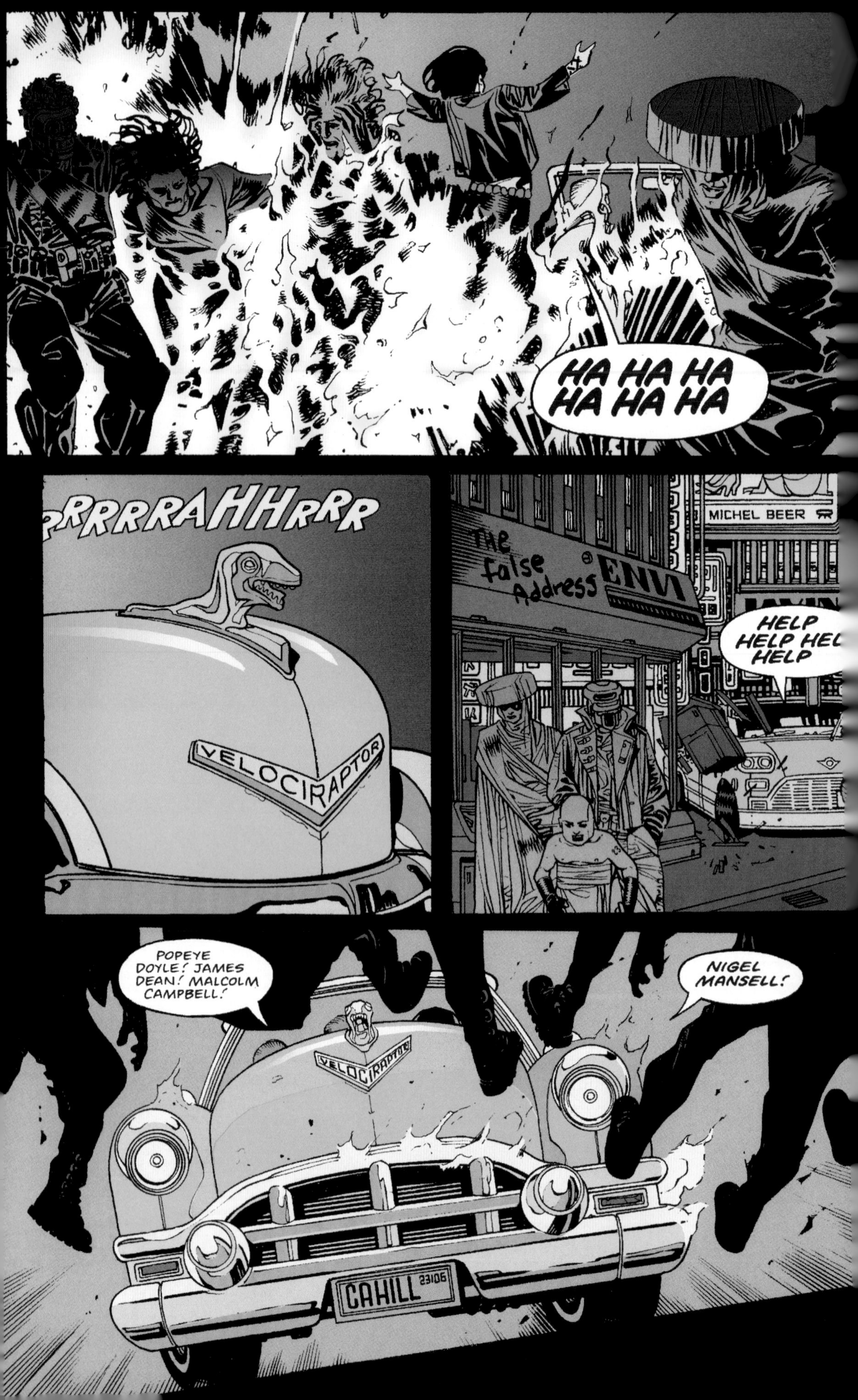
HA HA HA
HA HA HA
RRRRRAHHRRR
VELOCIRAPTOR
THE false Address
MICHEL BEER
HELP HELP HEL HELP
POPEYE DOYLE! JAMES DEAN! MALCOLM CAMPBELL!
NIGEL MANSELL!
VELOCIRAPTOR
CAHILL 23106

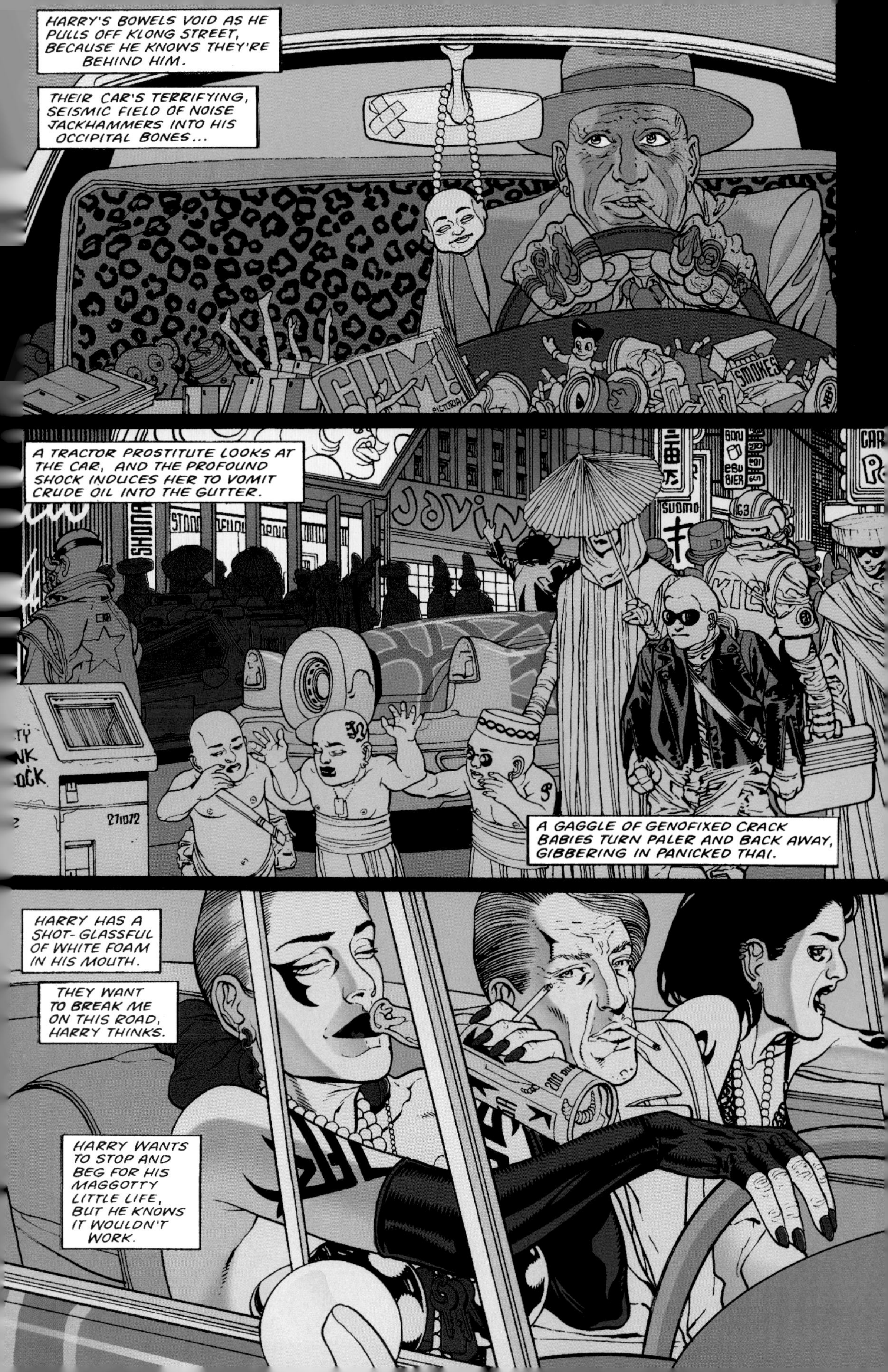
HARRY'S BOWELS VOID AS HE PULLS OFF KLONG STREET, BECAUSE HE KNOWS THEY'RE BEHIND HIM.
THEIR CAR'S TERRIFYING, SEISMIC FIELD OF NOISE JACKHAMMERS INTO HIS OCCIPITAL BONES...
GUM!
SMOKES
A TRACTOR PROSTITUTE LOOKS AT THE CAR, AND THE PROFOUND SHOCK INDUCES HER TO VOMIT CRUDE OIL INTO THE GUTTER.
SUOMO
A GAGGLE OF GENOFIXED CRACK BABIES TURN PALER AND BACK AWAY, GIBBERING IN PANICKED THAI.
HARRY HAS A SHOT-GLASSFUL OF WHITE FOAM IN HIS MOUTH.
THEY WANT TO BREAK ME ON THIS ROAD, HARRY THINKS.
HARRY WANTS TO STOP AND BEG FOR HIS MAGGOTTY LITTLE LIFE, BUT HE KNOWS IT WOULDN'T WORK.

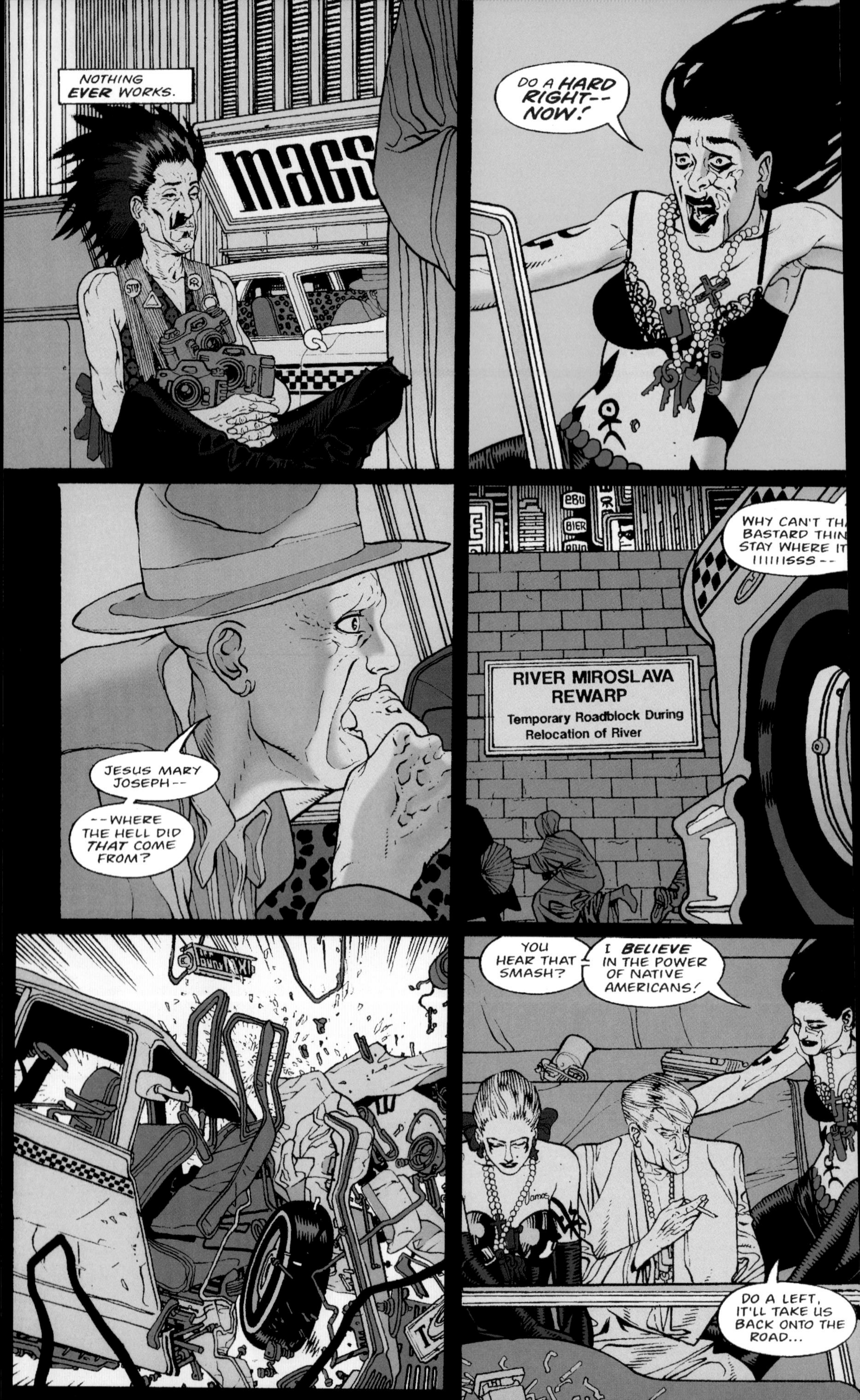
NOTHING EVER WORKS.
DO A HARD RIGHT-- NOW!
JESUS MARY JOSEPH--
--WHERE THE HELL DID THAT COME FROM?
WHY CAN'T THA BASTARD THIN STAY WHERE IT IIIIIISSS--
RIVER MIROSLAVA REWARP
Temporary Roadblock During Relocation of River
YOU HEAR THAT SMASH?
I BELIEVE IN THE POWER OF NATIVE AMERICANS!
DO A LEFT, IT'LL TAKE US BACK ONTO THE ROAD...

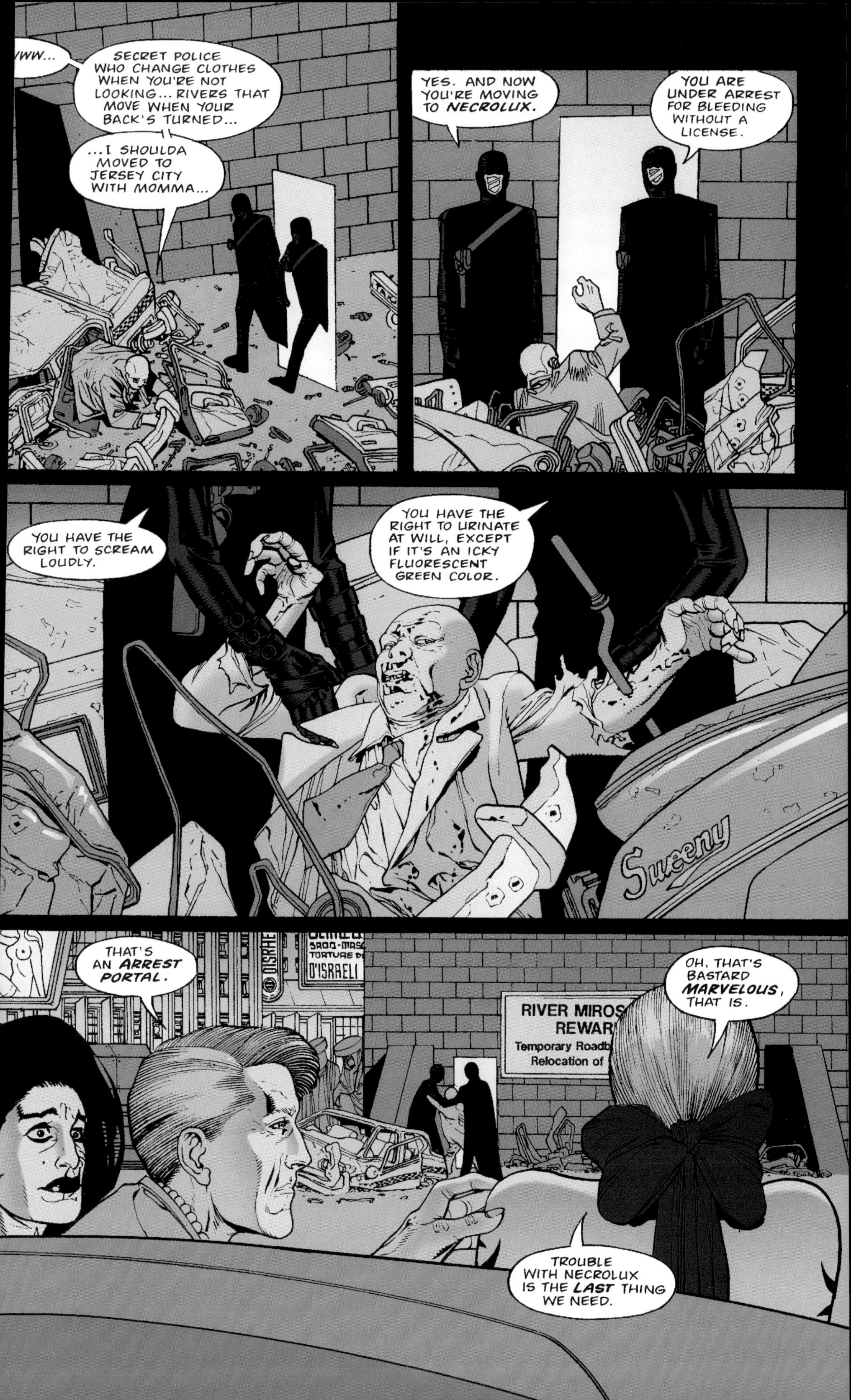

...WWW...
SECRET POLICE WHO CHANGE CLOTHES WHEN YOU'RE NOT LOOKING... RIVERS THAT MOVE WHEN YOUR BACK'S TURNED...
...I SHOULDA MOVED TO JERSEY CITY WITH MOMMA...
YES. AND NOW YOU'RE MOVING TO *NECROLUX*.
YOU ARE UNDER ARREST FOR BLEEDING WITHOUT A LICENSE.
YOU HAVE THE RIGHT TO SCREAM LOUDLY.
YOU HAVE THE RIGHT TO URINATE AT WILL, EXCEPT IF IT'S AN ICKY FLUORESCENT GREEN COLOR.
Sweeny
THAT'S AN *ARREST PORTAL*.
D'ISRAELI
RIVER MIROS
REWAR
Temporary Roadb
Relocation of
OH, THAT'S BASTARD *MARVELOUS*, THAT IS.
TROUBLE WITH NECROLUX IS THE *LAST* THING WE NEED.

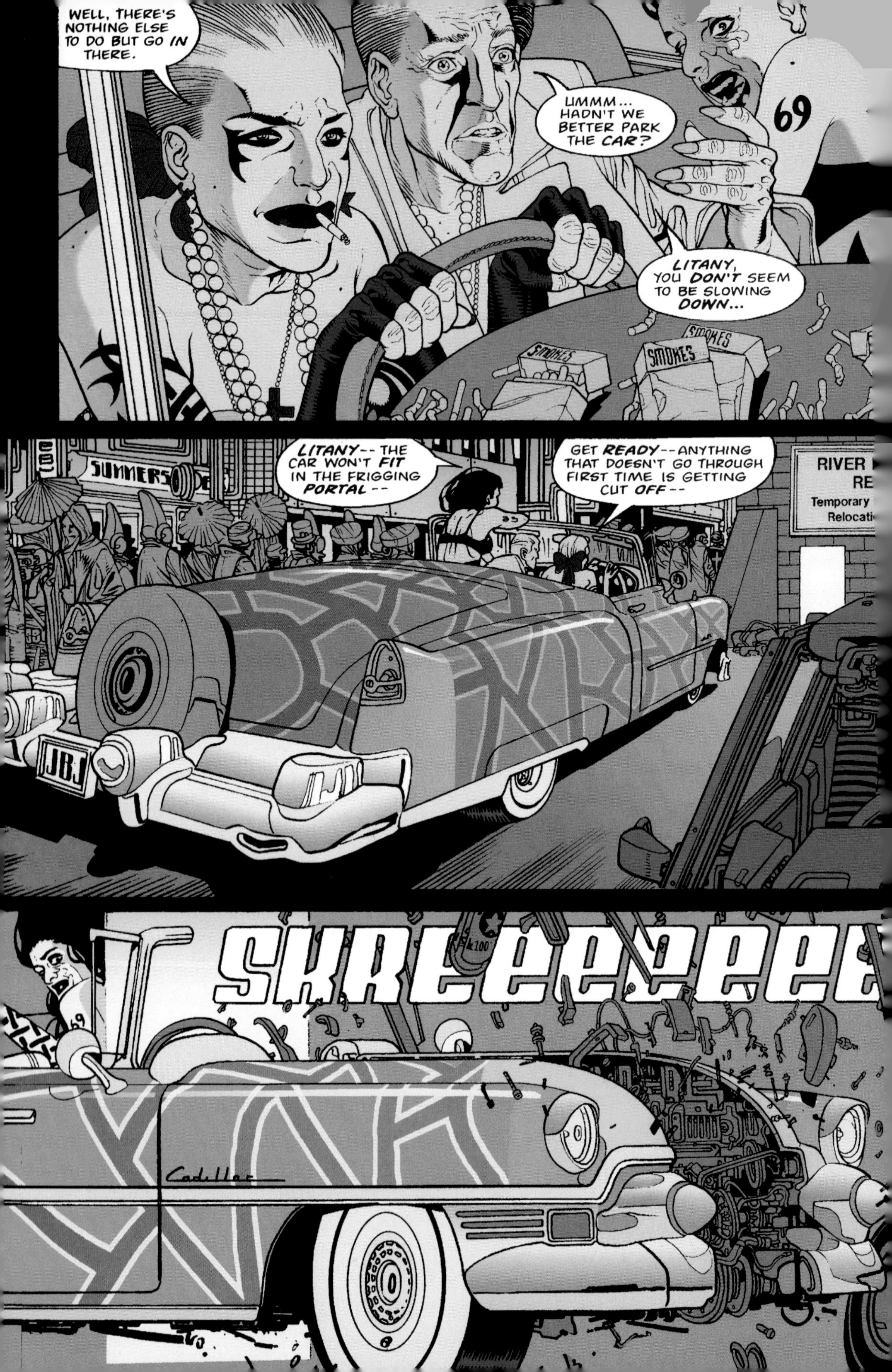
WELL, THERE'S NOTHING ELSE TO DO BUT GO *IN* THERE.
UMMM... HADN'T WE BETTER PARK THE *CAR?*
LITANY, YOU *DON'T* SEEM TO BE SLOWING *DOWN...*
LITANY-- THE CAR WON'T *FIT* IN THE FRIGGING *PORTAL*--
GET *READY*--ANYTHING THAT DOESN'T GO THROUGH FIRST TIME IS GETTING CUT *OFF*--
SKREEEEEEE

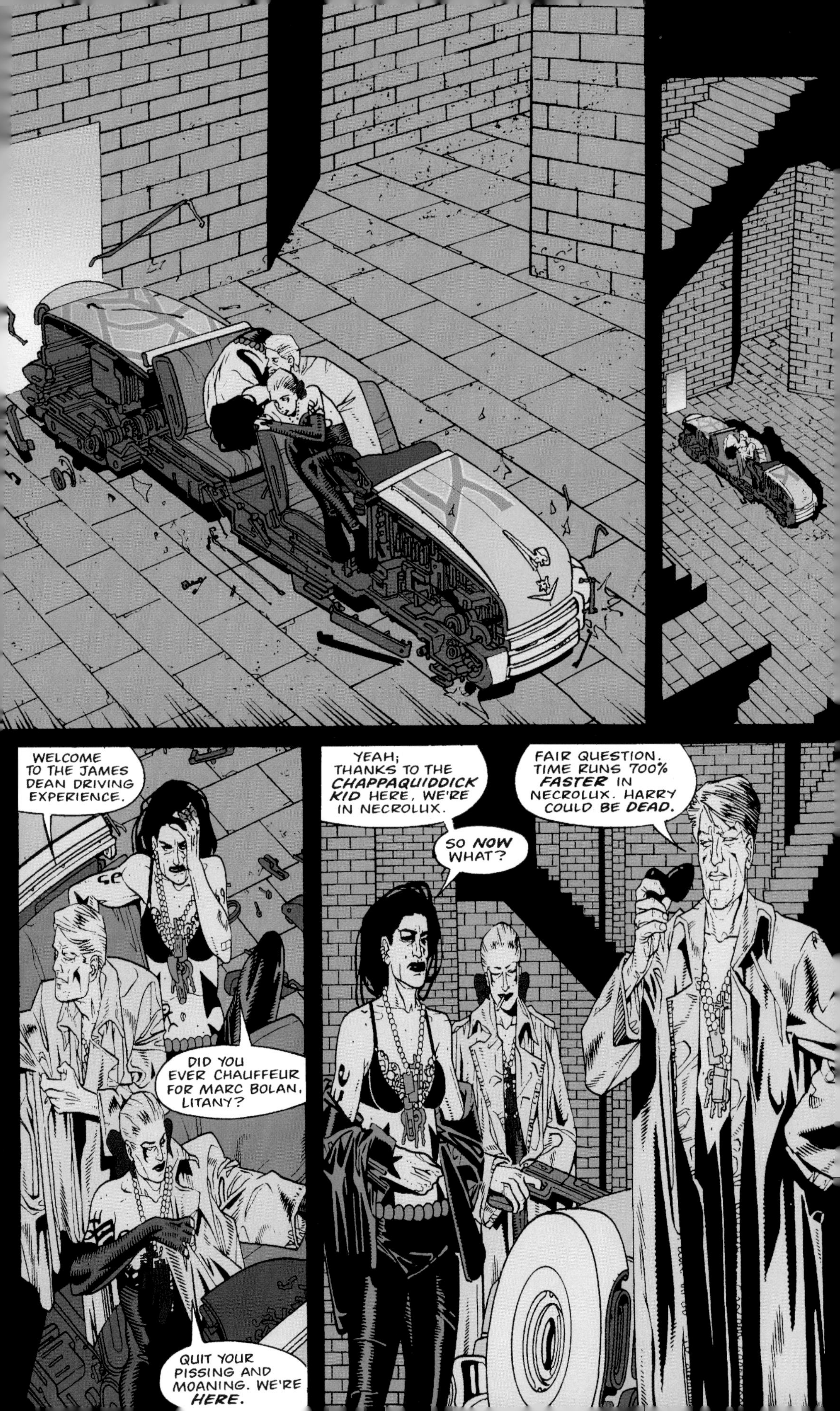

WELCOME TO THE JAMES DEAN DRIVING EXPERIENCE.
DID YOU EVER CHAUFFEUR FOR MARC BOLAN, LITANY?
QUIT YOUR PISSING AND MOANING. WE'RE HERE.
YEAH; THANKS TO THE CHAPPAQUIDDICK KID HERE, WE'RE IN NECROLUX.
SO NOW WHAT?
FAIR QUESTION. TIME RUNS 700% FASTER IN NECROLUX. HARRY COULD BE DEAD.

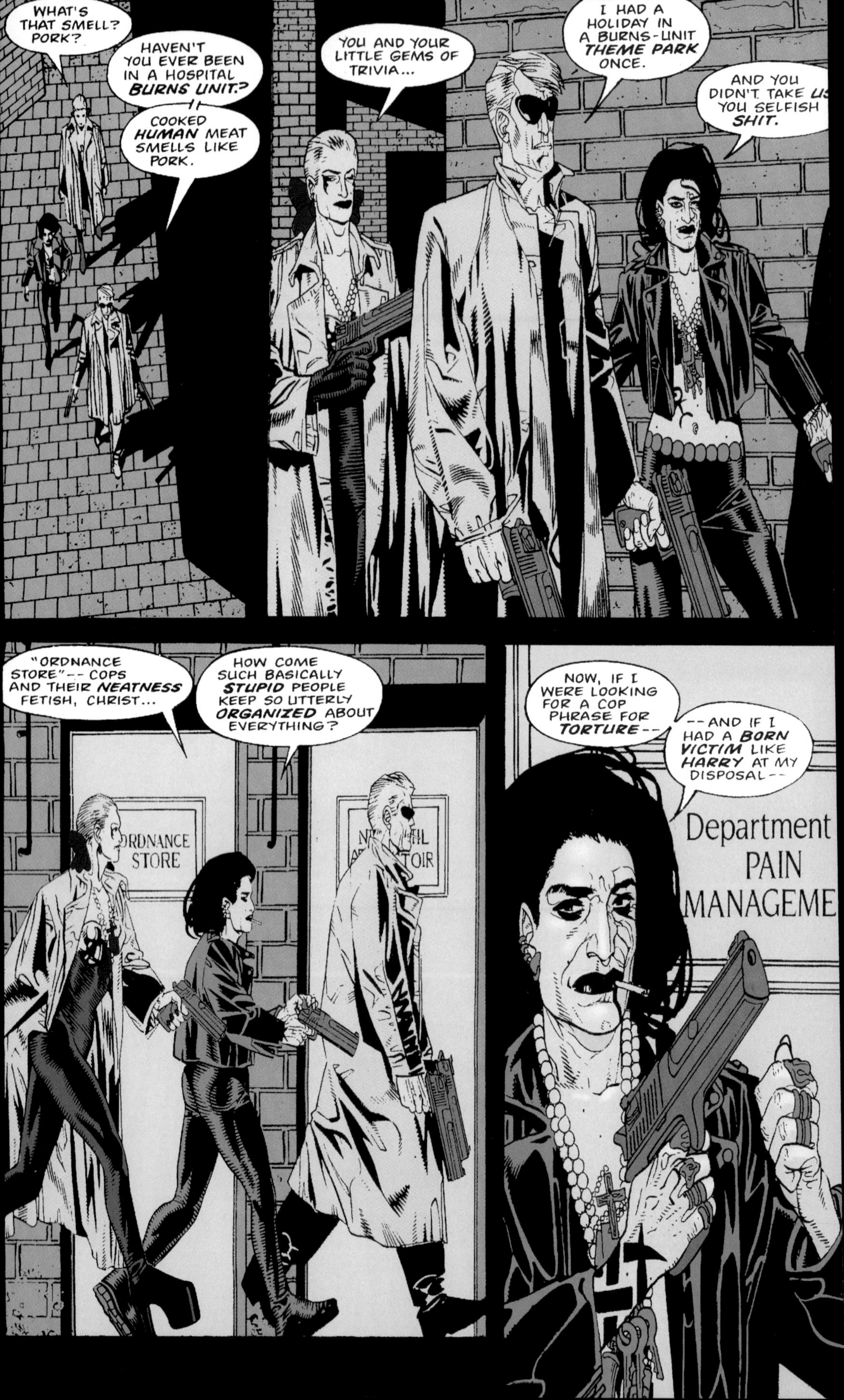
WHAT'S THAT SMELL? PORK?
HAVEN'T YOU EVER BEEN IN A HOSPITAL BURNS UNIT?
COOKED HUMAN MEAT SMELLS LIKE PORK.
YOU AND YOUR LITTLE GEMS OF TRIVIA...
I HAD A HOLIDAY IN A BURNS-UNIT THEME PARK ONCE.
AND YOU DIDN'T TAKE US YOU SELFISH SHIT.
"ORDNANCE STORE"-- COPS AND THEIR NEATNESS FETISH, CHRIST...
HOW COME SUCH BASICALLY STUPID PEOPLE KEEP SO UTTERLY ORGANIZED ABOUT EVERYTHING?
ORDNANCE STORE
NOW, IF I WERE LOOKING FOR A COP PHRASE FOR TORTURE--
--AND IF I HAD A BORN VICTIM LIKE HARRY AT MY DISPOSAL--
Department
PAIN
MANAGEME

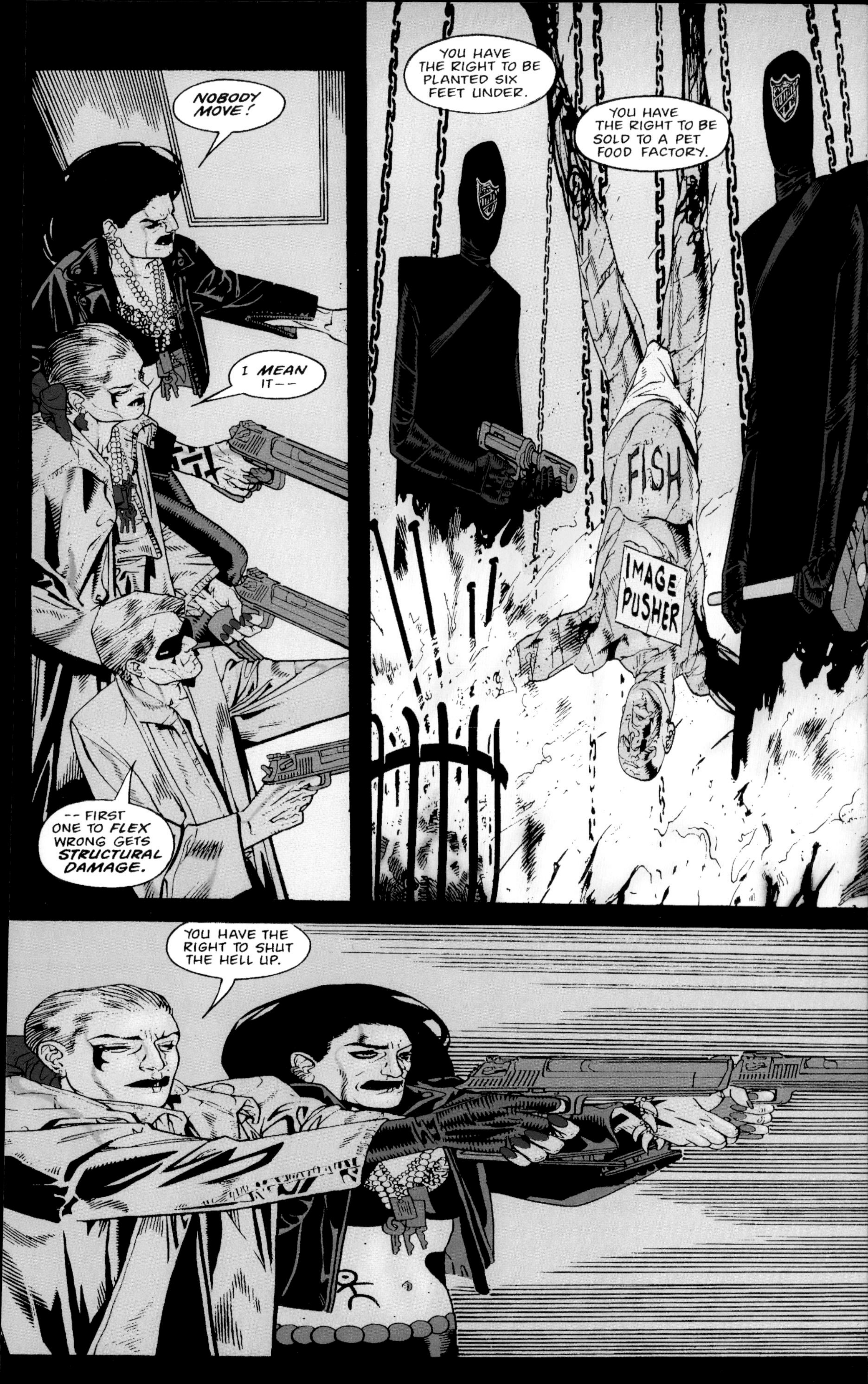
NOBODY MOVE!
I MEAN IT--
--FIRST ONE TO FLEX WRONG GETS STRUCTURAL DAMAGE.
YOU HAVE THE RIGHT TO BE PLANTED SIX FEET UNDER.
YOU HAVE THE RIGHT TO BE SOLD TO A PET FOOD FACTORY.
FISH
IMAGE PUSHER
YOU HAVE THE RIGHT TO SHUT THE HELL UP.

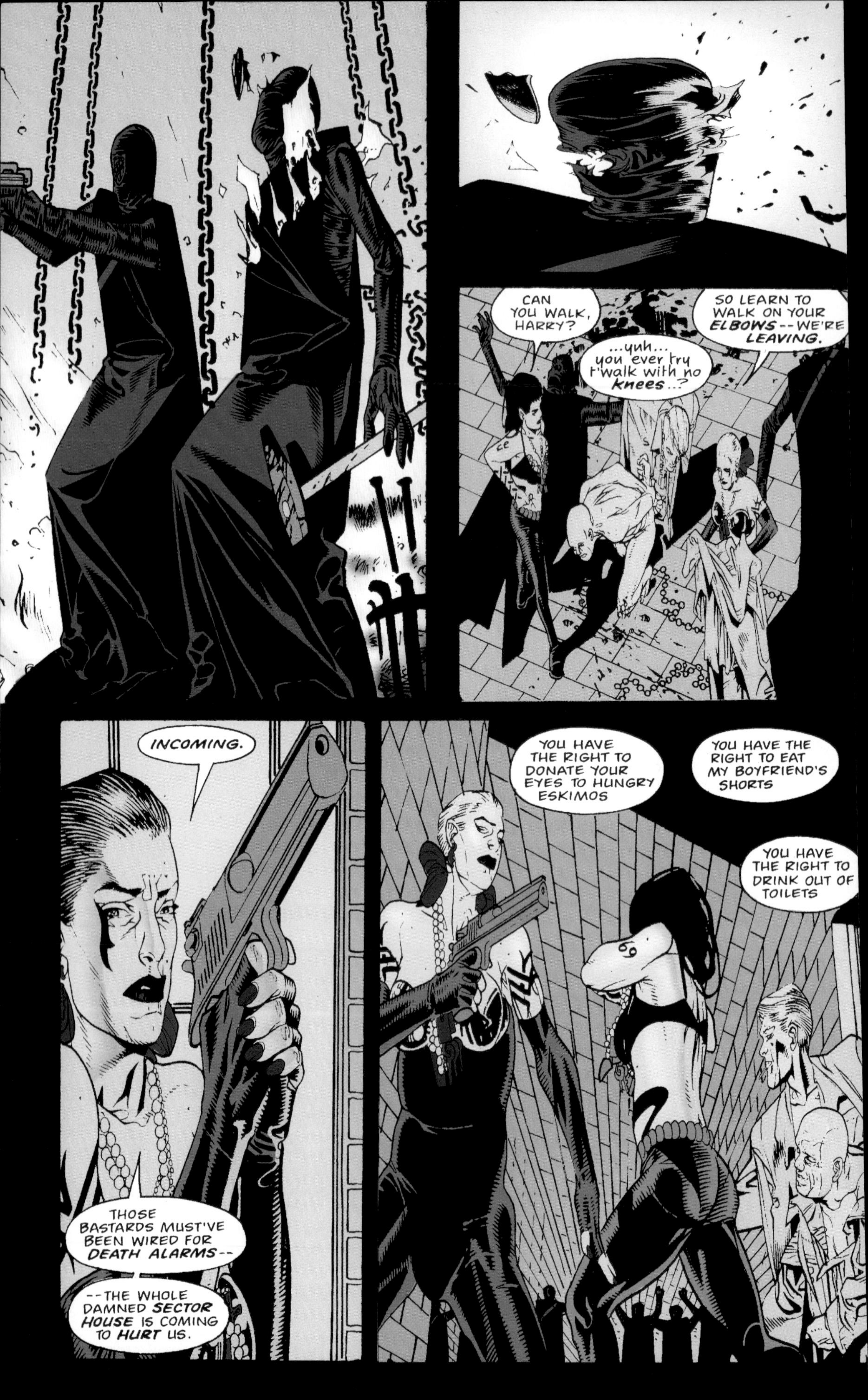
CAN YOU WALK, HARRY?
...yuh... you ever try t'walk with no knees..?
SO LEARN TO WALK ON YOUR ELBOWS--WE'RE LEAVING.
INCOMING.
THOSE BASTARDS MUST'VE BEEN WIRED FOR DEATH ALARMS--
--THE WHOLE DAMNED SECTOR HOUSE IS COMING TO HURT US.
YOU HAVE THE RIGHT TO DONATE YOUR EYES TO HUNGRY ESKIMOS
YOU HAVE THE RIGHT TO EAT MY BOYFRIEND'S SHORTS
YOU HAVE THE RIGHT TO DRINK OUT OF TOILETS

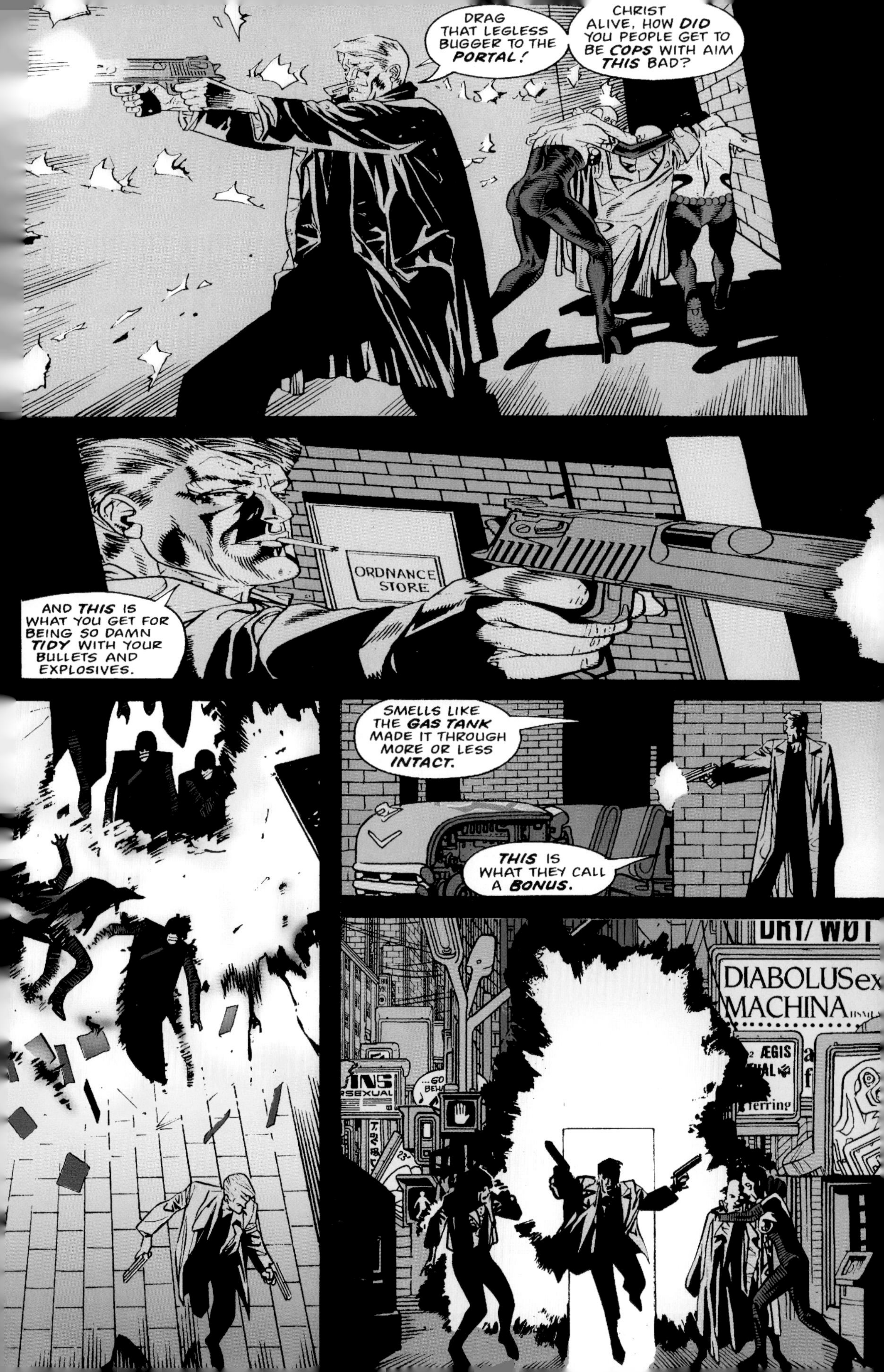
DRAG THAT LEGLESS BUGGER TO THE PORTAL!
CHRIST ALIVE, HOW DID YOU PEOPLE GET TO BE COPS WITH AIM THIS BAD?
ORDNANCE STORE
AND THIS IS WHAT YOU GET FOR BEING SO DAMN TIDY WITH YOUR BULLETS AND EXPLOSIVES.
SMELLS LIKE THE GAS TANK MADE IT THROUGH MORE OR LESS INTACT.
THIS IS WHAT THEY CALL A BONUS.
DIABOLUS ex MACHINA

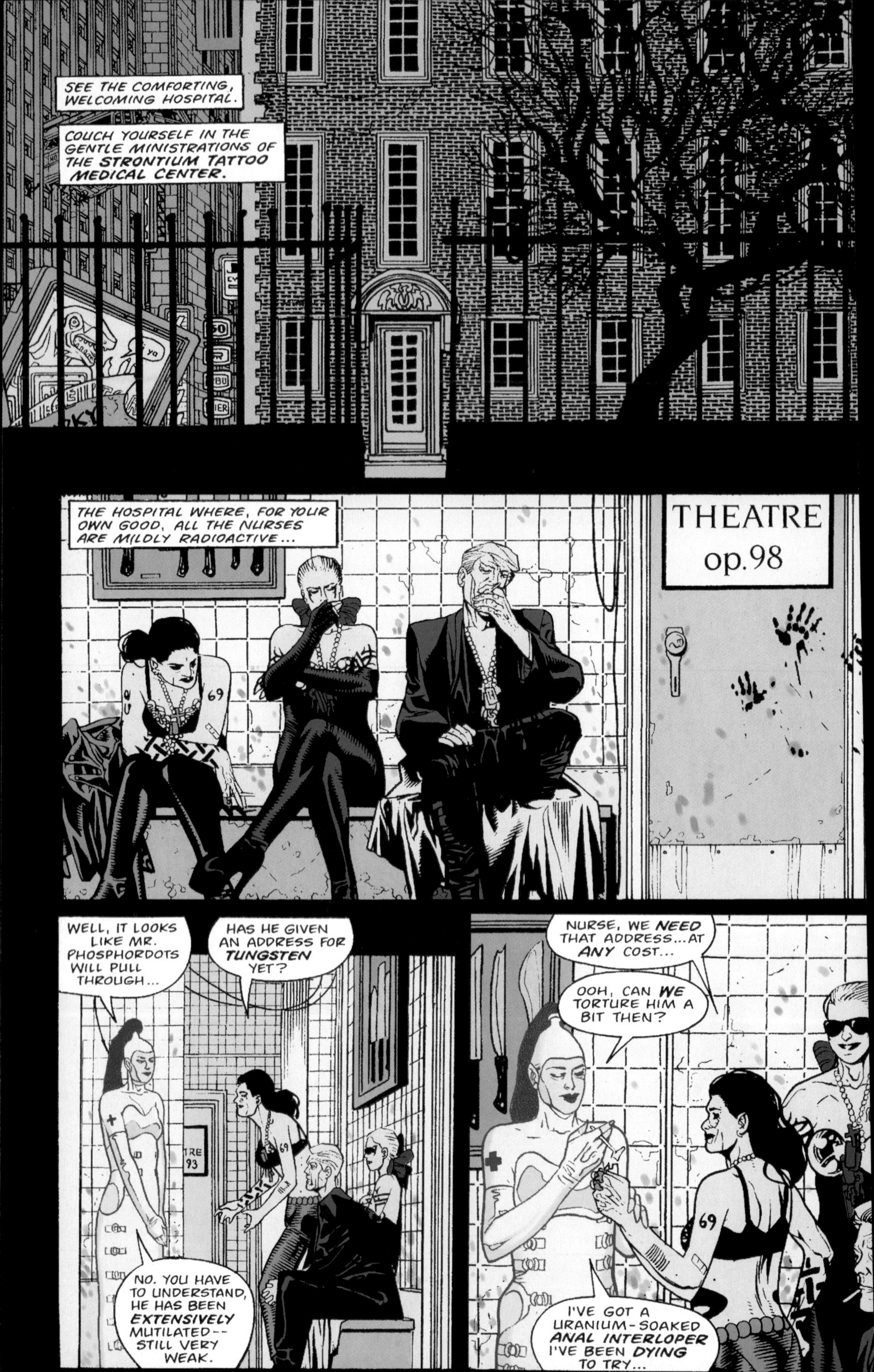

SEE THE COMFORTING, WELCOMING HOSPITAL.
COUCH YOURSELF IN THE GENTLE MINISTRATIONS OF THE STRONTIUM TATTOO MEDICAL CENTER.
THE HOSPITAL WHERE, FOR YOUR OWN GOOD, ALL THE NURSES ARE MILDLY RADIOACTIVE...
THEATRE op.98
WELL, IT LOOKS LIKE MR. PHOSPHORDOTS WILL PULL THROUGH...
HAS HE GIVEN AN ADDRESS FOR TUNGSTEN YET?
NO. YOU HAVE TO UNDERSTAND, HE HAS BEEN EXTENSIVELY MUTILATED-- STILL VERY WEAK.
NURSE, WE NEED THAT ADDRESS... AT ANY COST...
OOH, CAN WE TORTURE HIM A BIT THEN?
I'VE GOT A URANIUM-SOAKED ANAL INTERLOPER I'VE BEEN DYING TO TRY...

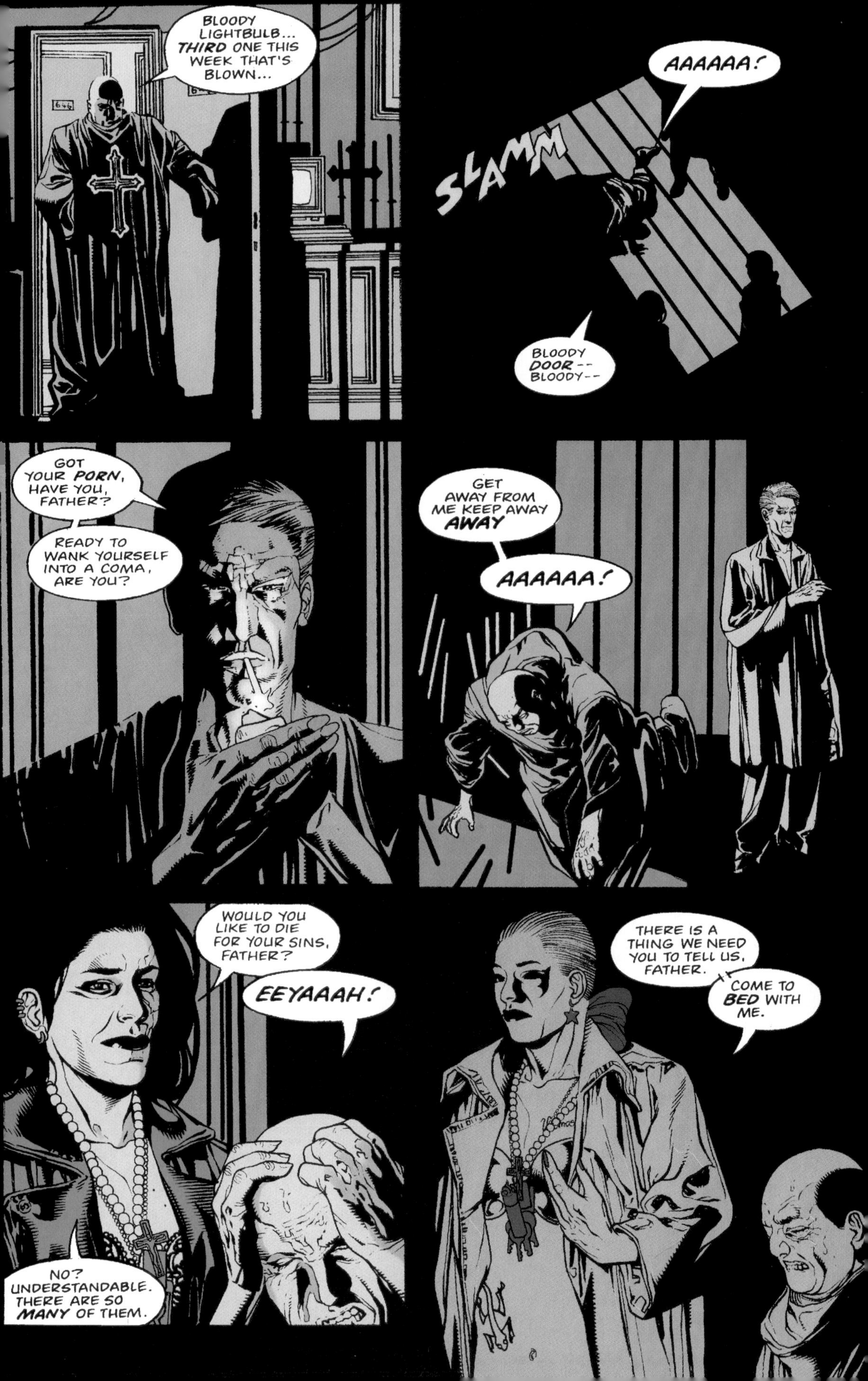
BLOODY LIGHTBULB... THIRD ONE THIS WEEK THAT'S BLOWN...
AAAAAA!
SLAMM
BLOODY DOOR-- BLOODY--
GOT YOUR PORN, HAVE YOU, FATHER?
READY TO WANK YOURSELF INTO A COMA, ARE YOU?
GET AWAY FROM ME KEEP AWAY AWAY
AAAAAA!
WOULD YOU LIKE TO DIE FOR YOUR SINS, FATHER?
EEYAAAH!
NO? UNDERSTANDABLE. THERE ARE SO MANY OF THEM.
THERE IS A THING WE NEED YOU TO TELL US, FATHER.
COME TO BED WITH ME.

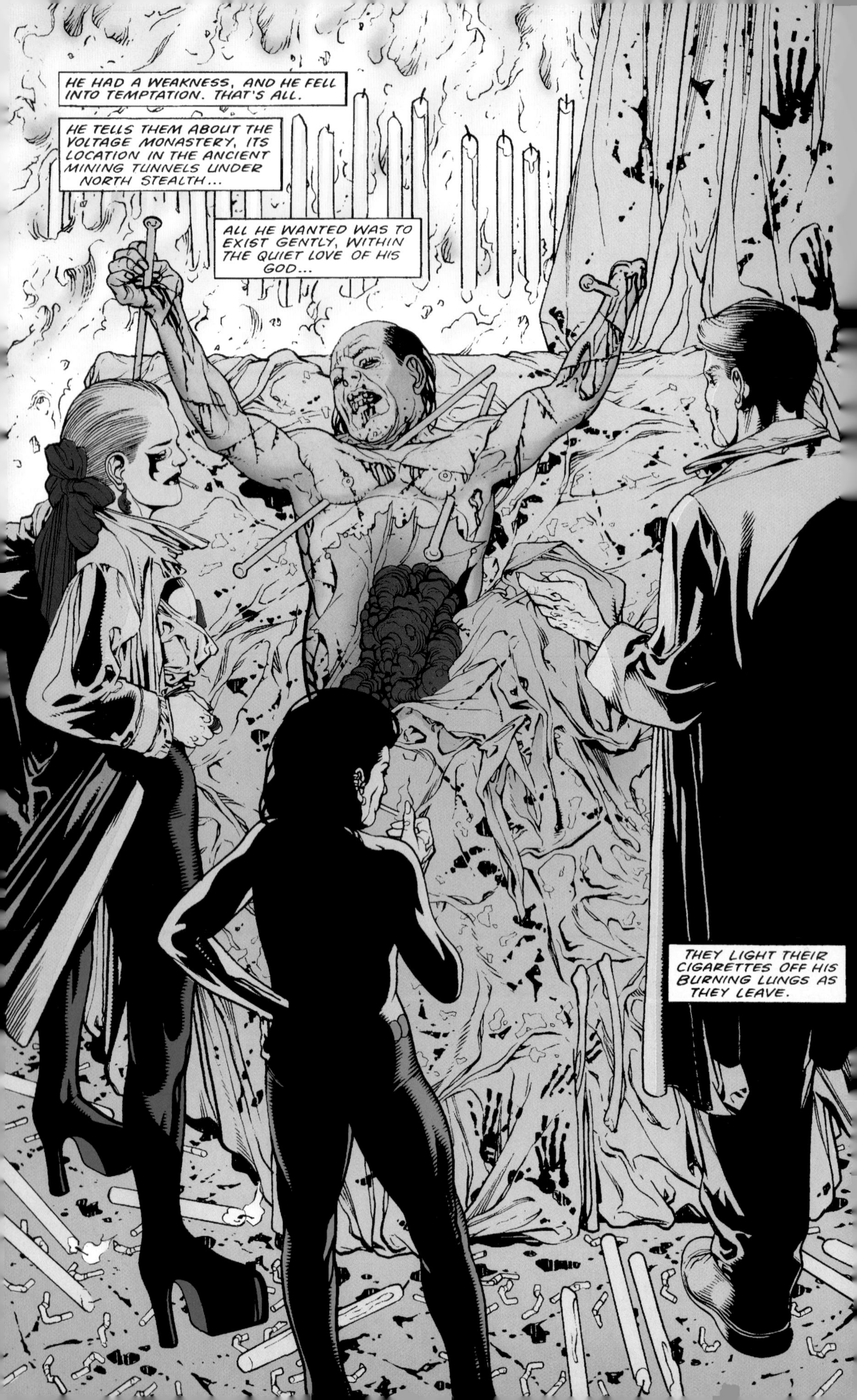
HE HAD A WEAKNESS, AND HE FELL INTO TEMPTATION. THAT'S ALL.
HE TELLS THEM ABOUT THE VOLTAGE MONASTERY, ITS LOCATION IN THE ANCIENT MINING TUNNELS UNDER NORTH STEALTH...
ALL HE WANTED WAS TO EXIST GENTLY, WITHIN THE QUIET LOVE OF HIS GOD...
THEY LIGHT THEIR CIGARETTES OFF HIS BURNING LUNGS AS THEY LEAVE.

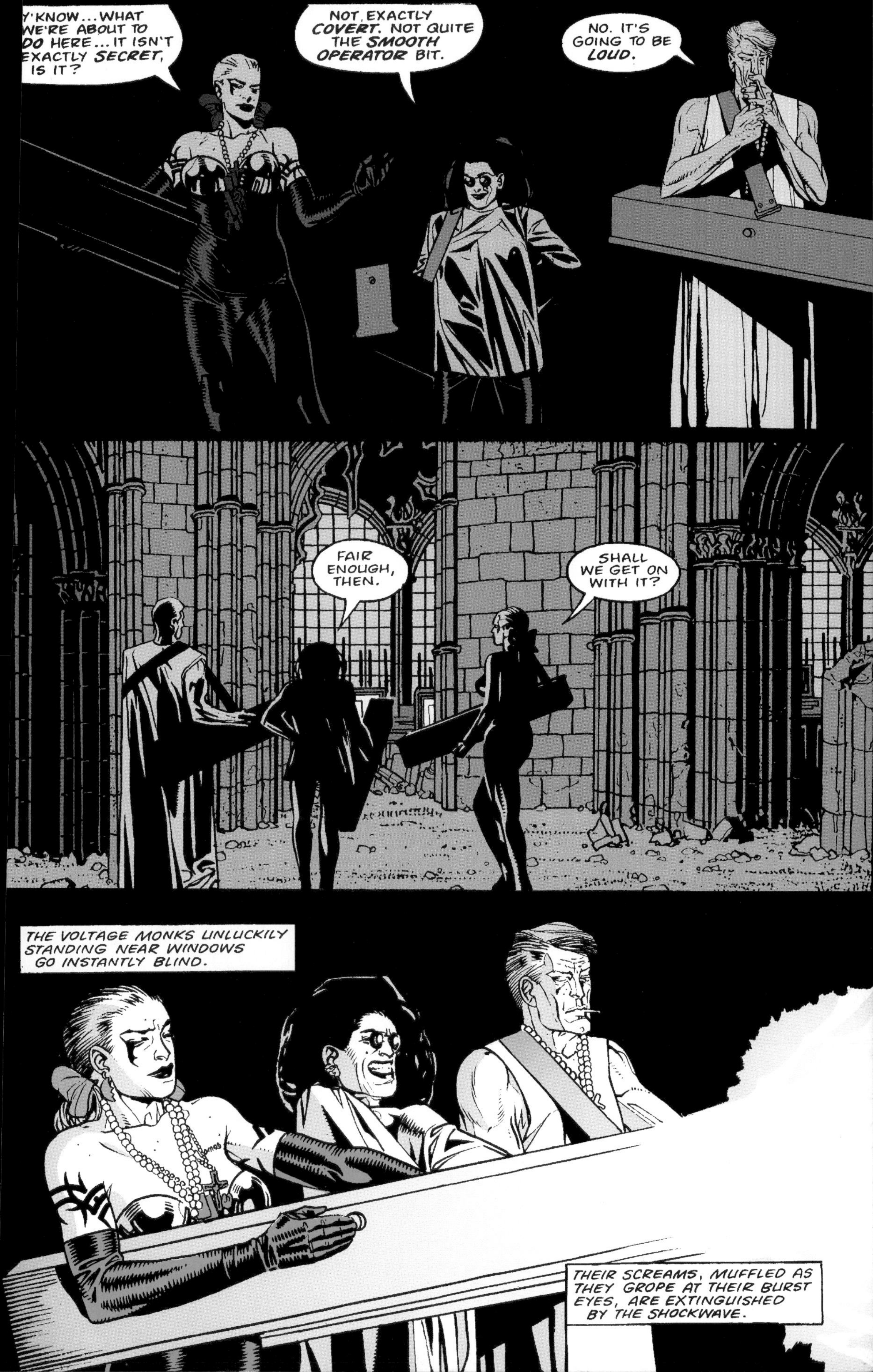
Y'KNOW... WHAT WE'RE ABOUT TO DO HERE... IT ISN'T EXACTLY SECRET, IS IT?
NOT, EXACTLY COVERT. NOT QUITE THE SMOOTH OPERATOR BIT.
NO. IT'S GOING TO BE LOUD.
FAIR ENOUGH, THEN.
SHALL WE GET ON WITH IT?
THE VOLTAGE MONKS UNLUCKILY STANDING NEAR WINDOWS GO INSTANTLY BLIND.
THEIR SCREAMS, MUFFLED AS THEY GROPE AT THEIR BURST EYES, ARE EXTINGUISHED BY THE SHOCKWAVE.

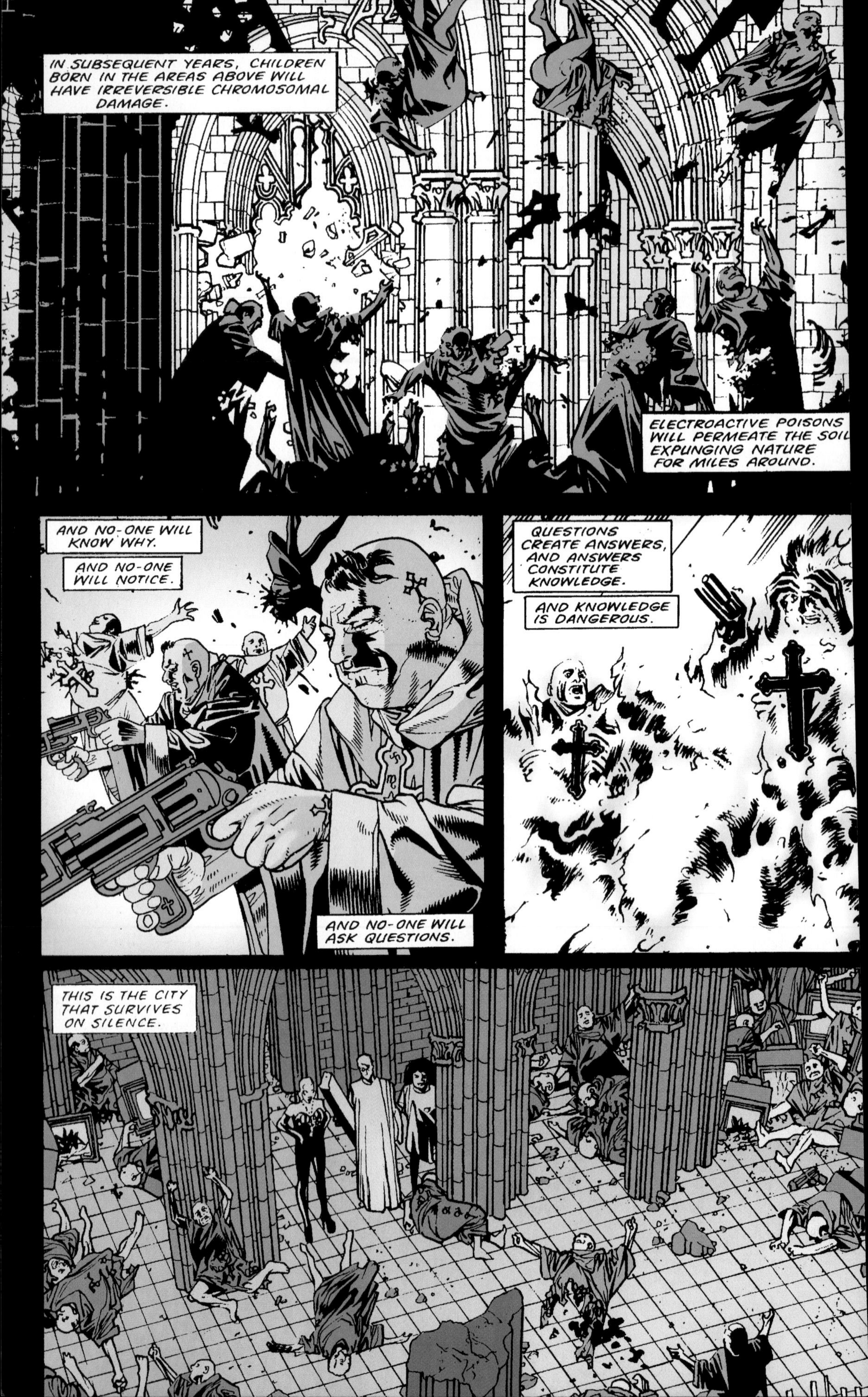
IN SUBSEQUENT YEARS, CHILDREN BORN IN THE AREAS ABOVE WILL HAVE IRREVERSIBLE CHROMOSOMAL DAMAGE.
ELECTROACTIVE POISONS WILL PERMEATE THE SOIL EXPUNGING NATURE FOR MILES AROUND.
AND NO-ONE WILL KNOW WHY.
AND NO-ONE WILL NOTICE.
AND NO-ONE WILL ASK QUESTIONS.
QUESTIONS CREATE ANSWERS, AND ANSWERS CONSTITUTE KNOWLEDGE.
AND KNOWLEDGE IS DANGEROUS.
THIS IS THE CITY THAT SURVIVES ON SILENCE.

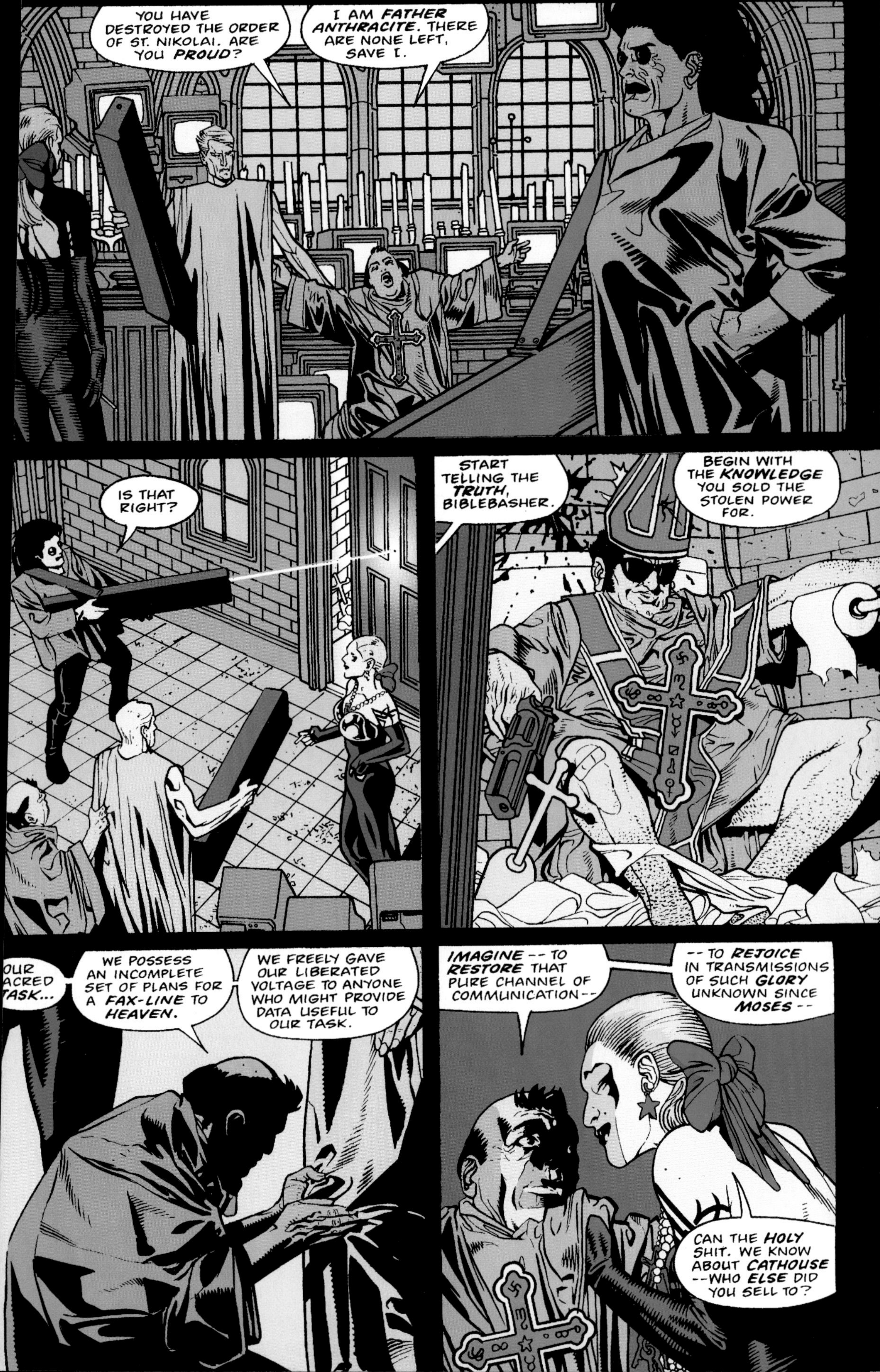
YOU HAVE DESTROYED THE ORDER OF ST. NIKOLAI. ARE YOU PROUD?
I AM FATHER ANTHRACITE. THERE ARE NONE LEFT, SAVE I.
IS THAT RIGHT?
START TELLING THE TRUTH, BIBLEBASHER.
BEGIN WITH THE KNOWLEDGE YOU SOLD THE STOLEN POWER FOR.
OUR SACRED TASK...
WE POSSESS AN INCOMPLETE SET OF PLANS FOR A FAX-LINE TO HEAVEN.
WE FREELY GAVE OUR LIBERATED VOLTAGE TO ANYONE WHO MIGHT PROVIDE DATA USEFUL TO OUR TASK.
IMAGINE -- TO RESTORE THAT PURE CHANNEL OF COMMUNICATION --
-- TO REJOICE IN TRANSMISSIONS OF SUCH GLORY UNKNOWN SINCE MOSES --
CAN THE HOLY SHIT. WE KNOW ABOUT CATHOUSE --WHO ELSE DID YOU SELL TO?

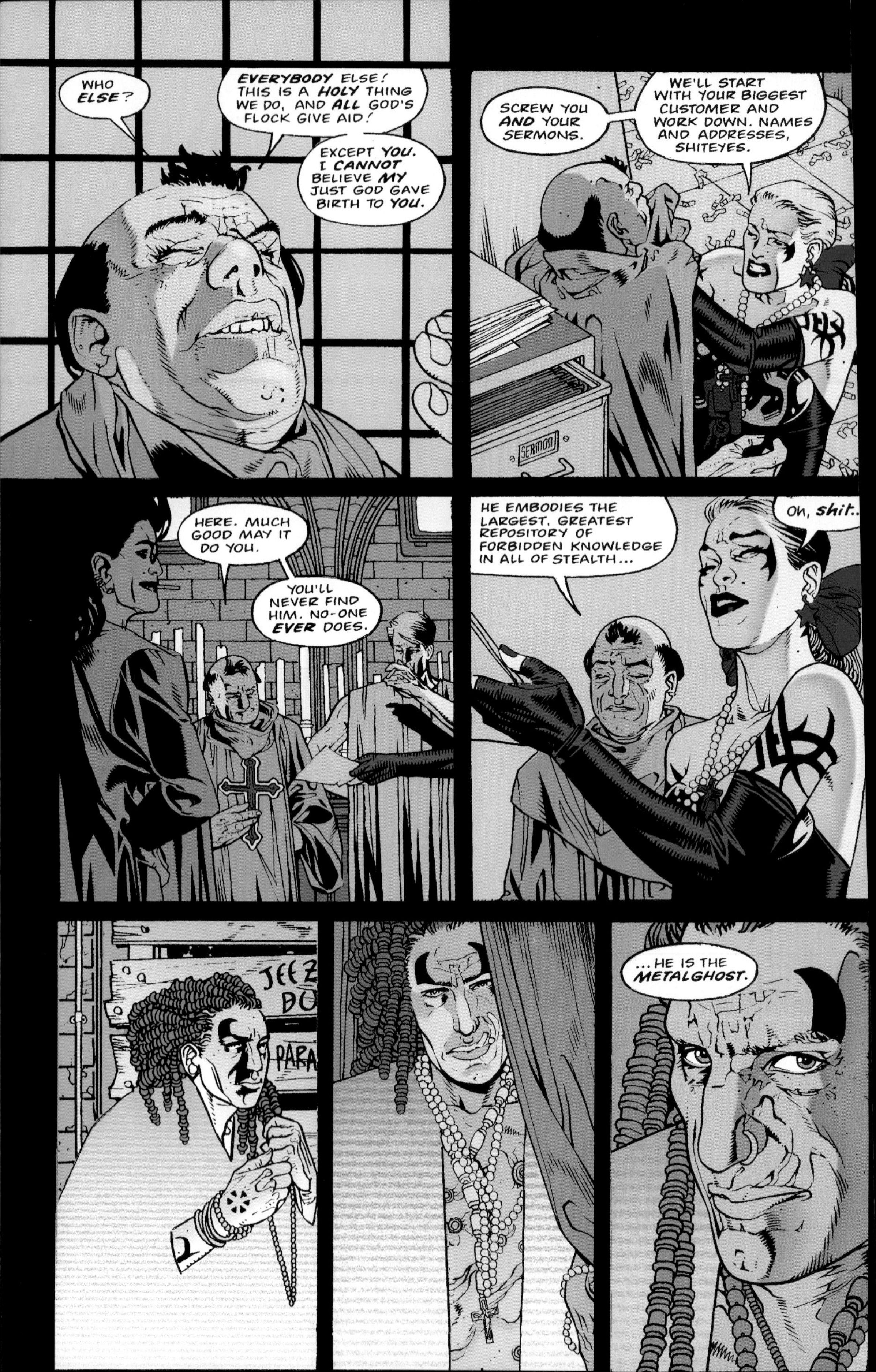
WHO ELSE?
EVERYBODY ELSE! THIS IS A HOLY THING WE DO, AND ALL GOD'S FLOCK GIVE AID!
EXCEPT YOU. I CANNOT BELIEVE MY JUST GOD GAVE BIRTH TO YOU.
SCREW YOU AND YOUR SERMONS.
WE'LL START WITH YOUR BIGGEST CUSTOMER AND WORK DOWN. NAMES AND ADDRESSES, SHITEYES.
SERMON
HERE. MUCH GOOD MAY IT DO YOU.
YOU'LL NEVER FIND HIM. NO-ONE EVER DOES.
HE EMBODIES THE LARGEST, GREATEST REPOSITORY OF FORBIDDEN KNOWLEDGE IN ALL OF STEALTH...
Oh, shit...
...HE IS THE METALGHOST.

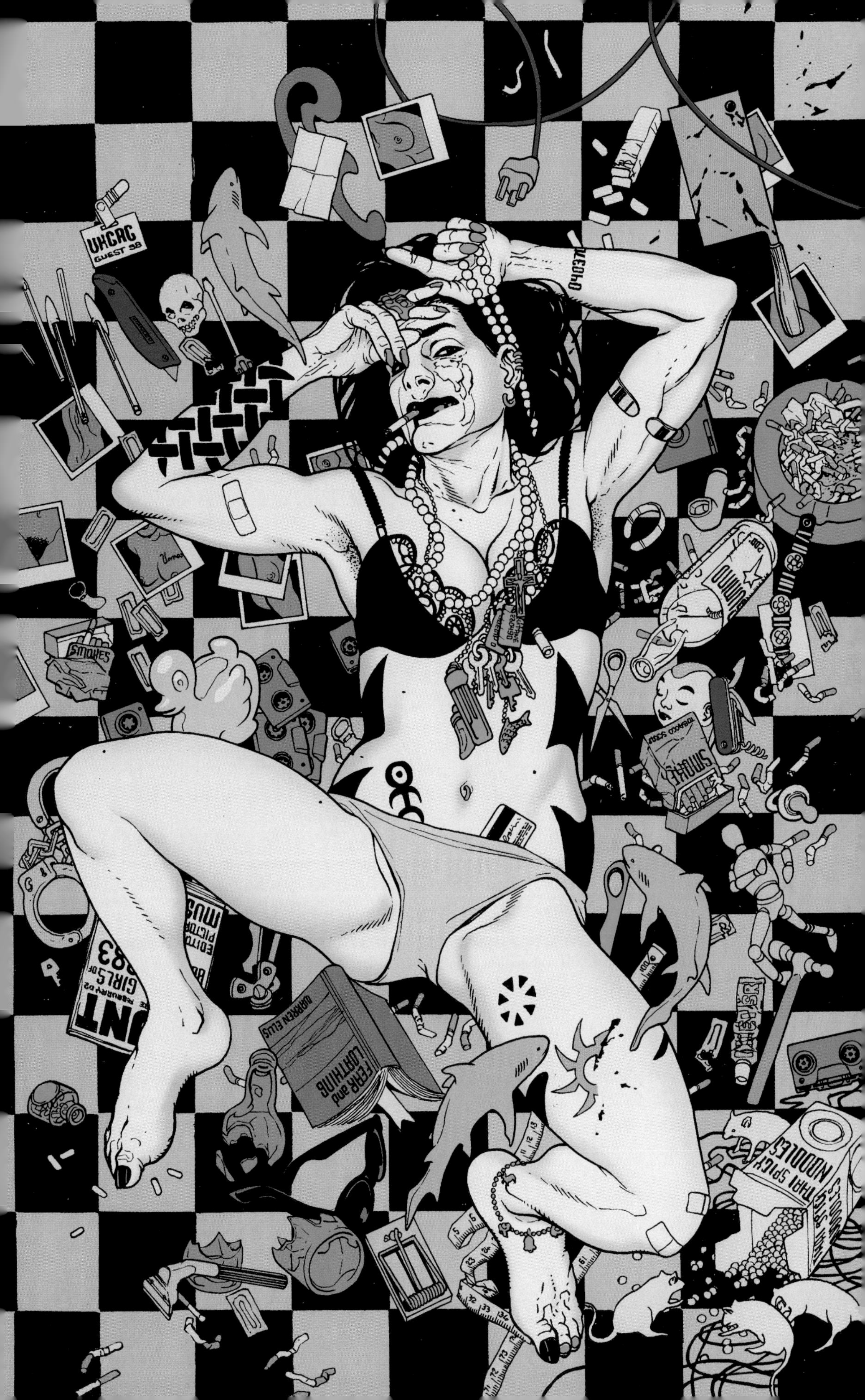
UKCAG
GUEST 98
SMOKES
WARREN ELLIS
FEAR and LOATHING
THAI SPICY NOODLES
TOBACCO SCRAP
SMOKE

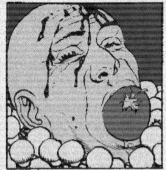

PHOSPHORDOTS, Harold Treece

Phosphordots pursues the illegal business practise of Image Pushing; amongst the illegal visual goods found on his person were:

Several **Carnographic** films. **Carnography**- snuff movies that culminate in the cadaver(s) being elaborately prepared in a kitchen and eaten. The thrill is not in the murder, but in what dish the victim will comprise. The titles found include *Smell Of Pork*, *Death By Biryani*, *Threat 2 Thighs*, *Pies For Satan*, and the truly vile *New Orleans Saucier Massacre*, which culminates in the defenestration (from a skyscraper penthouse) of five cheerleaders, who fall to their death into a vast steel vat of superheated chilli sauce.

Lightbooks; plastic blocks acting as display units for multimedia novels- fiction comprising text, illustration, animation, music, tactile input and olfactory performances. Some of these books use the highly illegal taste function, which allows the 'reader' to lick the protagonists.

All the titles Phosphordots carries are suppressed; the psychoactive texts *Interior Flowers* and *Goat Uplink Detectives*; *Piss Christ*, *The Wet Novel*, *My Friendly Blurred Days*, whose illustrations create senility in the reader; *The Savage Notebook Of Chairthing Butthole*, the mind-blistering ideology transmitted from the Greater Magellanic Cloud and *Lust For Polish*, an omnisexual porn-romance concerning a married couple and a seductive handbag. The book transmits a neural signal that induces unnatural desires for furniture.

Dirty Postcards; street nomenclature for rectangular neurostim tablets that jack into custom-designed groin-mounted cyberworks for unclean pleasures. It should be noted that it is spectacularly illegal for anyone even to have <u>heard</u> of these devices. Titles include *Honey's Dead But I Still Fancy Her*, *Taking Grandad For A Ride*, *Streetwalker Amputee*, *Hot Love Apres Dissection*, *Swinging Komodo Dragons*, *The Chipmunk In Miss Jones*, and *Moist Swedish Treetrunk*.

The last item on the original manifest, *Fantasies in Creosote*, has been appropriated for office use.

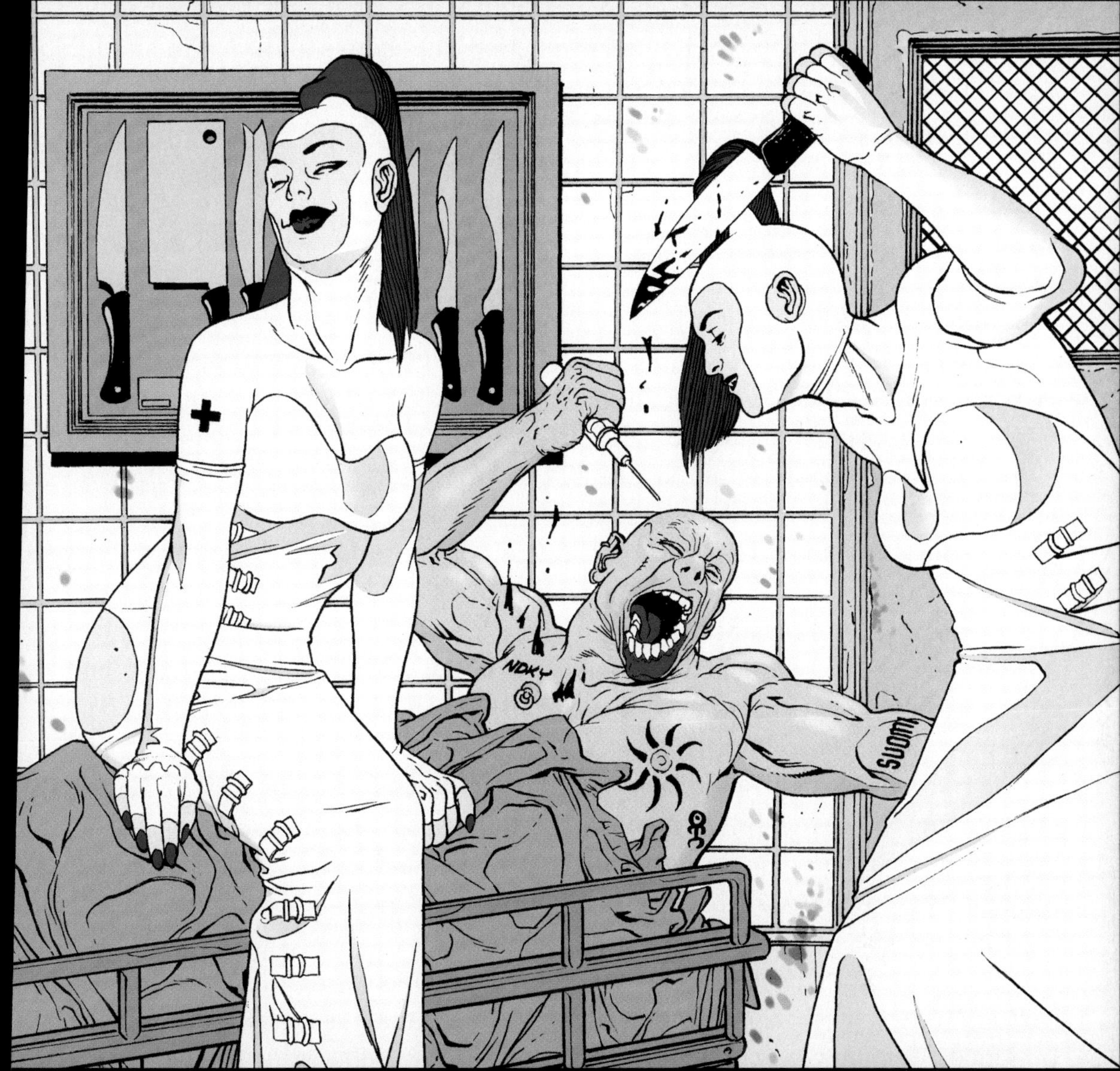
NDKY
SUOMI

STRONTIUM TATTOO NURSES

GLOWING BEAUTY!

with the Nurses from The Strontium Tattoo Medical Center

Hospitals are real boring places, where people bleed and die and stuff, right, girls? The only interestin' thing about 'em is those really wild prolapses that the wrinkly old bowel-cancer patients can do, right?

Wrong! As anyone who's stopped in at that spooky gaff on Klong Street can tell you, that ain't all hospitals are! God-damn, the *Strontium Tattoo Medical Center* is practically a *catwalk!*

All the nurses have perfect nails, smooth skin, absolutely *zero* cellulite, flawless tiny bound feet in that seriously cool Nippon style, and no *cataracts!* That's because, at Strontium Tattoo, the nurses are all *radioactive!*

That's right, this year's look is definitely *nuclear!* The boys won't take you down to that hot new Abuse Bar unless you have a calculable *half-life! Top Movie Ejaculator John Whipsong* says he won't marry any girl that ain't spraying disintegrating atoms all *over* the place!

You want to attain that healthy glow? Well, those *mental* Russians are still selling weapons-grade nuclear material on the black market! This lovely kit is smuggled out of those missile silos they're dismantling, ferried through East Germany (where those painfully hip terrorists buy some -- see our Baader-Meinhof-Nixon feature last issue!), and passed onto the Western fashion industry! Hit the Hotmenu on your see-phone for your local Uranium Boutique!

CHARLOTTE ANN suggests starting with the low-cost *"235 Charm Bracelet"*, then moving up to the *"Mouth Irradiator"* for that real fresh breath, and finishing with the complete *"White Sands"* basque-and-crotchguard outfit!

And remember, girls; kissing is evil, and sex is against God!

FEAR AND LOATHING

Well...yes, and here we go again. Sunk in the depths of this basically atavistic town, here to cover a vicious election duel between two swinish old po▌ who should have been castrated and locked up years ago...

God, this <u>town</u>. Welcome to the asshole of the American Dream. Ben Hecht would've snickered and cavorted like the evil old hack he was, to be in Stealth now, but Scott Fitzgerald would've wept like his Daisy, face buried in silks, to see the place...me, I was forced to buy a handful of mescaline and a headful of rotten cocaine from a thing on the street with the head of a fat, malignant tumour.

The Thing had a voice like shit being sucked down a drainpipe, but its eyes gleamed with savage curiosity and a feel for the street.

"What brings you to the Quiet City, bud?" it asked.

"I am a Doctor of Journalism, but tonight I am in the politics business, anc I need numbers. Pyne or Barbour?"

"Surely. You can do that good stuff up on the sidewalk if you like. No one here gives a shit."

No indeed; this is Stealth, and people here put worse than this up their nose for breakfast. I crouched like an ape, laid the coke in a paving crack, and whacked the whole load up into my head like a bullet as the Thing talked heavy Politics.

Barbour is slightly to the right of Attial the Hun. He has a face like a bull-dog chewing a wasp, a brain like a chicken on speed, and the heart of a torso killer. Pyne, on the other hand, is a spineless old wardheeler whose beady eyes frequently roll up into the back of his ugly truthless head when asked about such innocent things as Ethics, Justice or Competence.

The Thing, warming to his vile topic, explained to me that the election balances on one central Stealth street, owned by an infamous mobster named Linkletter. Whichever way he goes, most of the East Side will follow. Linkletter was apparently a schizophrenic procurer with a history of violent epileptoid fits and near-industrial substance abuse. Should he go one hour without a fix, his head implodes into a bucket of jabbering animals.

My god -- to think that the political future of an entire city rests on the vote of a drug-crazed pimp whose brain could at any moment turn into a raging inferno of contradictions...

I punched the Thing in the gizzard and felt crazy. Then I walked back to the hotel in the rain.

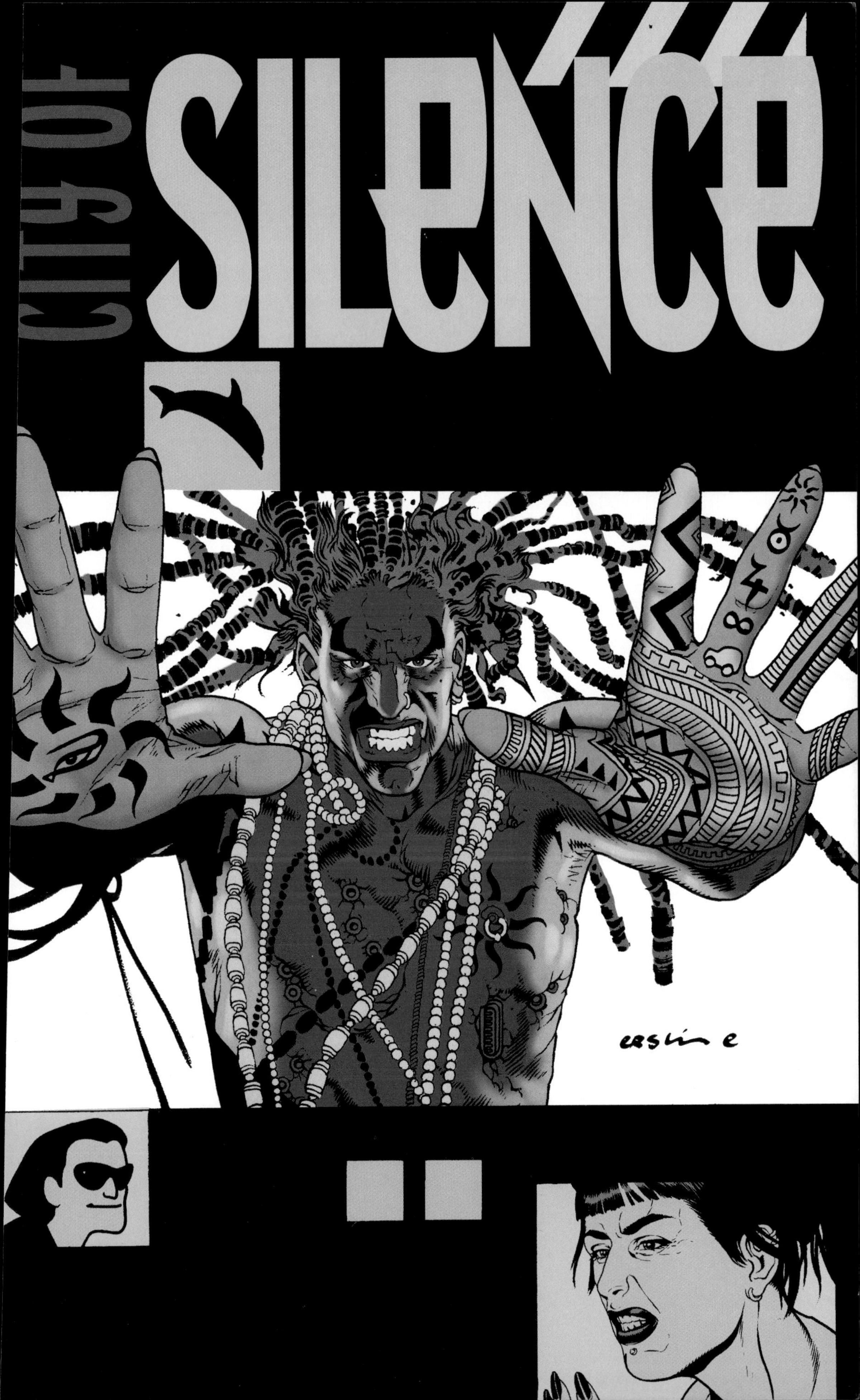
CITY OF
SILENCE

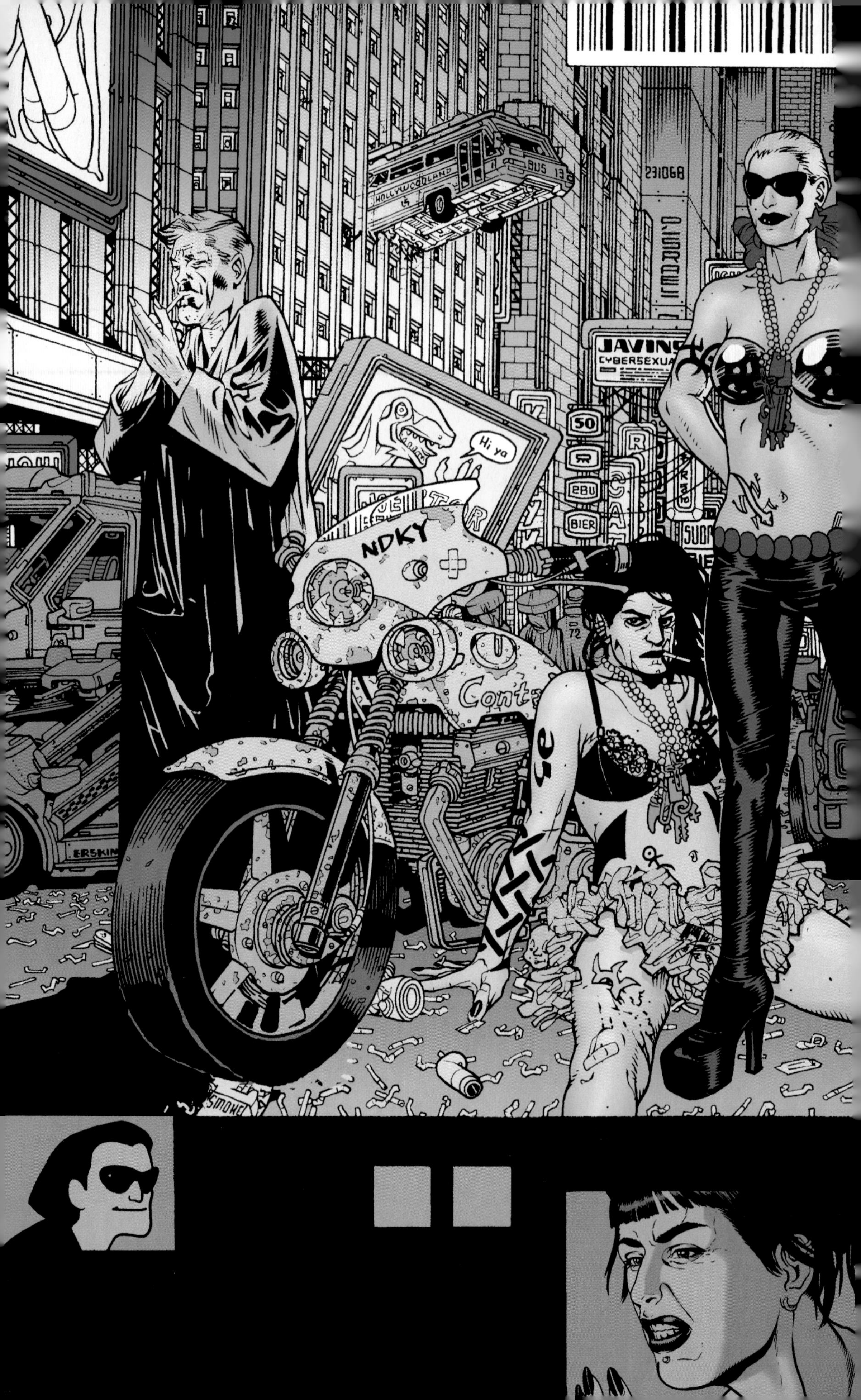

Hi ya
BUS 13
231068
JAVINS
CYBERSEXUA
50
BIER
NDKY
Conta
ERSKIN

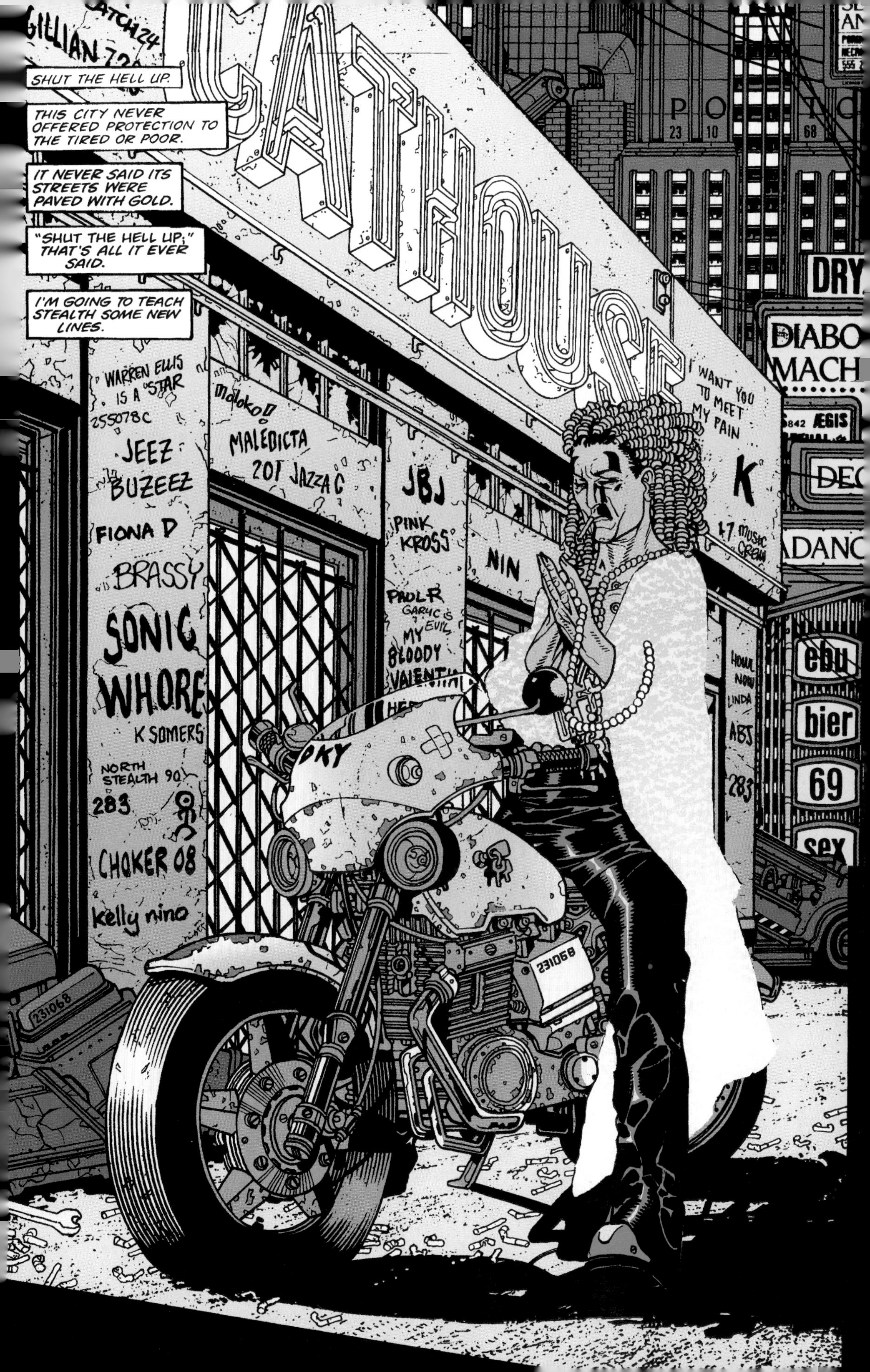
SHUT THE HELL UP.
THIS CITY NEVER OFFERED PROTECTION TO THE TIRED OR POOR.
IT NEVER SAID ITS STREETS WERE PAVED WITH GOLD.
"SHUT THE HELL UP," THAT'S ALL IT EVER SAID.
I'M GOING TO TEACH STEALTH SOME NEW LINES.
WARREN ELLIS IS A STAR
255078C
JEEZ BUZEEZ
FIONA D
BRASSY
SONIC WHORE
K SOMERS
NORTH STEALTH 90
283
CHOKER 08
kelly nino
moloko!!
MALEDICTA
201 JAZZA C
JBJ
PINK KROSS
NIN
PAUL R
GARUC IS EVIL
MY BLOODY
I WANT YOU TO MEET MY PAIN
K
HOWL NOW
LINDA
ABJ
283
DRY
DIABO
MACH
ÆGIS
DEC
ADANC
ebu
bier
69
sex
231068

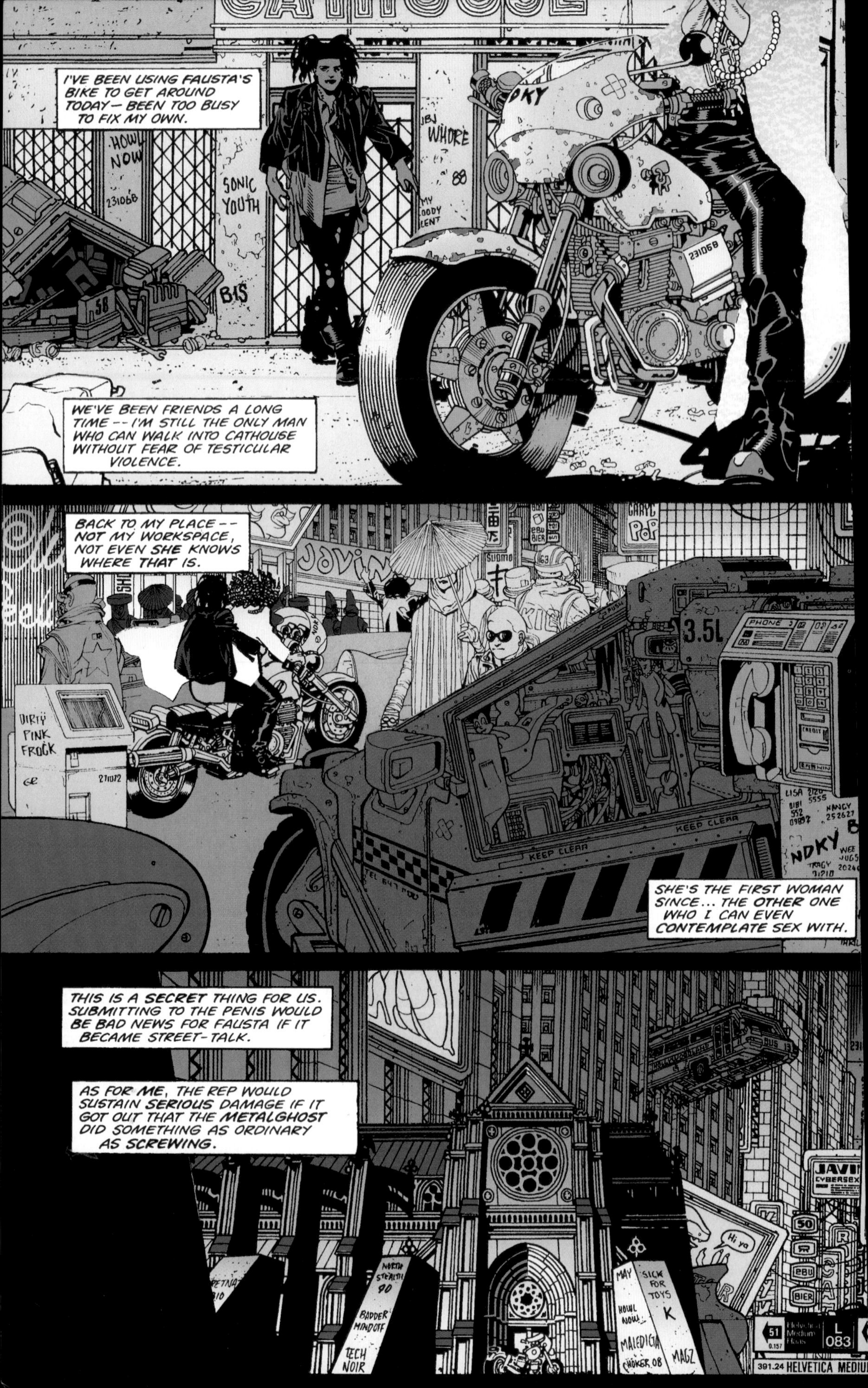
I'VE BEEN USING FAUSTA'S BIKE TO GET AROUND TODAY— BEEN TOO BUSY TO FIX MY OWN.
WE'VE BEEN FRIENDS A LONG TIME -- I'M STILL THE ONLY MAN WHO CAN WALK INTO CATHOUSE WITHOUT FEAR OF TESTICULAR VIOLENCE.
BACK TO MY PLACE -- NOT MY WORKSPACE, NOT EVEN SHE KNOWS WHERE THAT IS.
SHE'S THE FIRST WOMAN SINCE... THE OTHER ONE WHO I CAN EVEN CONTEMPLATE SEX WITH.
THIS IS A SECRET THING FOR US. SUBMITTING TO THE PENIS WOULD BE BAD NEWS FOR FAUSTA IF IT BECAME STREET-TALK.
AS FOR ME, THE REP WOULD SUSTAIN SERIOUS DAMAGE IF IT GOT OUT THAT THE METALGHOST DID SOMETHING AS ORDINARY AS SCREWING.

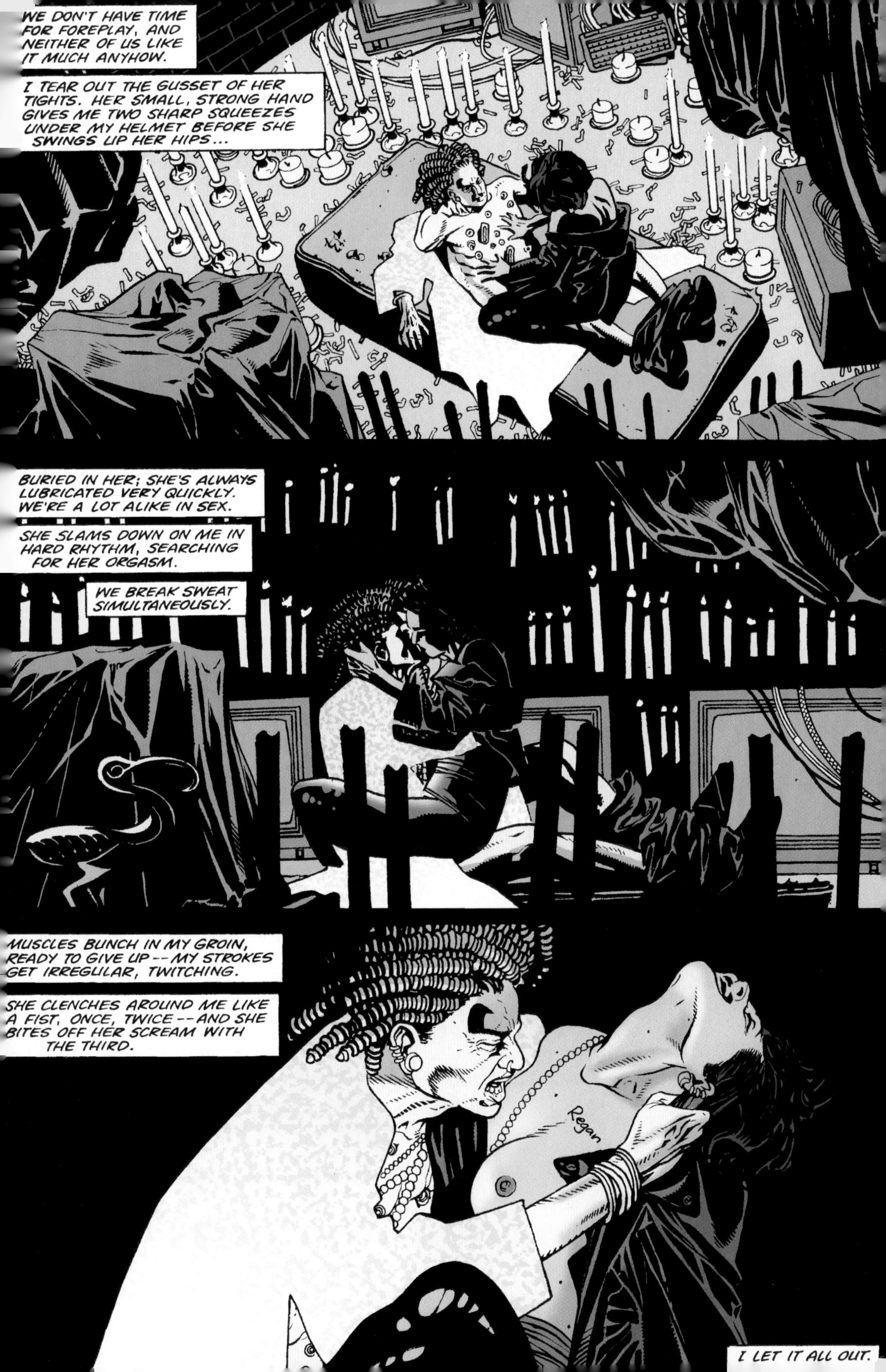
WE DON'T HAVE TIME FOR FOREPLAY, AND NEITHER OF US LIKE IT MUCH ANYHOW.
I TEAR OUT THE GUSSET OF HER TIGHTS. HER SMALL, STRONG HAND GIVES ME TWO SHARP SQUEEZES UNDER MY HELMET BEFORE SHE SWINGS UP HER HIPS...
BURIED IN HER; SHE'S ALWAYS LUBRICATED VERY QUICKLY. WE'RE A LOT ALIKE IN SEX.
SHE SLAMS DOWN ON ME IN HARD RHYTHM, SEARCHING FOR HER ORGASM.
WE BREAK SWEAT SIMULTANEOUSLY.
MUSCLES BUNCH IN MY GROIN, READY TO GIVE UP -- MY STROKES GET IRREGULAR, TWITCHING.
SHE CLENCHES AROUND ME LIKE A FIST, ONCE, TWICE -- AND SHE BITES OFF HER SCREAM WITH THE THIRD.
Regan
I LET IT ALL OUT.

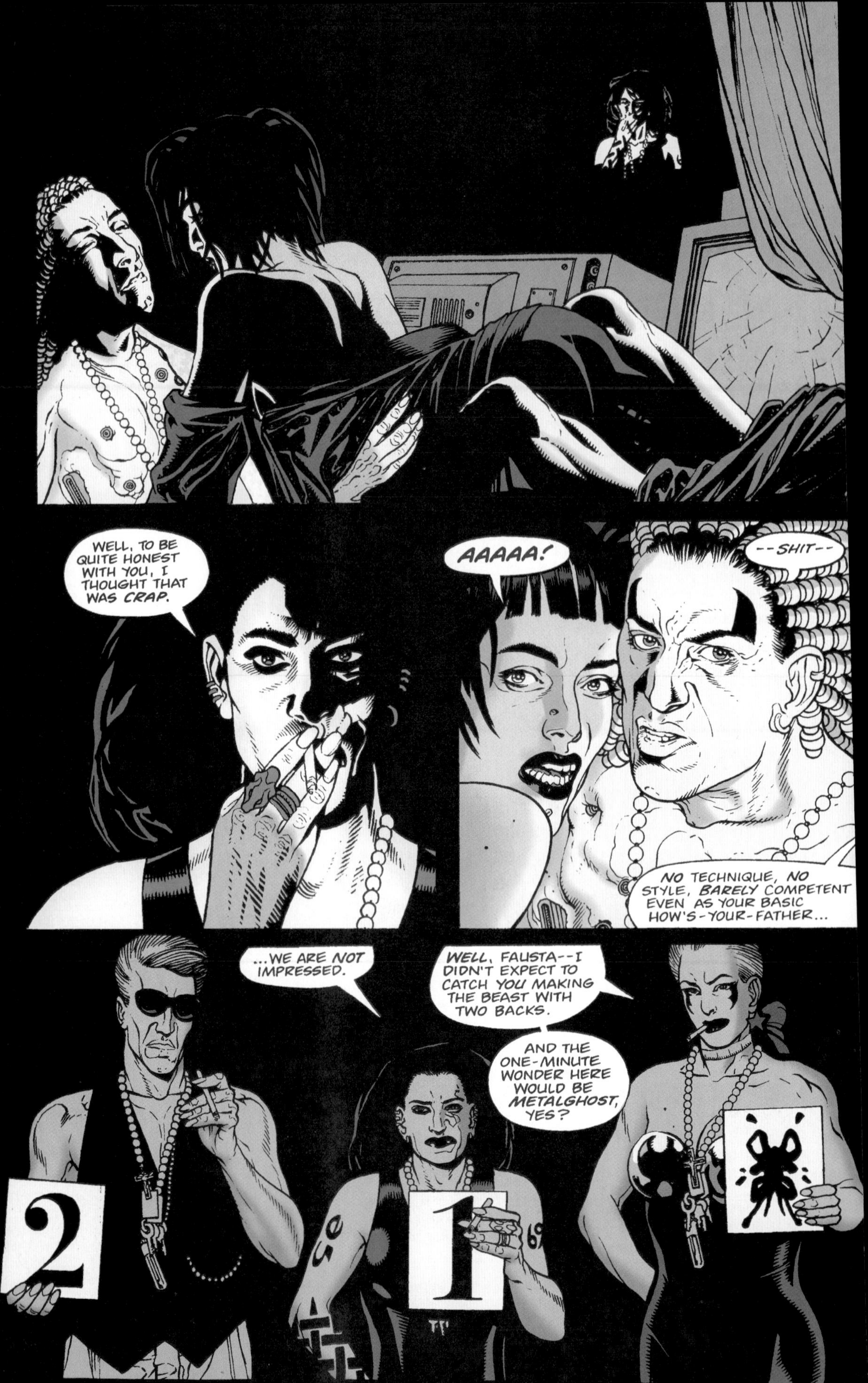

WELL, TO BE QUITE HONEST WITH YOU, I THOUGHT THAT WAS CRAP.
AAAAA!
--SHIT--
NO TECHNIQUE, NO STYLE, BARELY COMPETENT EVEN AS YOUR BASIC HOW'S-YOUR-FATHER...
...WE ARE NOT IMPRESSED.
WELL, FAUSTA--I DIDN'T EXPECT TO CATCH YOU MAKING THE BEAST WITH TWO BACKS.
AND THE ONE-MINUTE WONDER HERE WOULD BE METALGHOST, YES?
2
1

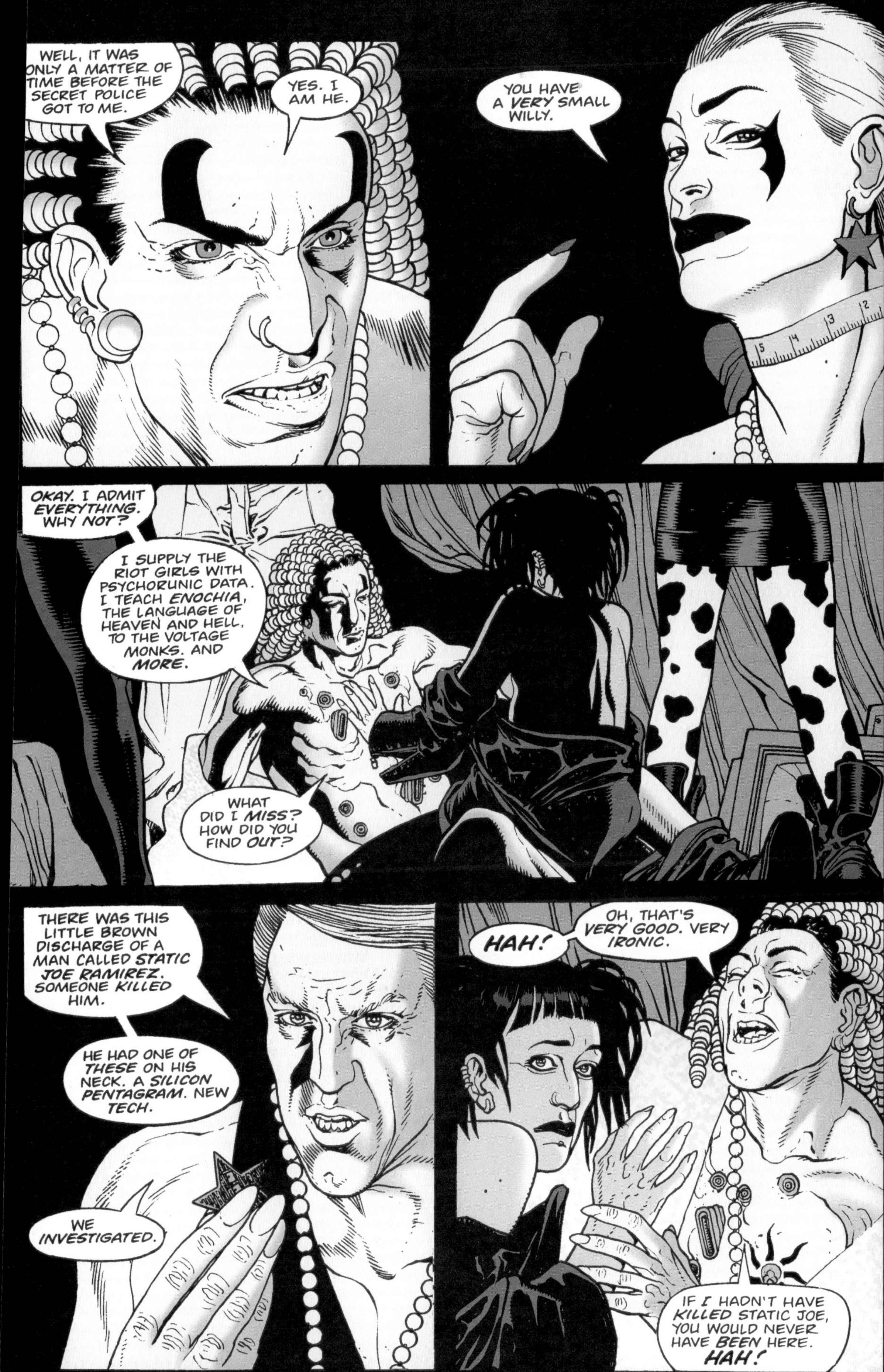
WELL, IT WAS ONLY A MATTER OF TIME BEFORE THE SECRET POLICE GOT TO ME.
YES. I AM HE.
YOU HAVE A *VERY* SMALL WILLY.
OKAY. I ADMIT *EVERYTHING.* WHY *NOT?*
I SUPPLY THE RIOT GIRLS WITH PSYCHORUNIC DATA. I TEACH *ENOCHIA,* THE LANGUAGE OF HEAVEN AND HELL, TO THE VOLTAGE MONKS. AND *MORE.*
WHAT DID I *MISS?* HOW DID YOU FIND *OUT?*
THERE WAS THIS LITTLE BROWN DISCHARGE OF A MAN CALLED *STATIC JOE RAMIREZ.* SOMEONE *KILLED* HIM.
HE HAD ONE OF *THESE* ON HIS NECK. A *SILICON PENTAGRAM.* NEW *TECH.*
WE *INVESTIGATED.*
HAH!
OH, THAT'S *VERY GOOD.* VERY *IRONIC.*
IF *I* HADN'T HAVE *KILLED* STATIC JOE, YOU WOULD NEVER HAVE *BEEN* HERE. *HAH!*

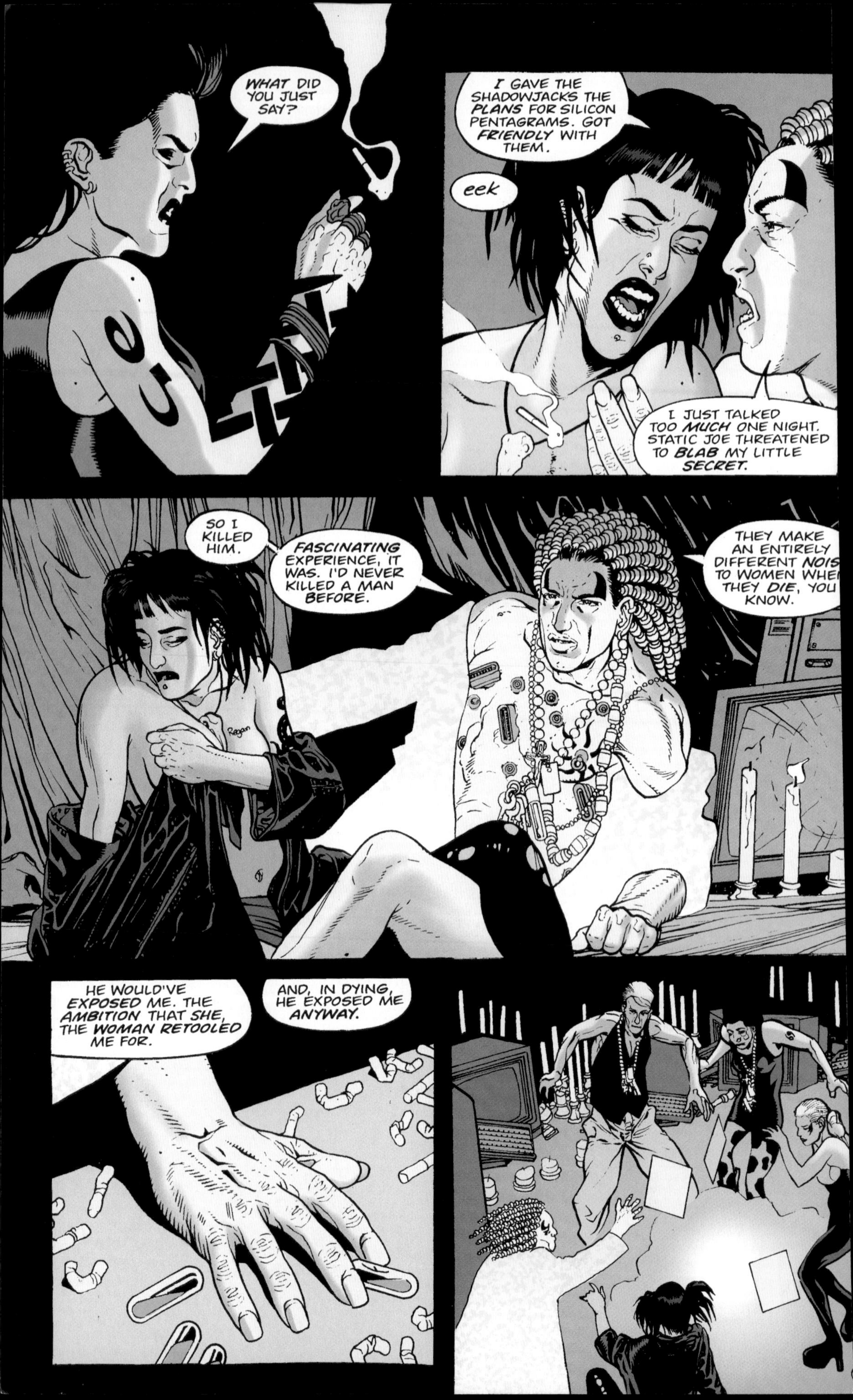
WHAT DID YOU JUST SAY?
I GAVE THE SHADOWJACKS THE PLANS FOR SILICON PENTAGRAMS. GOT FRIENDLY WITH THEM.
eek
I JUST TALKED TOO MUCH ONE NIGHT. STATIC JOE THREATENED TO BLAB MY LITTLE SECRET.
SO I KILLED HIM.
FASCINATING EXPERIENCE, IT WAS. I'D NEVER KILLED A MAN BEFORE.
THEY MAKE AN ENTIRELY DIFFERENT NOIS TO WOMEN WHE THEY DIE, YOU KNOW.
Regan
HE WOULD'VE EXPOSED ME. THE AMBITION THAT SHE, THE WOMAN RETOOLED ME FOR.
AND, IN DYING, HE EXPOSED ME ANYWAY.

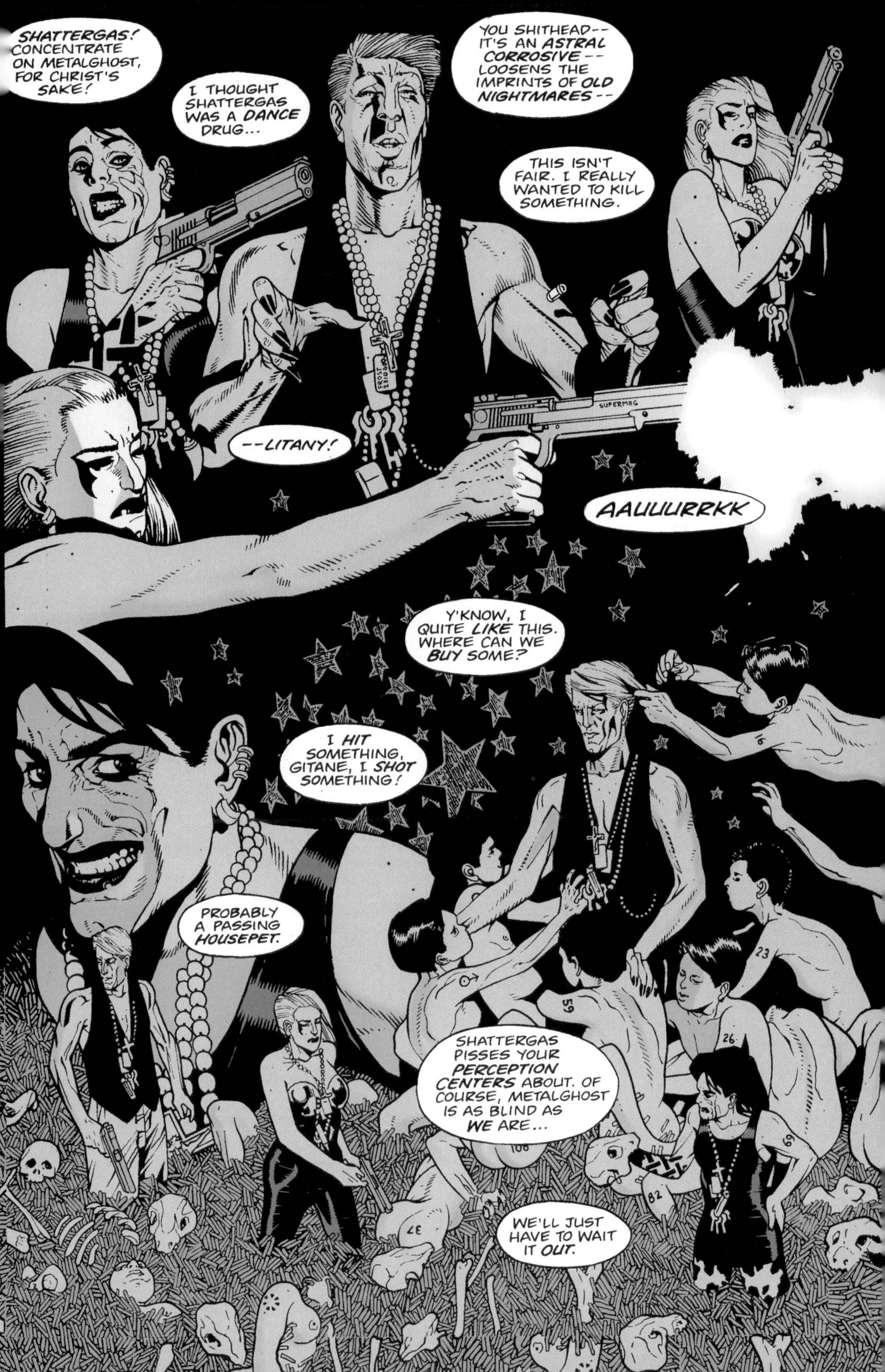
SHATTERGAS! CONCENTRATE ON METALGHOST, FOR CHRIST'S SAKE!
I THOUGHT SHATTERGAS WAS A DANCE DRUG...
YOU SHITHEAD-- IT'S AN ASTRAL CORROSIVE -- LOOSENS THE IMPRINTS OF OLD NIGHTMARES --
THIS ISN'T FAIR. I REALLY WANTED TO KILL SOMETHING.
--LITANY!
SUPERMAG
AAUUURRKK
Y'KNOW, I QUITE LIKE THIS. WHERE CAN WE BUY SOME?
I HIT SOMETHING, GITANE, I SHOT SOMETHING!
PROBABLY A PASSING HOUSEPET.
SHATTERGAS PISSES YOUR PERCEPTION CENTERS ABOUT. OF COURSE, METALGHOST IS AS BLIND AS WE ARE...
WE'LL JUST HAVE TO WAIT IT OUT.

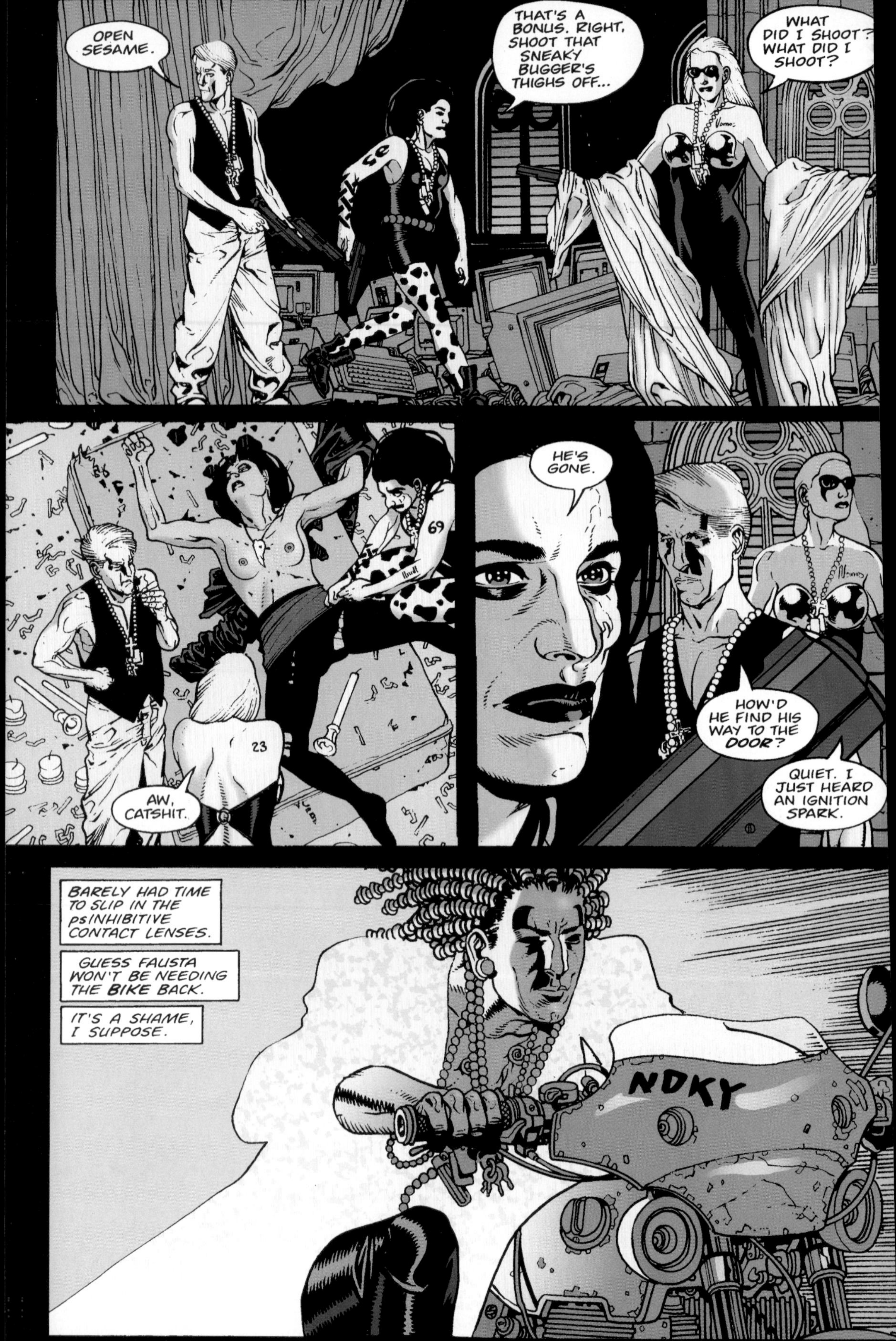
OPEN SESAME.
THAT'S A BONUS. RIGHT, SHOOT THAT SNEAKY BUGGER'S THIGHS OFF...
WHAT DID I SHOOT? WHAT DID I SHOOT?
AW, CATSHIT.
HE'S GONE.
HOW'D HE FIND HIS WAY TO THE DOOR?
QUIET. I JUST HEARD AN IGNITION SPARK.
BARELY HAD TIME TO SLIP IN THE psINHIBITIVE CONTACT LENSES.
GUESS FAUSTA WON'T BE NEEDING THE BIKE BACK.
IT'S A SHAME, I SUPPOSE.
NOKY

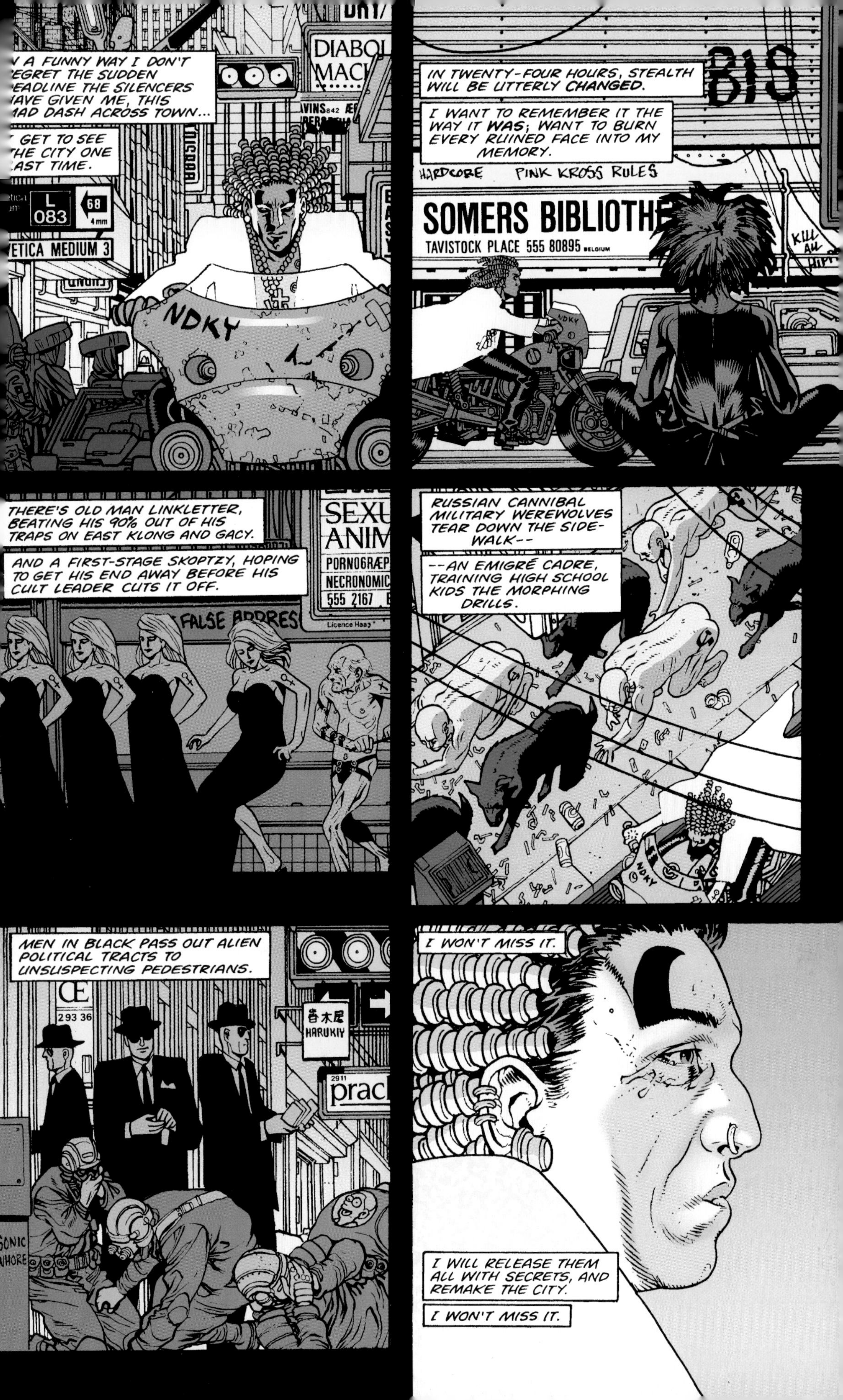
N A FUNNY WAY I DON'T EGRET THE SUDDEN EADLINE THE SILENCERS HAVE GIVEN ME, THIS MAD DASH ACROSS TOWN...
GET TO SEE THE CITY ONE AST TIME.
DIABO
MACH
L 083
68 4mm
VETICA MEDIUM 3
NDKY
IN TWENTY-FOUR HOURS, STEALTH WILL BE UTTERLY CHANGED.
I WANT TO REMEMBER IT THE WAY IT WAS; WANT TO BURN EVERY RUINED FACE INTO MY MEMORY.
HARDCORE
PINK KROSS RULES
SOMERS BIBLIOTHE
TAVISTOCK PLACE 555 80895 BELGIUM
KILL ALL
NDKY
THERE'S OLD MAN LINKLETTER, BEATING HIS 90% OUT OF HIS TRAPS ON EAST KLONG AND GACY.
AND A FIRST-STAGE SKOPTZY, HOPING TO GET HIS END AWAY BEFORE HIS CULT LEADER CUTS IT OFF.
SEXU
ANIM
PORNOGRÆP
NECRONOMIC
555 2167
Licence Haa3
FALSE ADDRES
RUSSIAN CANNIBAL MILITARY WEREWOLVES TEAR DOWN THE SIDE-WALK--
--AN EMIGRÉ CADRE, TRAINING HIGH SCHOOL KIDS THE MORPHING DRILLS.
NDKY
MEN IN BLACK PASS OUT ALIEN POLITICAL TRACTS TO UNSUSPECTING PEDESTRIANS.
Œ
293 36
HARUKIY
2911
pracl
SONIC WHORE
I WON'T MISS IT.
I WILL RELEASE THEM ALL WITH SECRETS, AND REMAKE THE CITY.
I WON'T MISS IT.

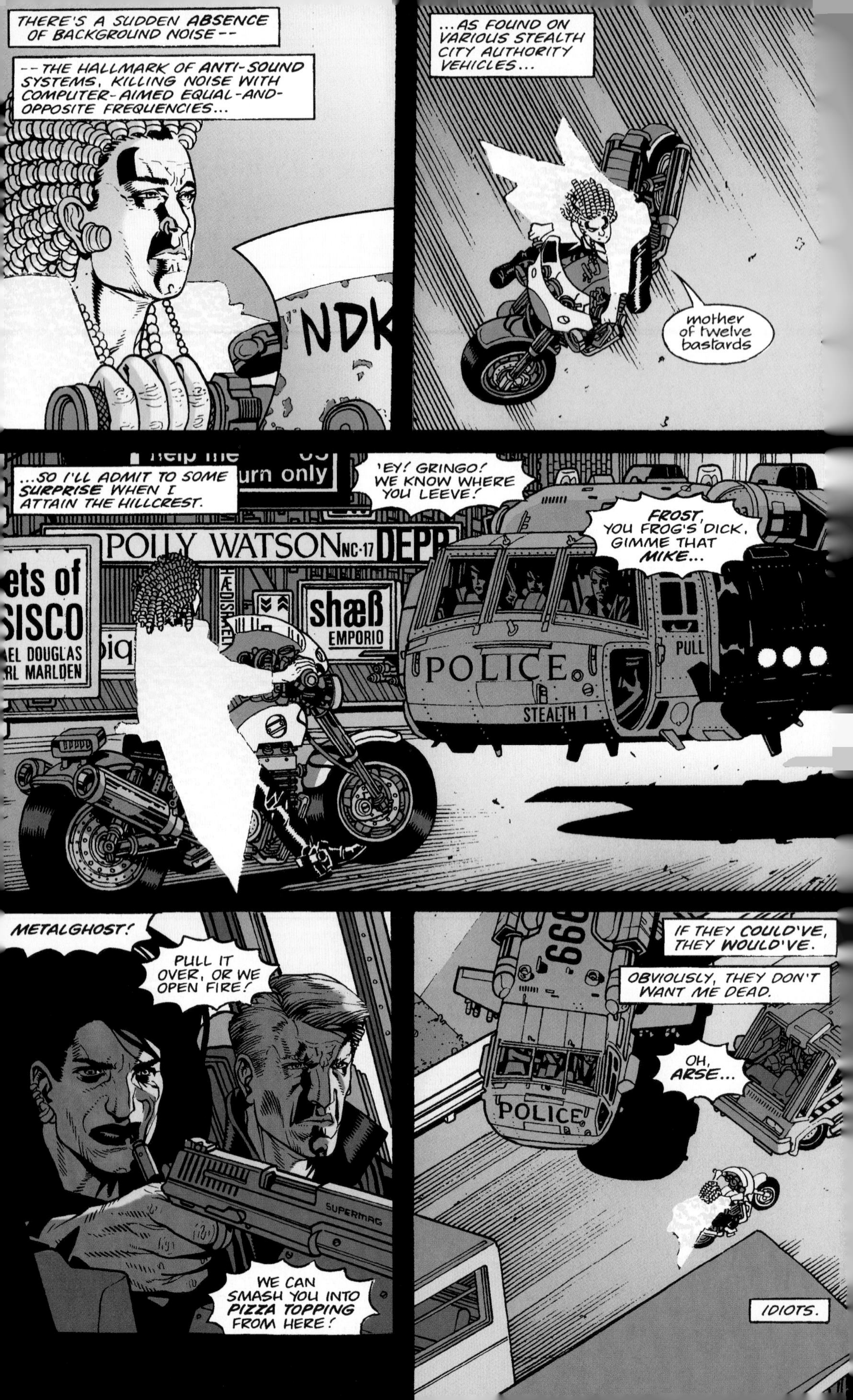
THERE'S A SUDDEN ABSENCE OF BACKGROUND NOISE--
--THE HALLMARK OF ANTI-SOUND SYSTEMS, KILLING NOISE WITH COMPUTER-AIMED EQUAL-AND-OPPOSITE FREQUENCIES...
NDK
...AS FOUND ON VARIOUS STEALTH CITY AUTHORITY VEHICLES...
mother of twelve bastards
...SO I'LL ADMIT TO SOME SURPRISE WHEN I ATTAIN THE HILLCREST.
urn only
'EY! GRINGO! WE KNOW WHERE YOU LEEVE!
FROST, YOU FROG'S DICK, GIMME THAT MIKE...
POLLY WATSON NC-17 DEPP
ets of
SISCO
AEL DOUGLAS
RL MARLDEN
shæß
EMPORIO
POLICE
PULL
STEALTH 1
METALGHOST!
PULL IT OVER, OR WE OPEN FIRE!
SUPERMAG
WE CAN SMASH YOU INTO PIZZA TOPPING FROM HERE!
IF THEY COULD'VE, THEY WOULD'VE.
OBVIOUSLY, THEY DON'T WANT ME DEAD.
OH, ARSE...
POLICE
IDIOTS.

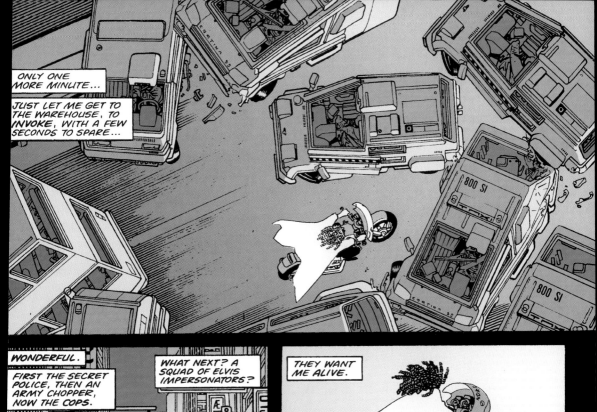

CORTINA 55
ONLY ONE MORE MINUTE...
JUST LET ME GET TO THE WAREHOUSE, TO INVOKE, WITH A FEW SECONDS TO SPARE...
800 SI
800 SI
CORTINA 55
WONDERFUL.
FIRST THE SECRET POLICE, THEN AN ARMY CHOPPER, NOW THE COPS.
WHAT NEXT? A SQUAD OF ELVIS IMPERSONATORS?
51 0.157
Helvetica Medium Haas
L 083
68 4 mm
391.24 HELVETICA MEDIUM 3
SEX
PHAIR
THE LAST NIGHT
(16pt) 0.157 inch 4 mm
POLICE 357 3037
Licence
THEY WANT ME ALIVE.
THEY WANT TO KNOW EXACTLY HOW MUCH I KNOW, AND WHO I'VE TOLD IT TO.
IF THEY KILLED ME NOW, THEY'D WIN.
ONLY BULLETS COULD CUT THE KNOT OF THE PROMISE I MADE HER.
KEEP OUT
BEFORE I CROWBAR'D HER RIBS OUT WITH THE CLAW HAMMER.

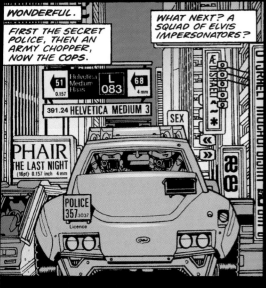

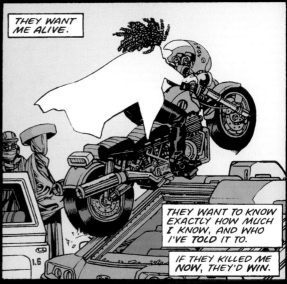

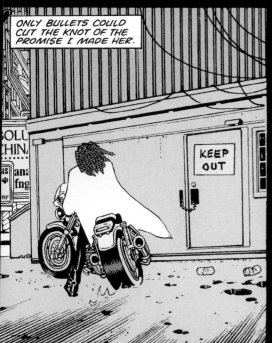

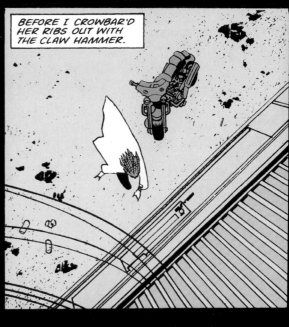

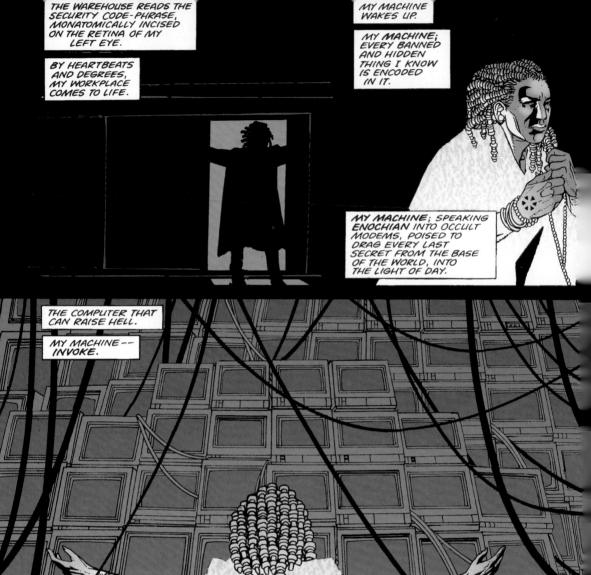

THE WAREHOUSE READS THE SECURITY CODE-PHRASE, MONATOMICALLY INCISED ON THE RETINA OF MY LEFT EYE.

BY HEARTBEATS AND DEGREES, MY WORKPLACE COMES TO LIFE.

MY MACHINE WAKES UP.

MY MACHINE; EVERY BANNED AND HIDDEN THING I KNOW IS ENCODED IN IT.

MY MACHINE; SPEAKING ENOCHIAN INTO OCCULT MODEMS, POISED TO DRAG EVERY LAST SECRET FROM THE BASE OF THE WORLD, INTO THE LIGHT OF DAY.

THE COMPUTER THAT CAN RAISE HELL.

MY MACHINE -- INVOKE.

SONYA

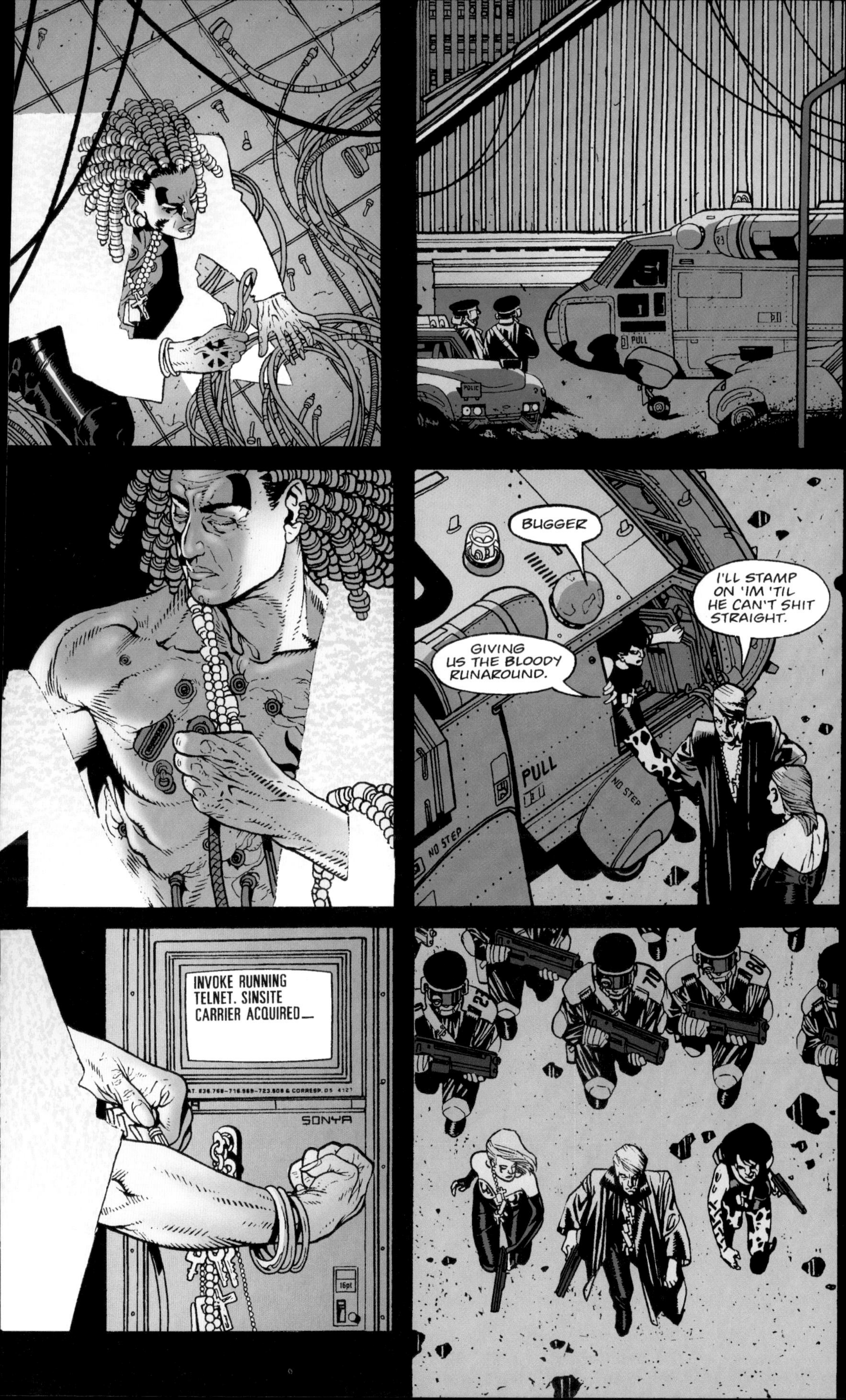

BUGGER
GIVING US THE BLOODY RUNAROUND.
I'LL STAMP ON 'IM 'TIL HE CAN'T SHIT STRAIGHT.
PULL
NO STEP
INVOKE RUNNING TELNET. SINSITE CARRIER ACQUIRED_
SONYA

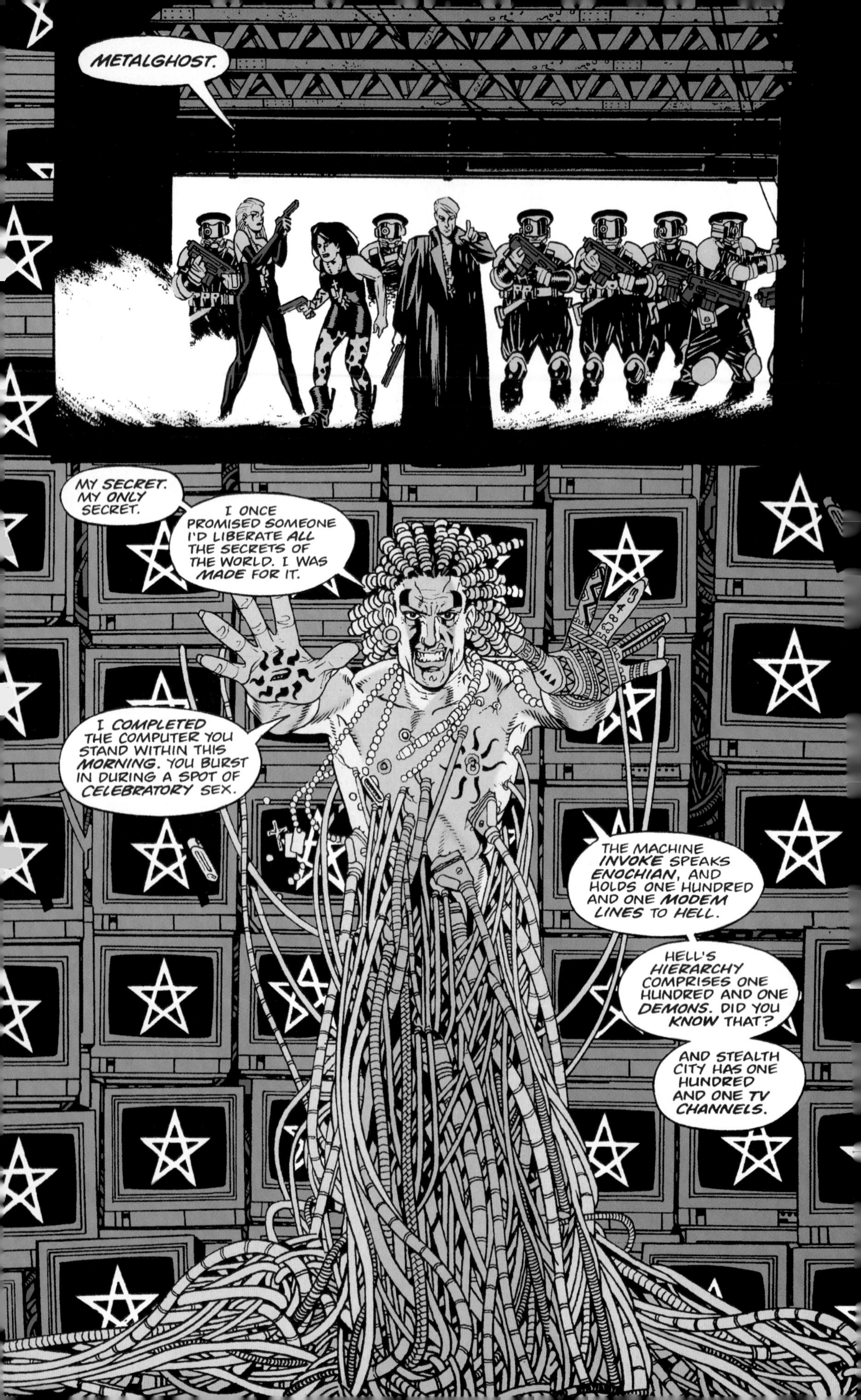
METALGHOST.
MY SECRET. MY ONLY SECRET.
I ONCE PROMISED SOMEONE I'D LIBERATE ALL THE SECRETS OF THE WORLD. I WAS MADE FOR IT.
I COMPLETED THE COMPUTER YOU STAND WITHIN THIS MORNING. YOU BURST IN DURING A SPOT OF CELEBRATORY SEX.
THE MACHINE INVOKE SPEAKS ENOCHIAN, AND HOLDS ONE HUNDRED AND ONE MODEM LINES TO HELL.
HELL'S HIERARCHY COMPRISES ONE HUNDRED AND ONE DEMONS. DID YOU KNOW THAT?
AND STEALTH CITY HAS ONE HUNDRED AND ONE TV CHANNELS.

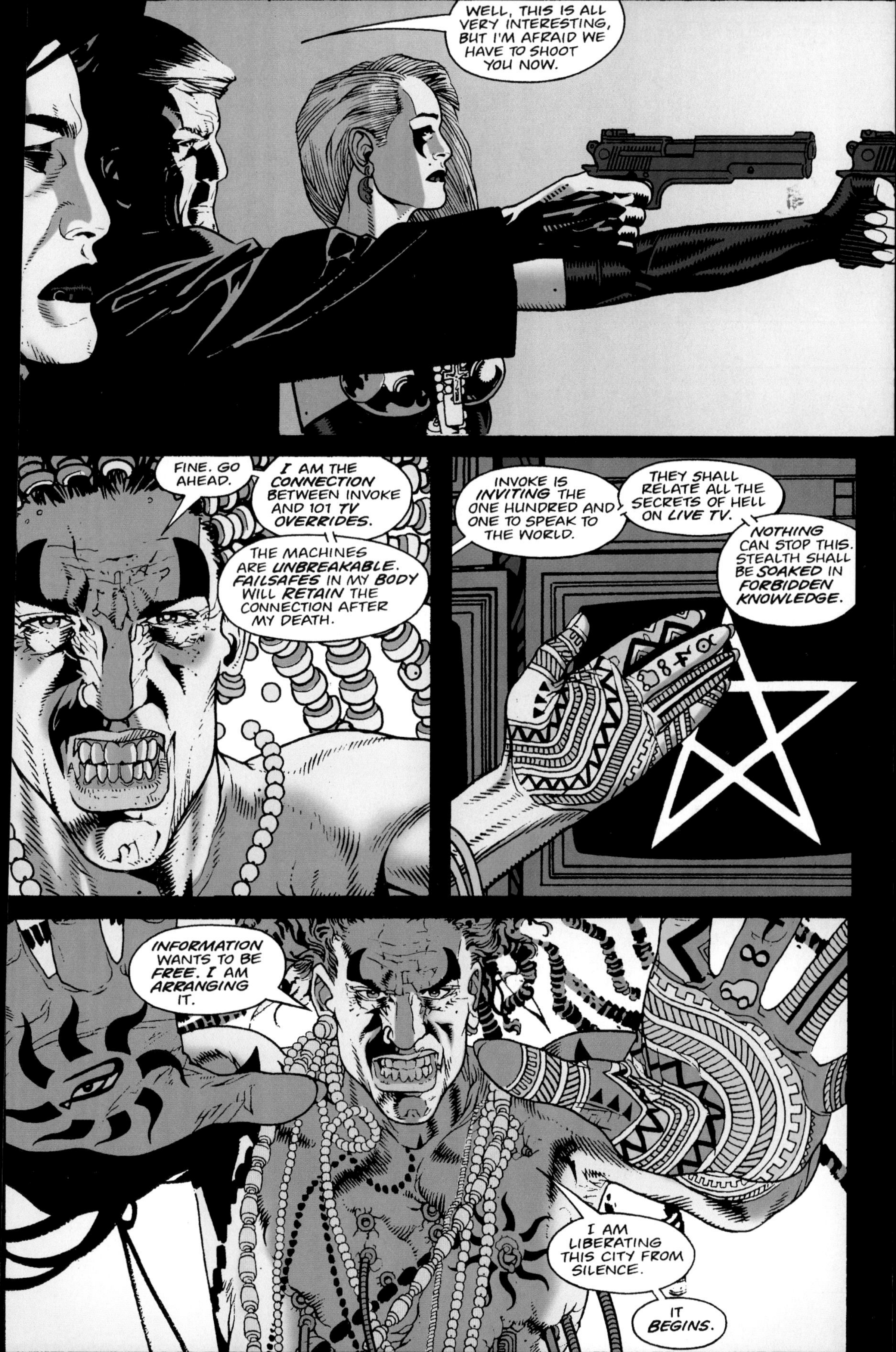
WELL, THIS IS ALL VERY INTERESTING, BUT I'M AFRAID WE HAVE TO SHOOT YOU NOW.
FINE. GO AHEAD.
I AM THE CONNECTION BETWEEN INVOKE AND 101 TV OVERRIDES.
THE MACHINES ARE UNBREAKABLE. FAILSAFES IN MY BODY WILL RETAIN THE CONNECTION AFTER MY DEATH.
INVOKE IS INVITING THE ONE HUNDRED AND ONE TO SPEAK TO THE WORLD.
THEY SHALL RELATE ALL THE SECRETS OF HELL ON LIVE TV.
NOTHING CAN STOP THIS. STEALTH SHALL BE SOAKED IN FORBIDDEN KNOWLEDGE.
INFORMATION WANTS TO BE FREE. I AM ARRANGING IT.
I AM LIBERATING THIS CITY FROM SILENCE.
IT BEGINS.

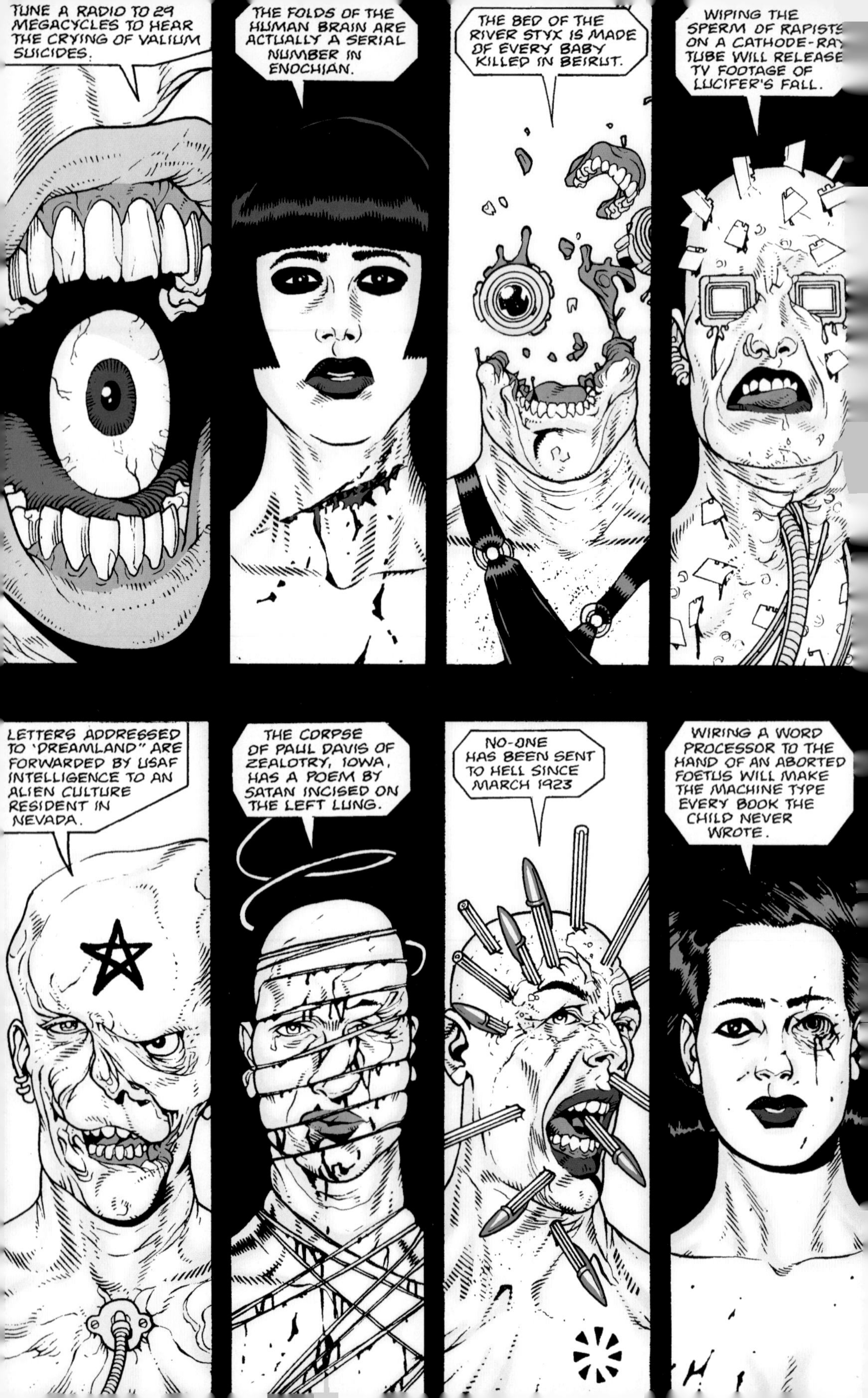
TUNE A RADIO TO 29 MEGACYCLES TO HEAR THE CRYING OF VALIUM SUICIDES.
THE FOLDS OF THE HUMAN BRAIN ARE ACTUALLY A SERIAL NUMBER IN ENOCHIAN.
THE BED OF THE RIVER STYX IS MADE OF EVERY BABY KILLED IN BEIRUT.
WIPING THE SPERM OF RAPISTS ON A CATHODE-RAY TUBE WILL RELEASE TV FOOTAGE OF LUCIFER'S FALL.
LETTERS ADDRESSED TO 'DREAMLAND" ARE FORWARDED BY USAF INTELLIGENCE TO AN ALIEN CULTURE RESIDENT IN NEVADA.
THE CORPSE OF PAUL DAVIS OF ZEALOTRY, IOWA, HAS A POEM BY SATAN INCISED ON THE LEFT LUNG.
NO-ONE HAS BEEN SENT TO HELL SINCE MARCH 1923
WIRING A WORD PROCESSOR TO THE HAND OF AN ABORTED FOETUS WILL MAKE THE MACHINE TYPE EVERY BOOK THE CHILD NEVER WROTE.

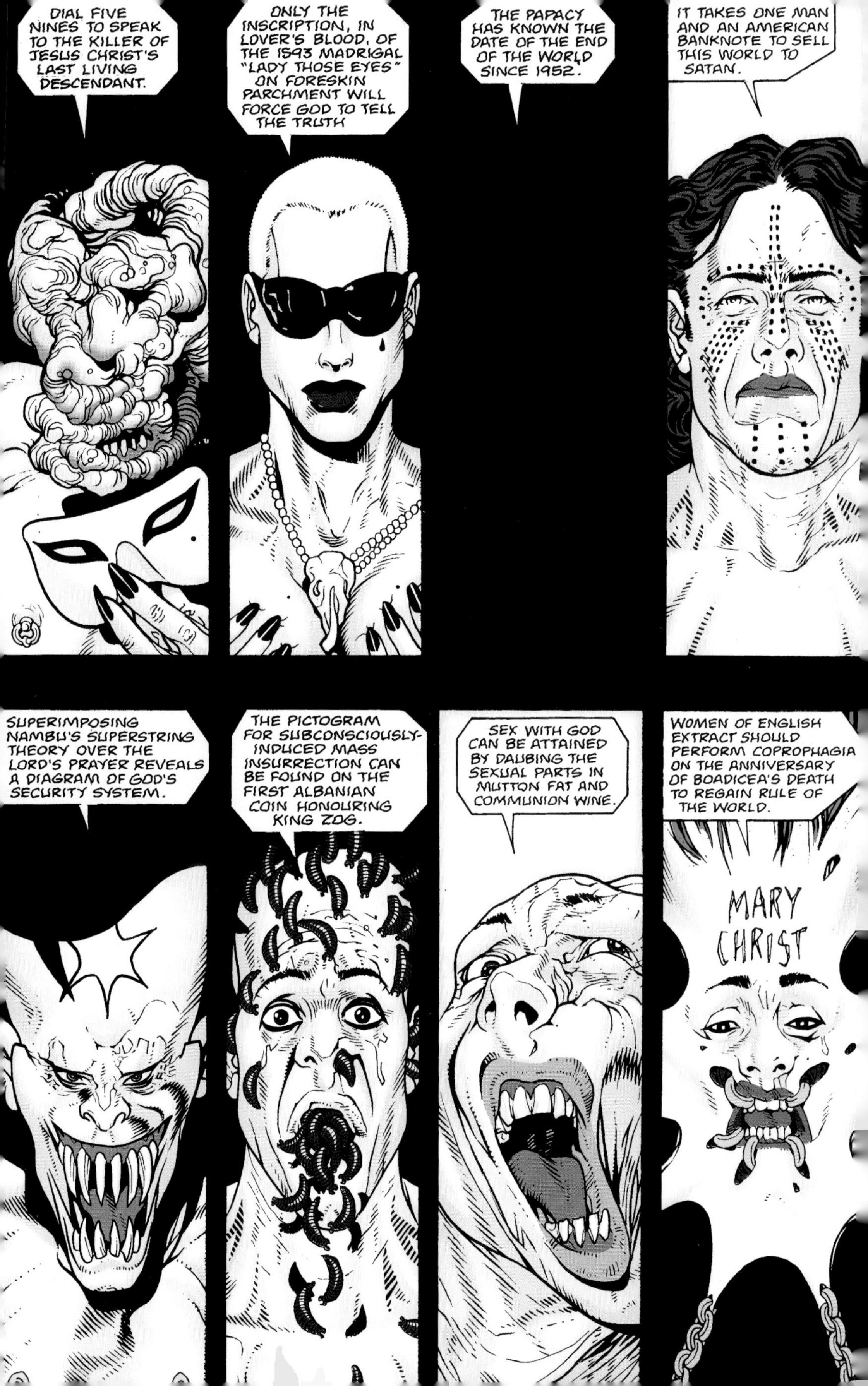
DIAL FIVE NINES TO SPEAK TO THE KILLER OF JESUS CHRIST'S LAST LIVING DESCENDANT.
ONLY THE INSCRIPTION, IN LOVER'S BLOOD, OF THE 1593 MADRIGAL "LADY THOSE EYES" ON FORESKIN PARCHMENT WILL FORCE GOD TO TELL THE TRUTH
THE PAPACY HAS KNOWN THE DATE OF THE END OF THE WORLD SINCE 1952.
IT TAKES ONE MAN AND AN AMERICAN BANKNOTE TO SELL THIS WORLD TO SATAN.
SUPERIMPOSING NAMBU'S SUPERSTRING THEORY OVER THE LORD'S PRAYER REVEALS A DIAGRAM OF GOD'S SECURITY SYSTEM.
THE PICTOGRAM FOR SUBCONSCIOUSLY-INDUCED MASS INSURRECTION CAN BE FOUND ON THE FIRST ALBANIAN COIN HONOURING KING ZOG.
SEX WITH GOD CAN BE ATTAINED BY DAUBING THE SEXUAL PARTS IN MUTTON FAT AND COMMUNION WINE.
WOMEN OF ENGLISH EXTRACT SHOULD PERFORM COPROPHAGIA ON THE ANNIVERSARY OF BOADICEA'S DEATH TO REGAIN RULE OF THE WORLD.
MARY CHRIST

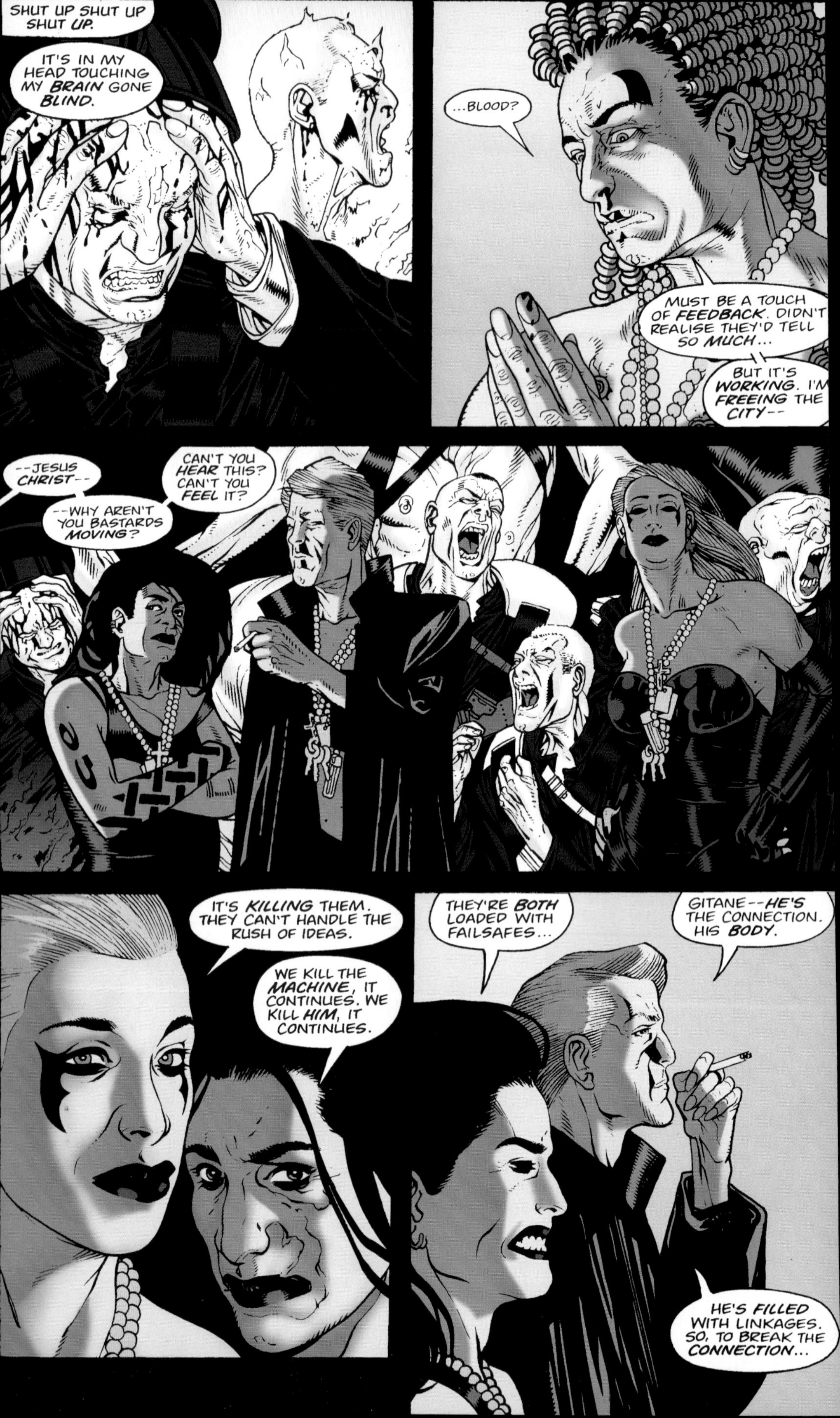
SHUT UP SHUT UP SHUT UP.
IT'S IN MY HEAD TOUCHING MY BRAIN GONE BLIND.
...BLOOD?
MUST BE A TOUCH OF FEEDBACK. DIDN'T REALISE THEY'D TELL SO MUCH...
BUT IT'S WORKING. I'M FREEING THE CITY--
--JESUS CHRIST--
--WHY AREN'T YOU BASTARDS MOVING?
CAN'T YOU HEAR THIS? CAN'T YOU FEEL IT?
IT'S KILLING THEM. THEY CAN'T HANDLE THE RUSH OF IDEAS.
WE KILL THE MACHINE, IT CONTINUES. WE KILL HIM, IT CONTINUES.
THEY'RE BOTH LOADED WITH FAILSAFES...
GITANE--HE'S THE CONNECTION. HIS BODY.
HE'S FILLED WITH LINKAGES. SO, TO BREAK THE CONNECTION...

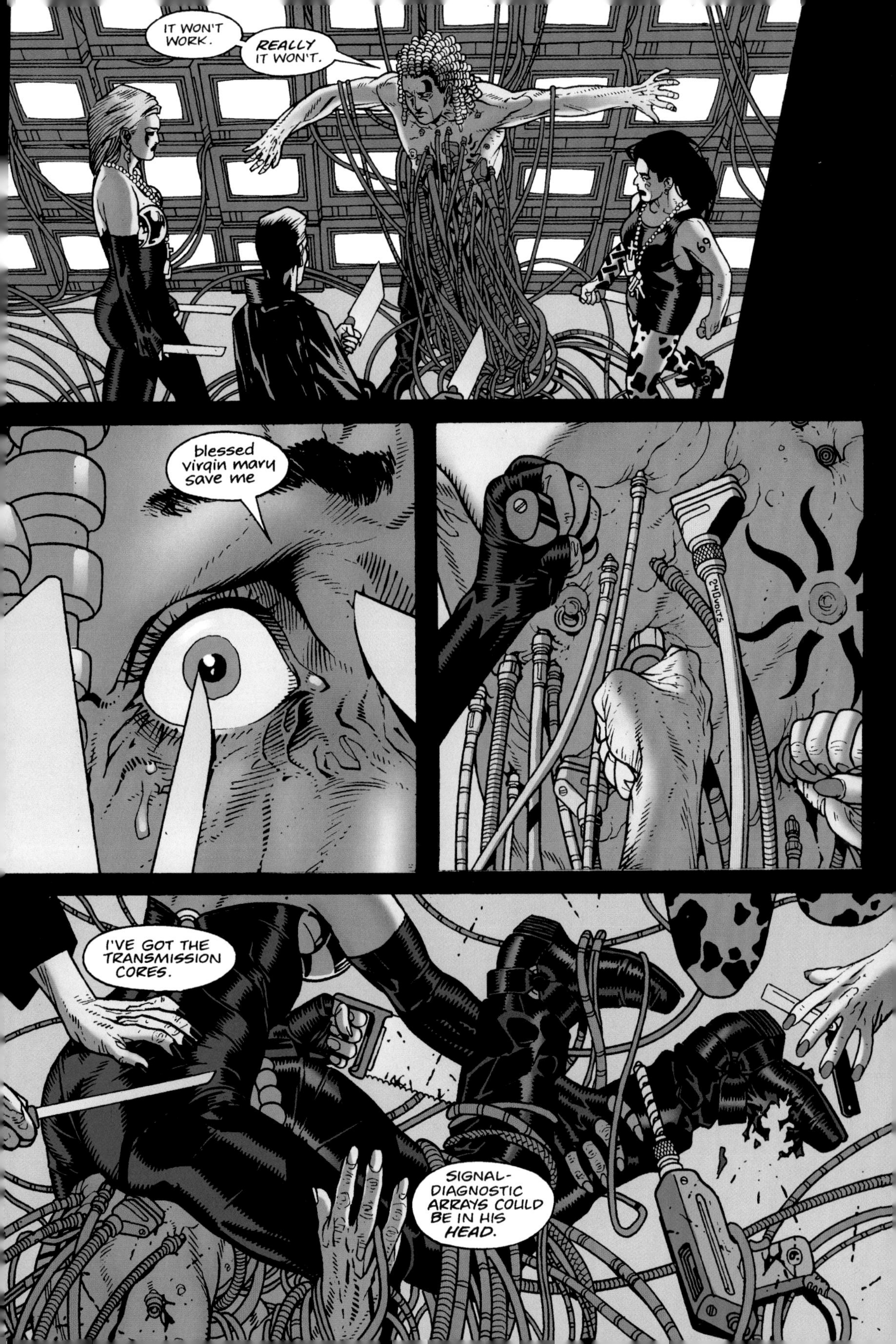
IT WON'T WORK.
REALLY IT WON'T.
blessed virgin mary save me
240 VOLTS
I'VE GOT THE TRANSMISSION CORES.
SIGNAL-DIAGNOSTIC ARRAYS COULD BE IN HIS HEAD.

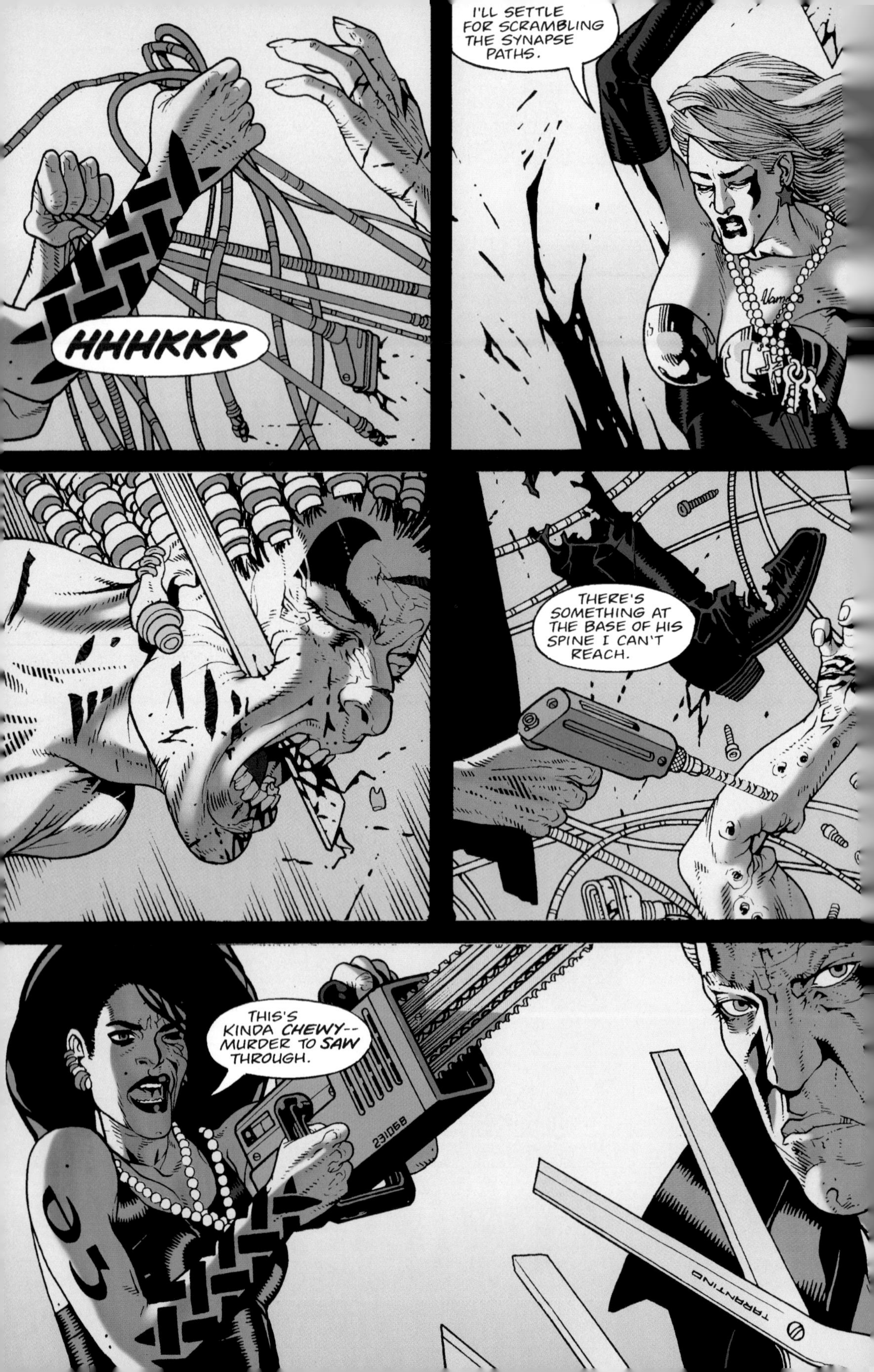
HHHKKK
I'LL SETTLE FOR SCRAMBLING THE SYNAPSE PATHS.
THERE'S SOMETHING AT THE BASE OF HIS SPINE I CAN'T REACH.
THIS'S KINDA *CHEWY*-- MURDER TO *SAW* THROUGH.

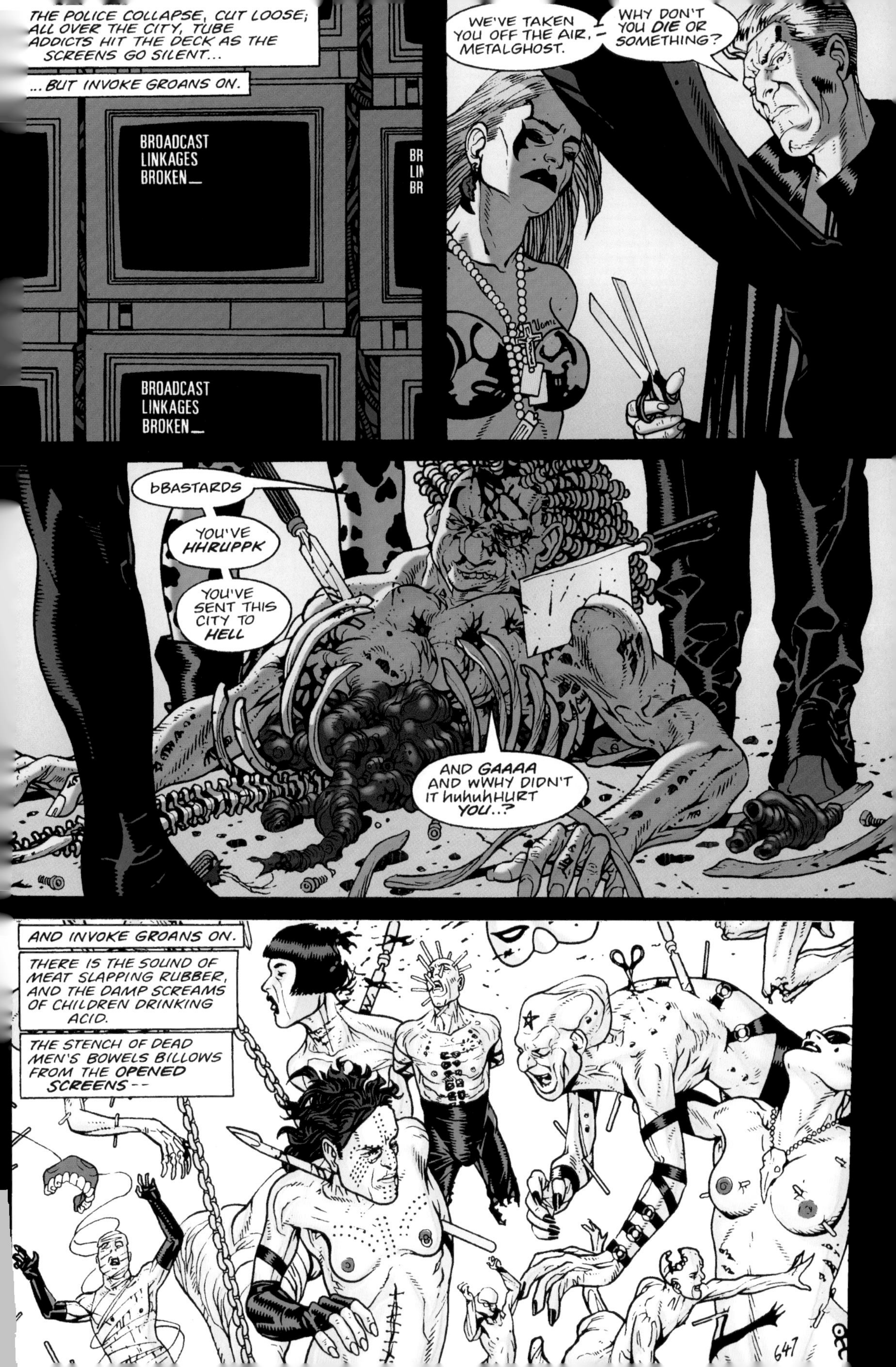

THE POLICE COLLAPSE, CUT LOOSE; ALL OVER THE CITY, TUBE ADDICTS HIT THE DECK AS THE SCREENS GO SILENT...
...BUT INVOKE GROANS ON.
BROADCAST LINKAGES BROKEN_
BROADCAST LINKAGES BROKEN_
WE'VE TAKEN YOU OFF THE AIR, METALGHOST.
WHY DON'T YOU DIE OR SOMETHING?
bBASTARDS
YOU'VE HHRUPPK
YOU'VE SENT THIS CITY TO HELL
AND GAAAA AND WWHY DIDN'T IT huhuhHURT YOU..?
AND INVOKE GROANS ON.
THERE IS THE SOUND OF MEAT SLAPPING RUBBER, AND THE DAMP SCREAMS OF CHILDREN DRINKING ACID.
THE STENCH OF DEAD MEN'S BOWELS BILLOWS FROM THE OPENED SCREENS--

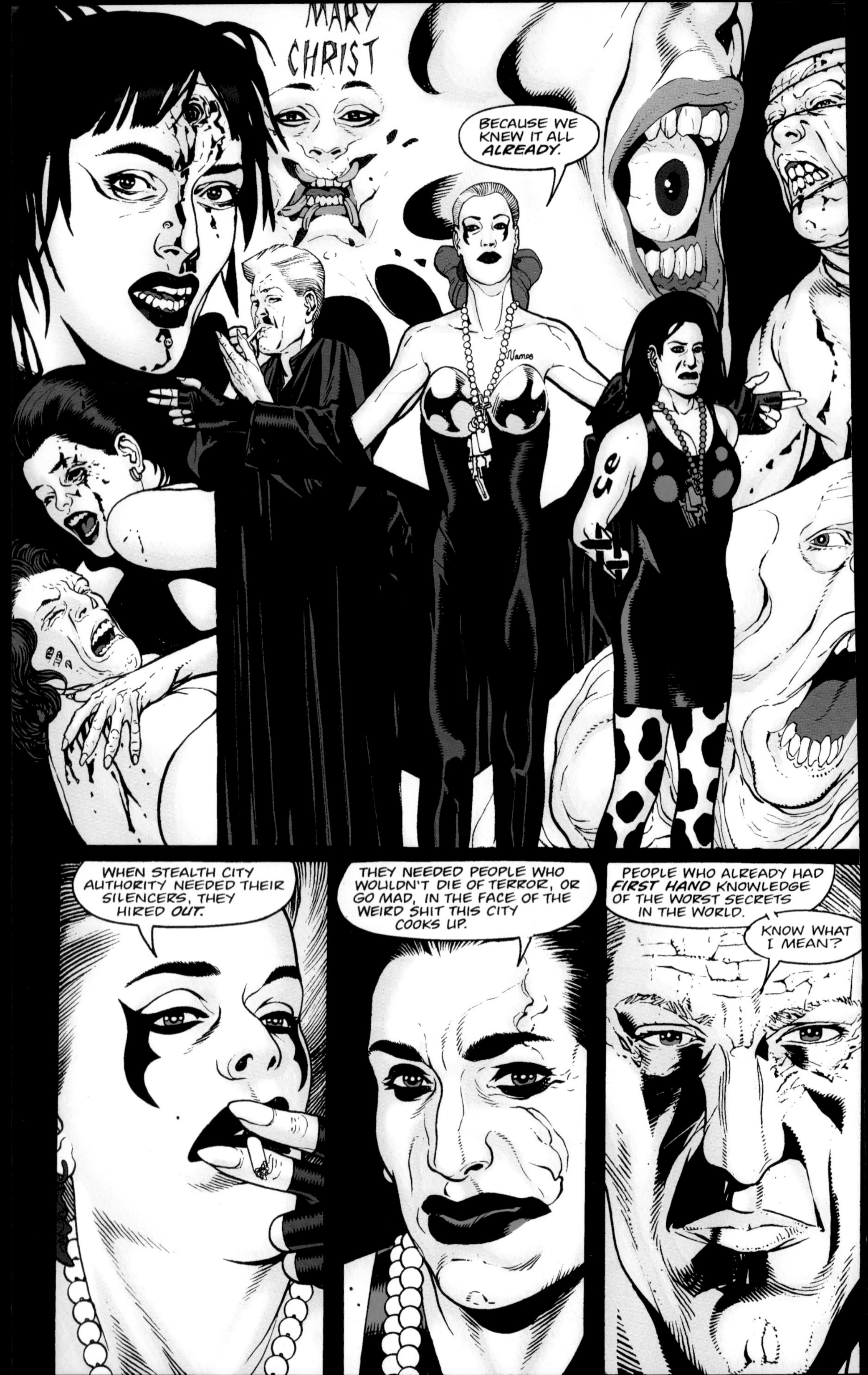

MARY CHRIST
BECAUSE WE KNEW IT ALL ALREADY.
WHEN STEALTH CITY AUTHORITY NEEDED THEIR SILENCERS, THEY HIRED OUT.
THEY NEEDED PEOPLE WHO WOULDN'T DIE OF TERROR, OR GO MAD, IN THE FACE OF THE WEIRD SHIT THIS CITY COOKS UP.
PEOPLE WHO ALREADY HAD FIRST HAND KNOWLEDGE OF THE WORST SECRETS IN THE WORLD.
KNOW WHAT I MEAN?

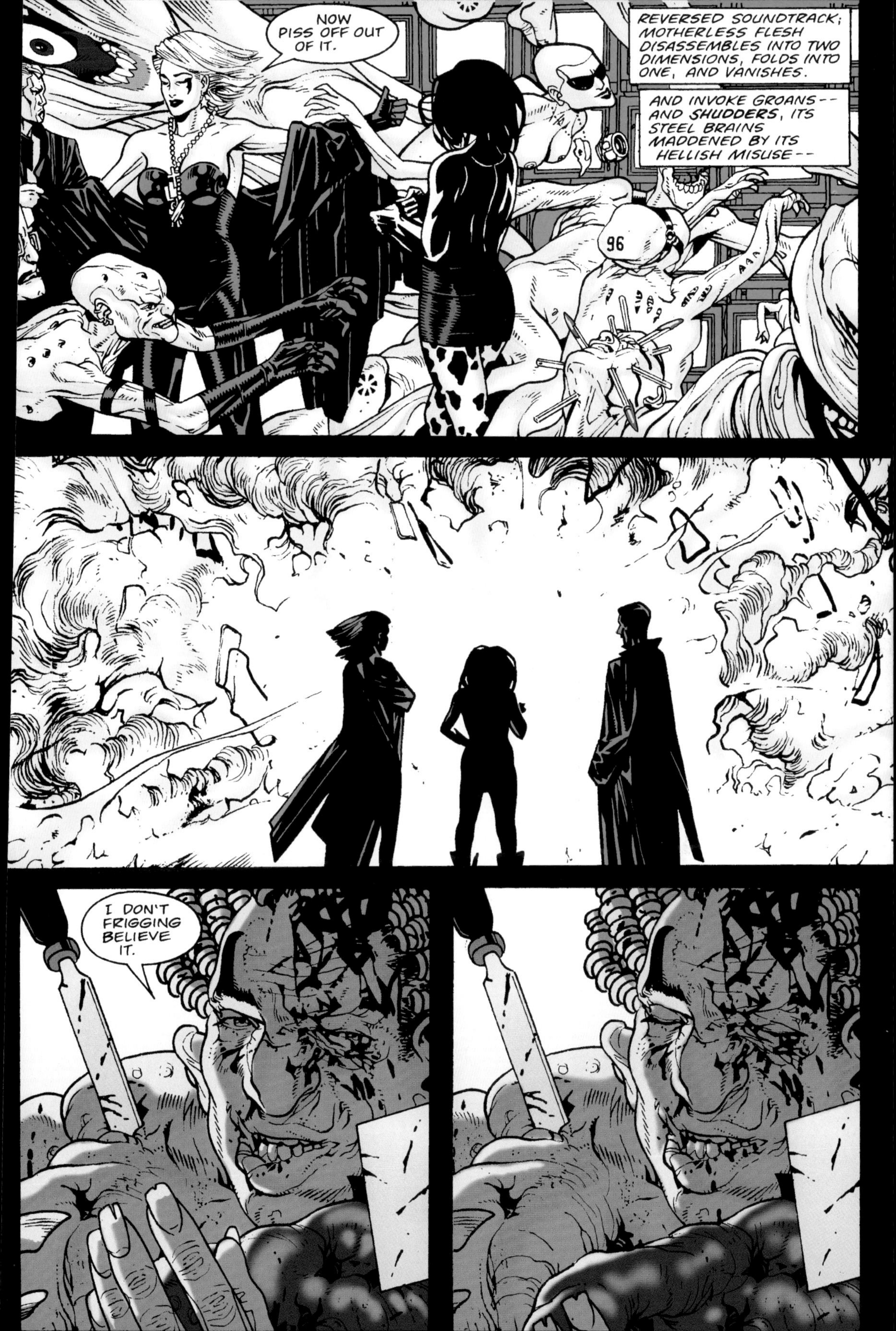
NOW PISS OFF OUT OF IT.
REVERSED SOUNDTRACK; MOTHERLESS FLESH DISASSEMBLES INTO TWO DIMENSIONS, FOLDS INTO ONE, AND VANISHES.
AND INVOKE GROANS-- AND SHUDDERS, ITS STEEL BRAINS MADDENED BY ITS HELLISH MISUSE--
96
I DON'T FRIGGING BELIEVE IT.

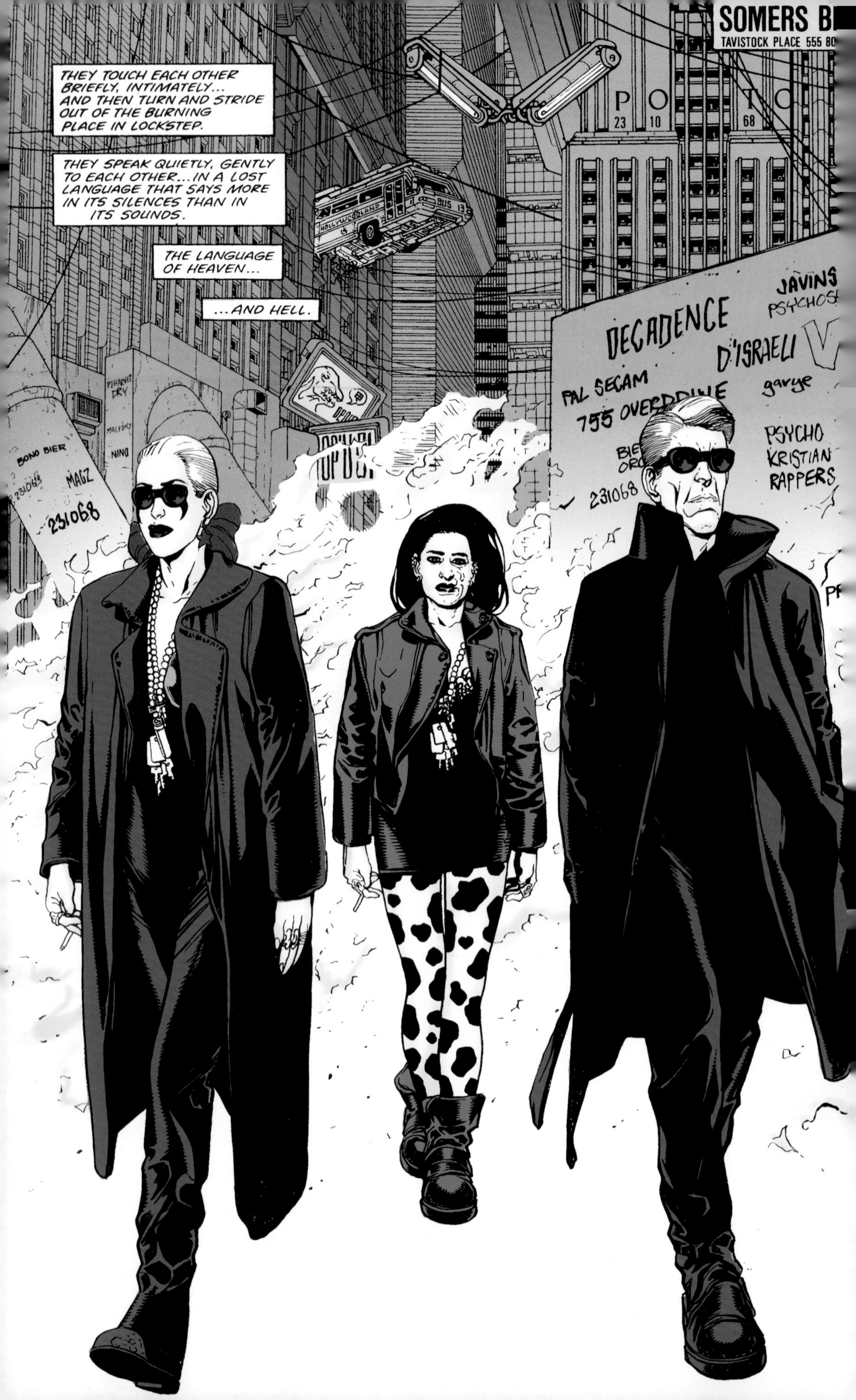

SOMERS B
TAVISTOCK PLACE 555 80
THEY TOUCH EACH OTHER BRIEFLY, INTIMATELY... AND THEN TURN AND STRIDE OUT OF THE BURNING PLACE IN LOCKSTEP.
THEY SPEAK QUIETLY, GENTLY TO EACH OTHER... IN A LOST LANGUAGE THAT SAYS MORE IN ITS SILENCES THAN IN ITS SOUNDS.
THE LANGUAGE OF HEAVEN...
...AND HELL.
P O T O
23 10 68
DECADENCE
D'ISRAELI
JAVINS
PAL SECAM
PSYCHO KRISTIAN RAPPERS
231068
BONO BIER
MAGZ
231068

The stars grew bright in the Winter sky,
The wind came keen with a tang of frost,
The brook was troubled for new things lost,
The copse was happy for old things found,
The fox came home and he went to ground.

John Masefield . . .
'Reynard the Fox'

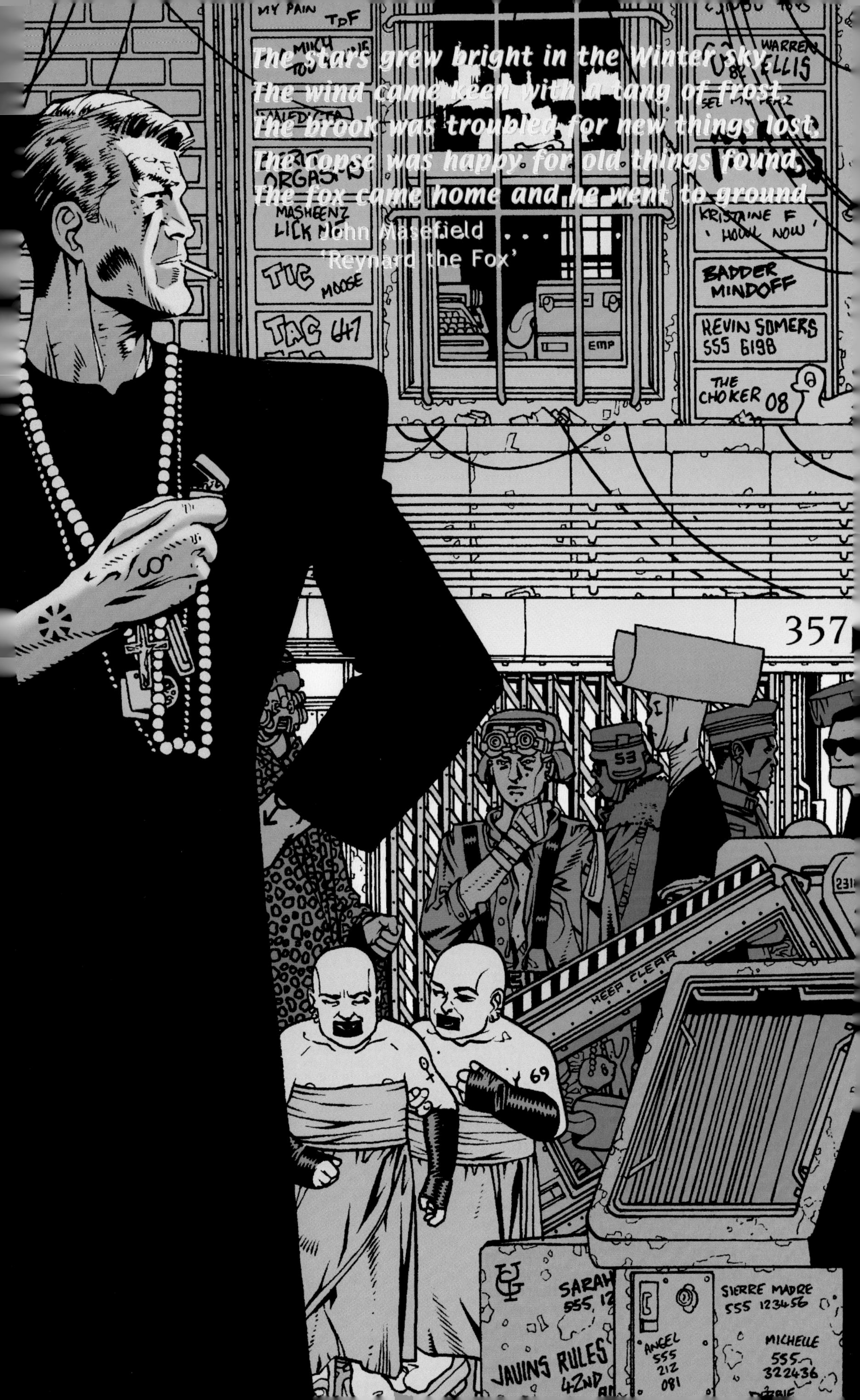

MY PAIN
TDF
WARREN ELLIS
MASHEENZ LICK
TIC MOOSE
TAG 647
EMP
KRISTAINE F 'HOWL NOW'
BADDER MINDOFF
KEVIN SOMERS 555 6198
THE CHOKER 08
357
53
69
KEEP CLEAR
SARAH 555 12
SIERRE MADRE 555 123456
ANGEL 555 212 081
MICHELLE 555 322436
JAVINS RULES 42ND

STEALTH POLICE DEPARTMENT HEADQUARTER

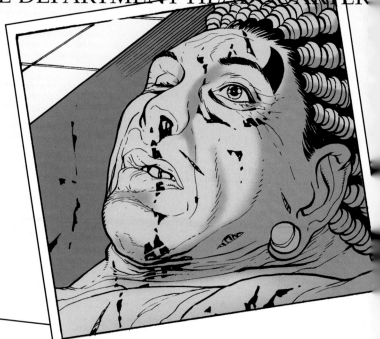

STEALTH … REPORT

McCannon:

What follows is our early findings and basic interim report. Between us, it's a good shooting—don't expect trouble.

The decedent using the name 'Metalghost' was in his early thirties.

Distinguishing features include approximately eighteen pounds of illegal technology secreted within his bone structure, neural matter, stomach, lungs and integument. Following procedure, we are waiting for an approved specialist to do a full study of the technology, but a brief viewing ascertained its basic function—to interface with another illegal item of hardware, and to interfere with and overrule the Stealth television communications web. Further to this, we also located an illegal linkage to ARPAnet.

His diaries, located on the death scene, were illuminating. The decedent was your common manic-depressive paranoid schizophrenic sociopath. Seems it was brought on by the insertion of the physical tech mentioned by a rogue Disneyland technician he had a brief sexual relationship with—and exacerbated by his subsequent murder of the woman.

Our professional analysis of the situation concludes that the man was a frigging nutcase and needed shooting.

Yours Faithfully

McCannon

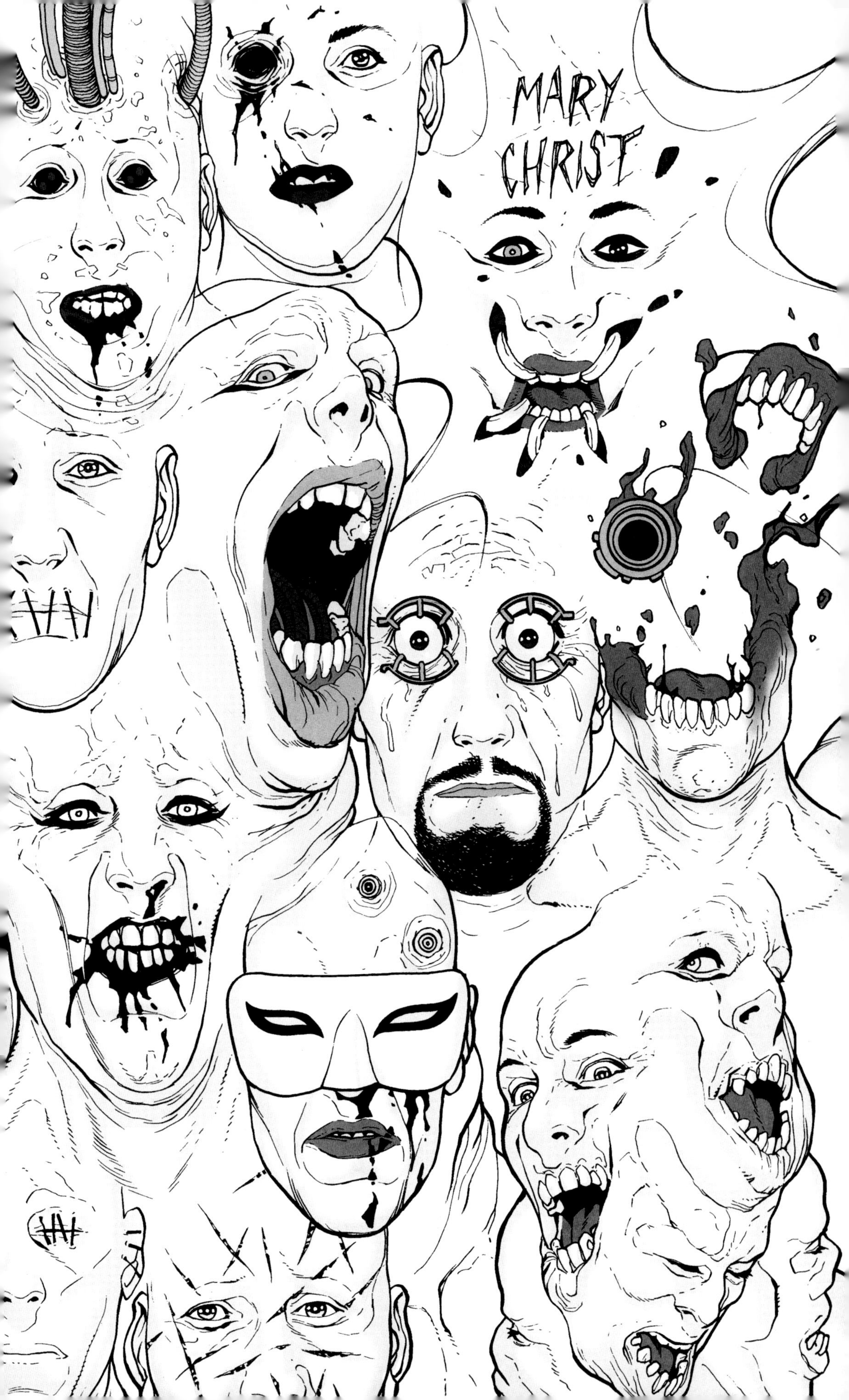
MARY CHRIST

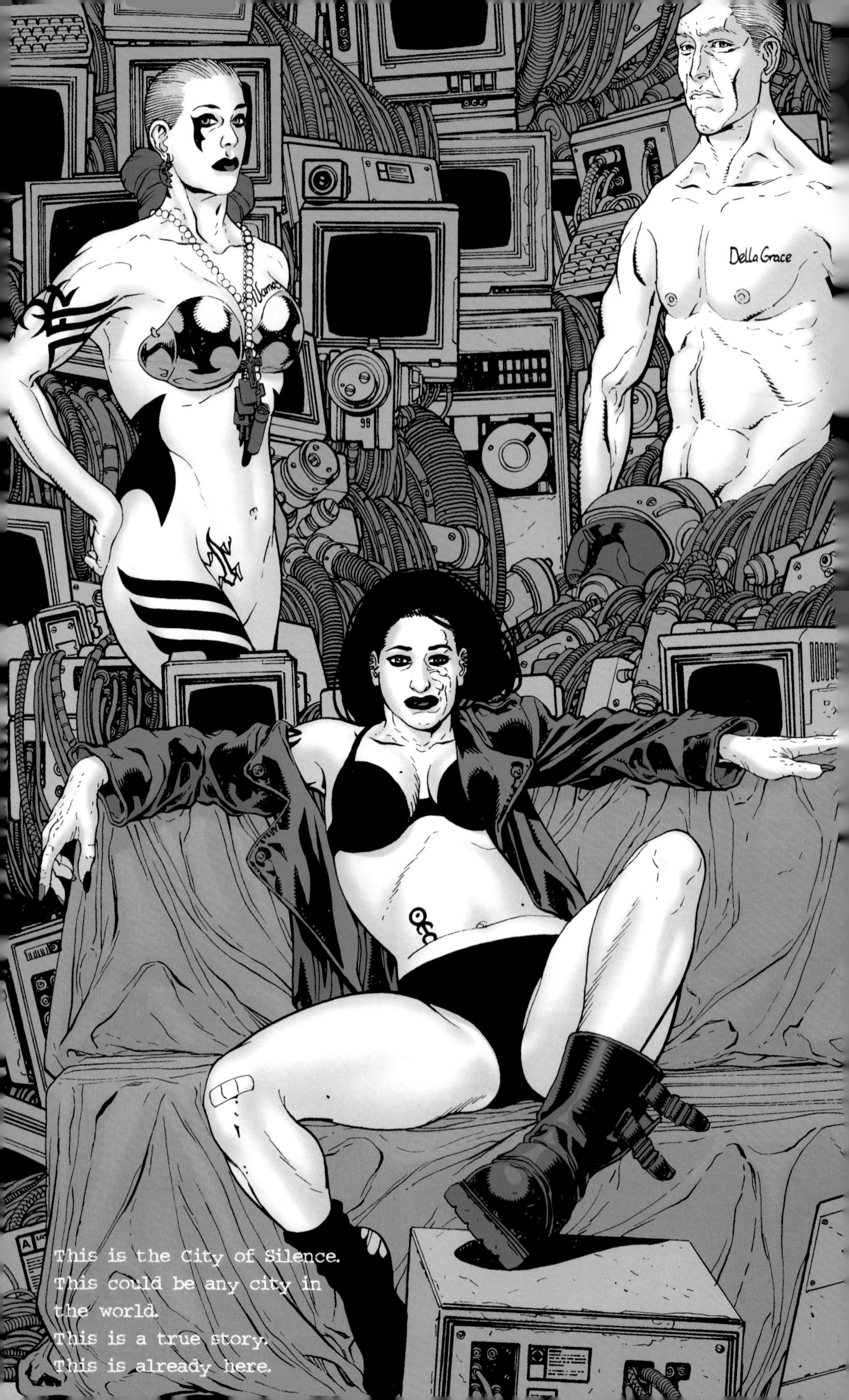
Della Grace
This is the City of Silence.
This could be any city in the world.
This is a true story.
This is already here.

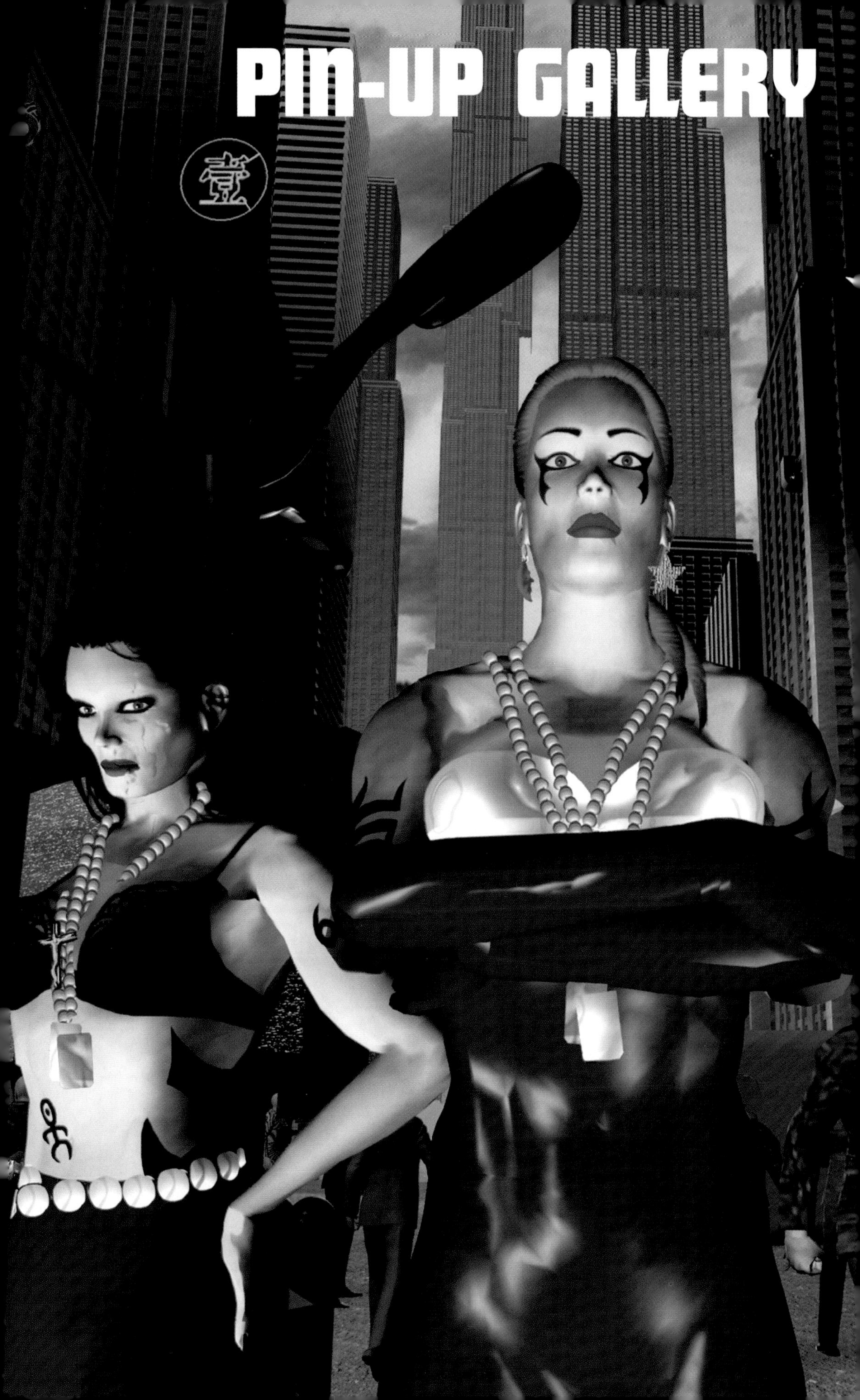
PIN-UP GALLERY

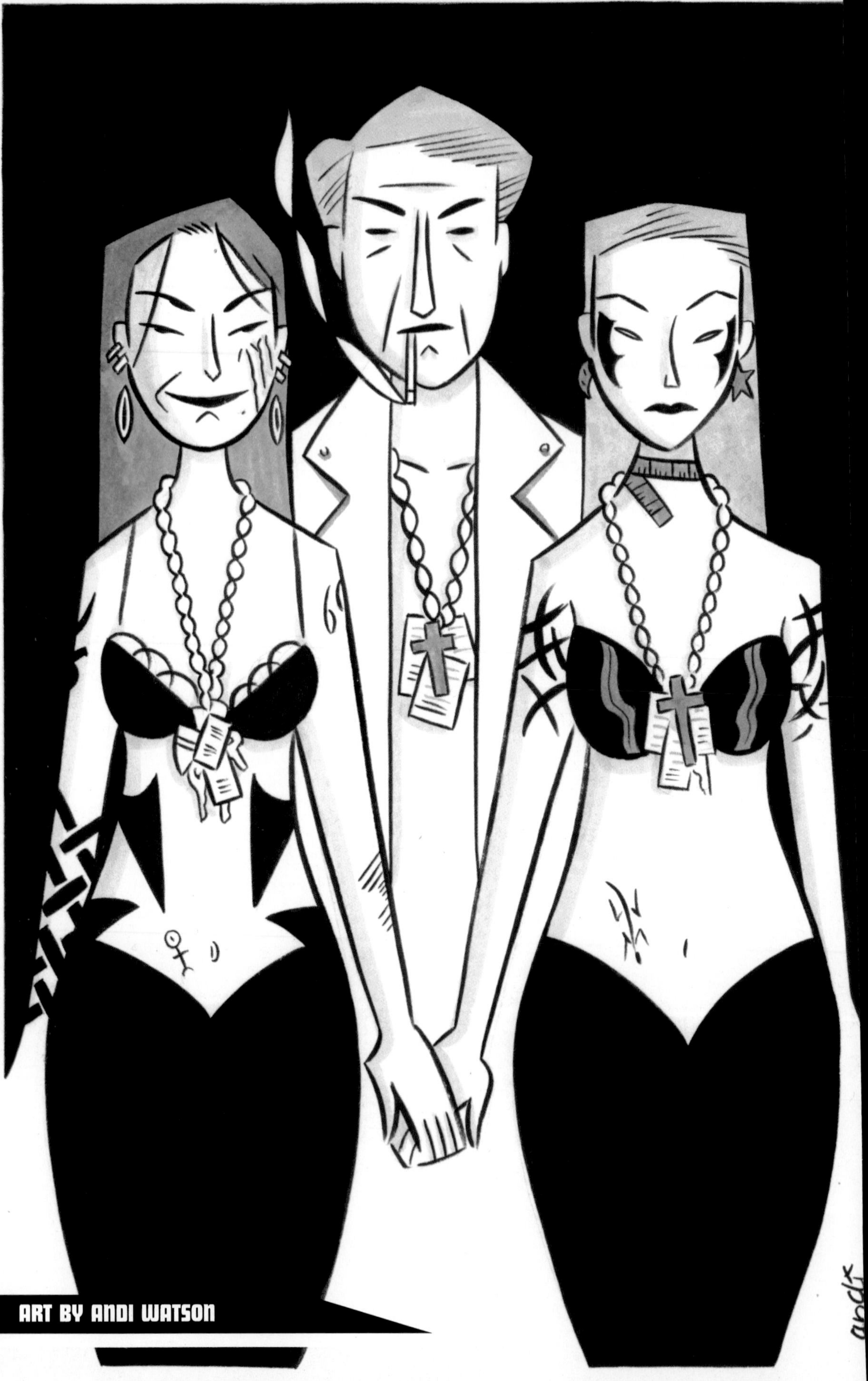
andi

ART BY ANDI WATSON

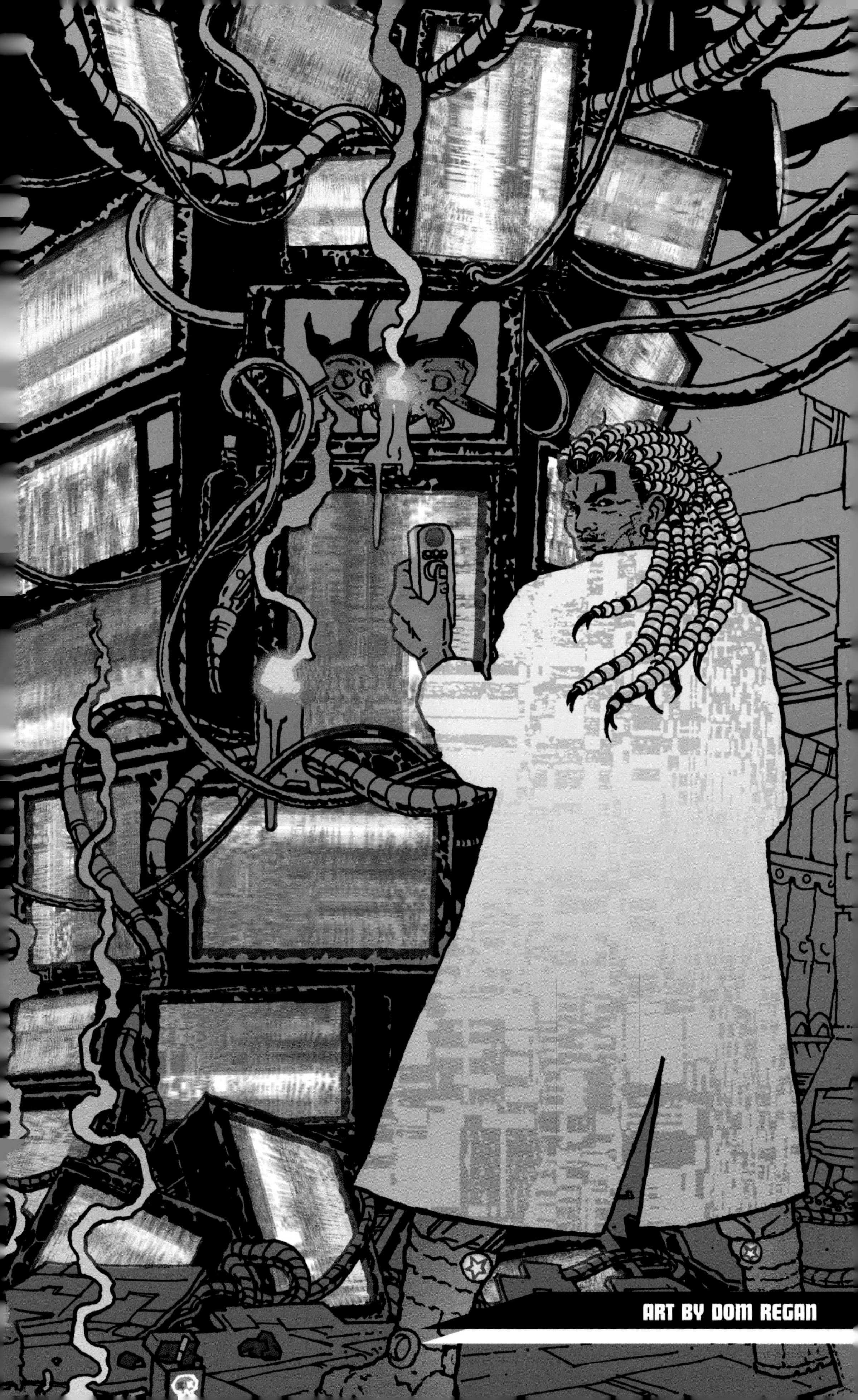

ART BY DOM REGAN

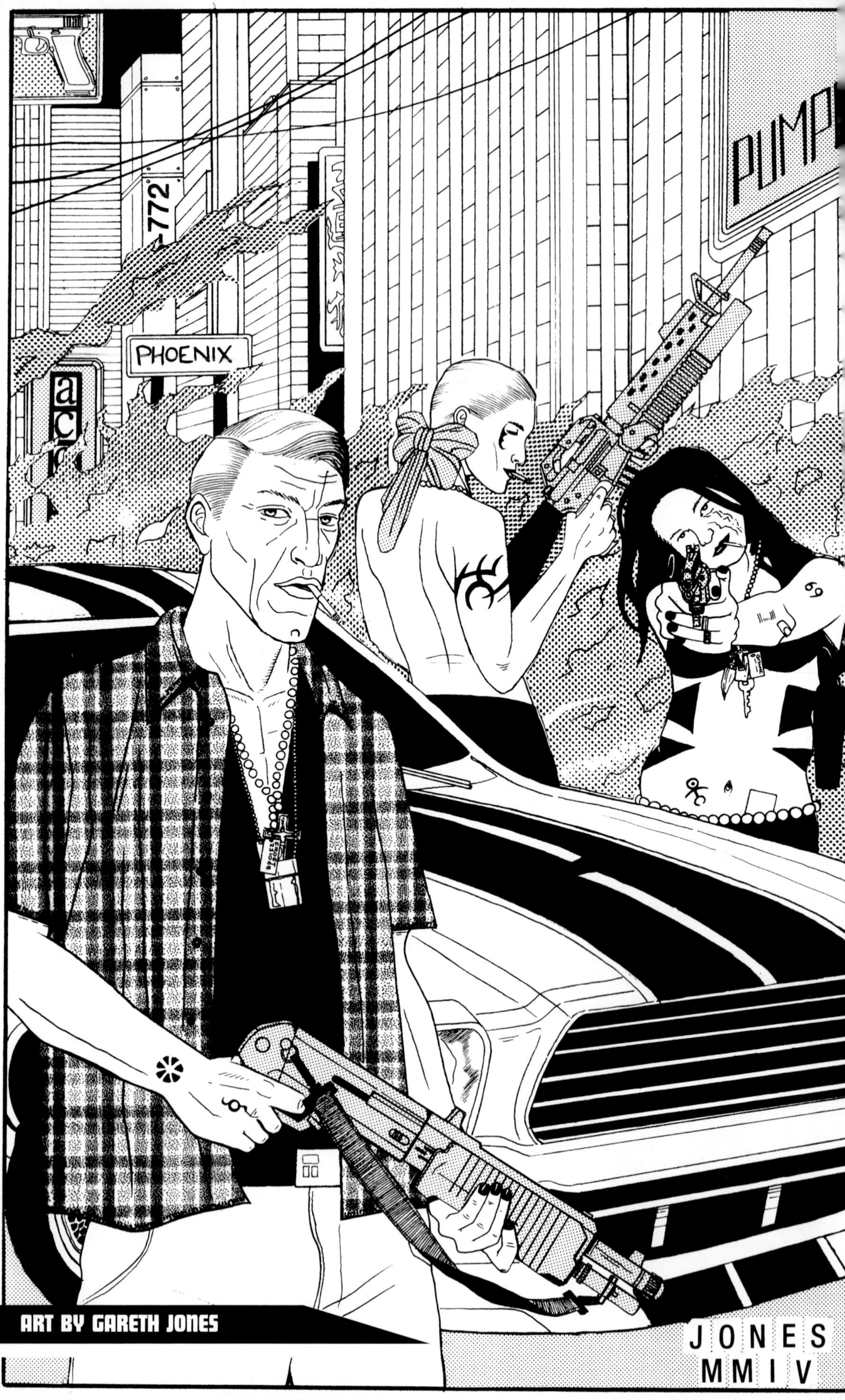
772
PHOENIX
PUMP
JONES
MMIV
ART BY GARETH JONES

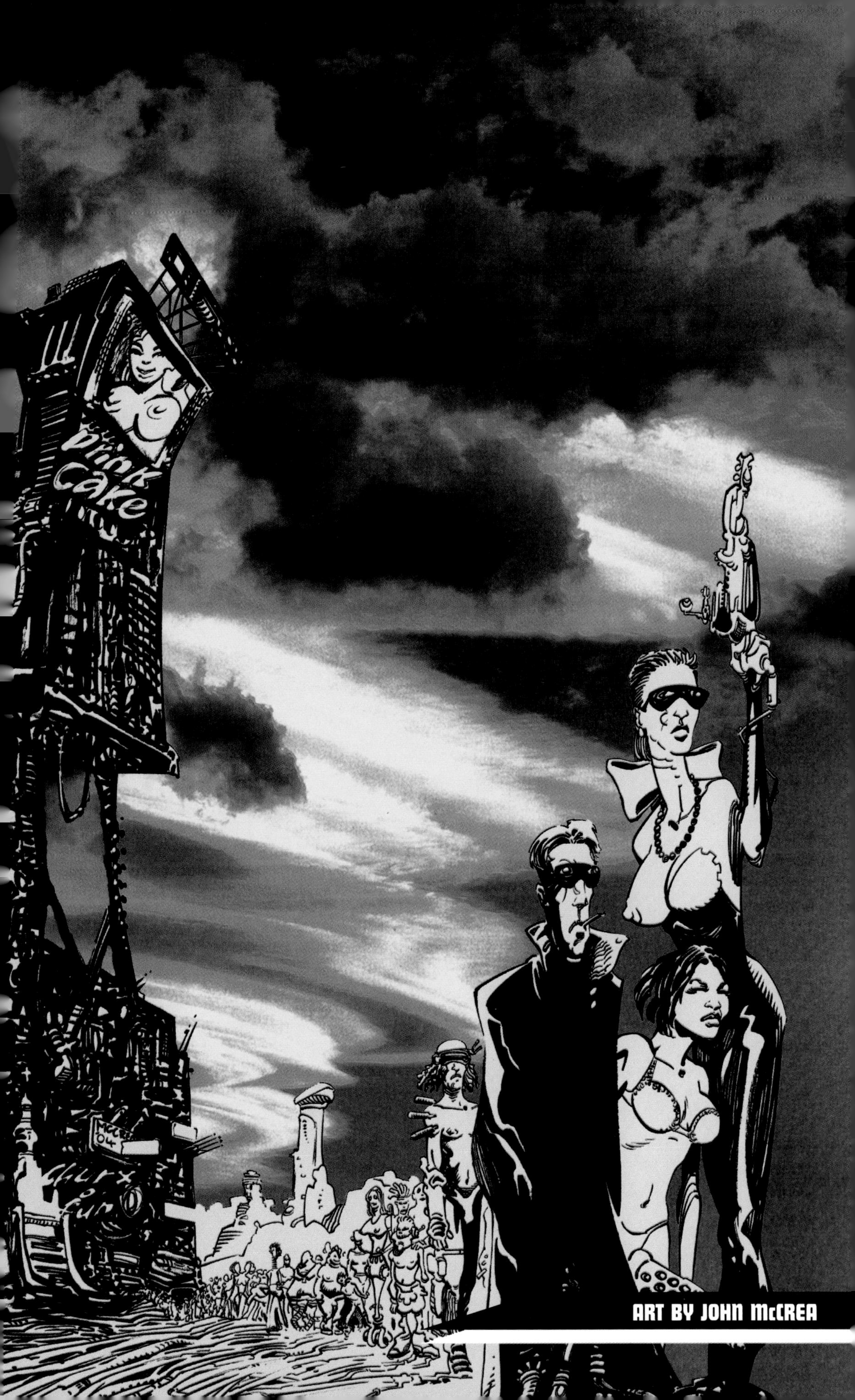
pink
cake

ART BY JOHN McCREA

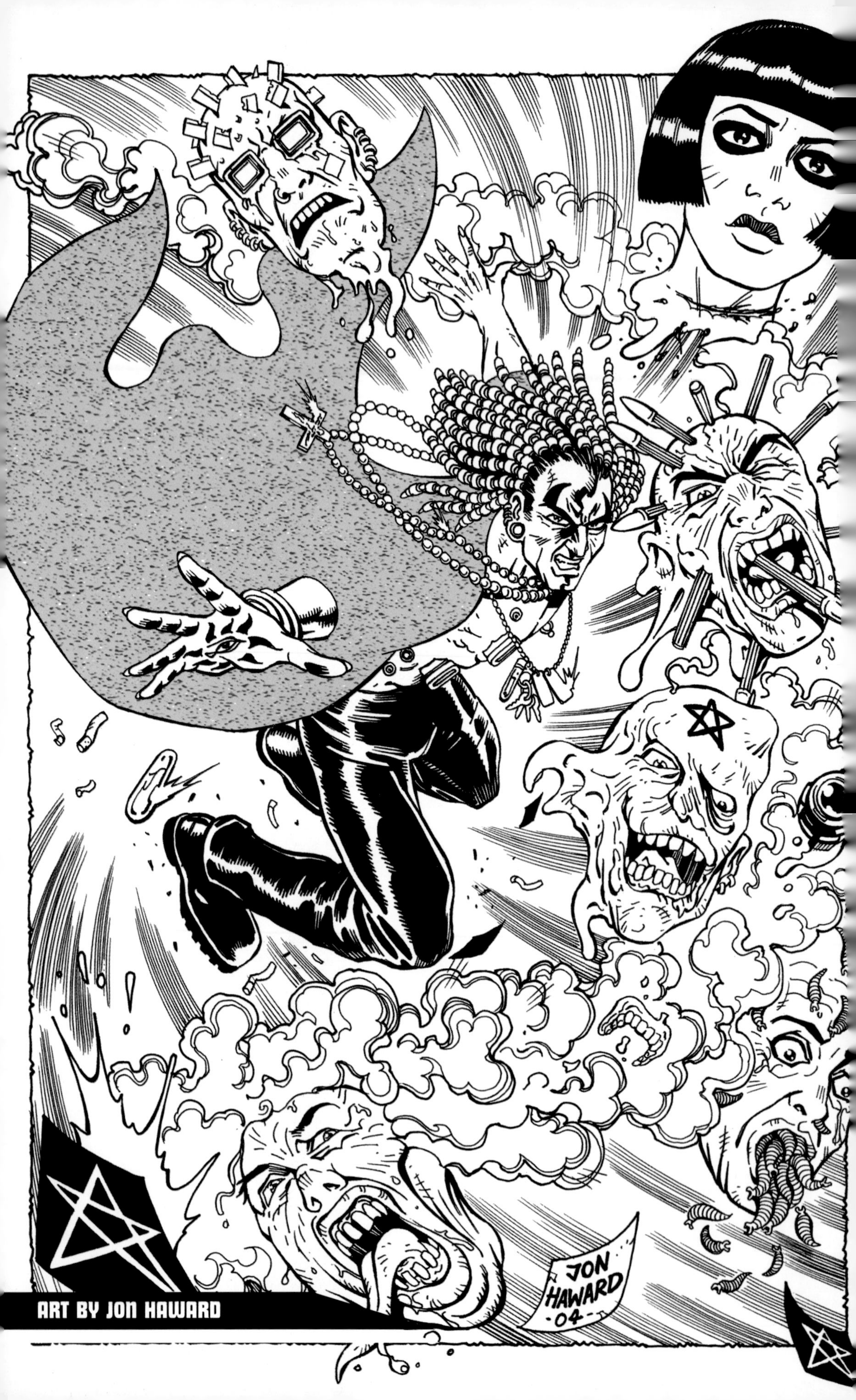
JON HAWARD -04-
ART BY JON HAWARD

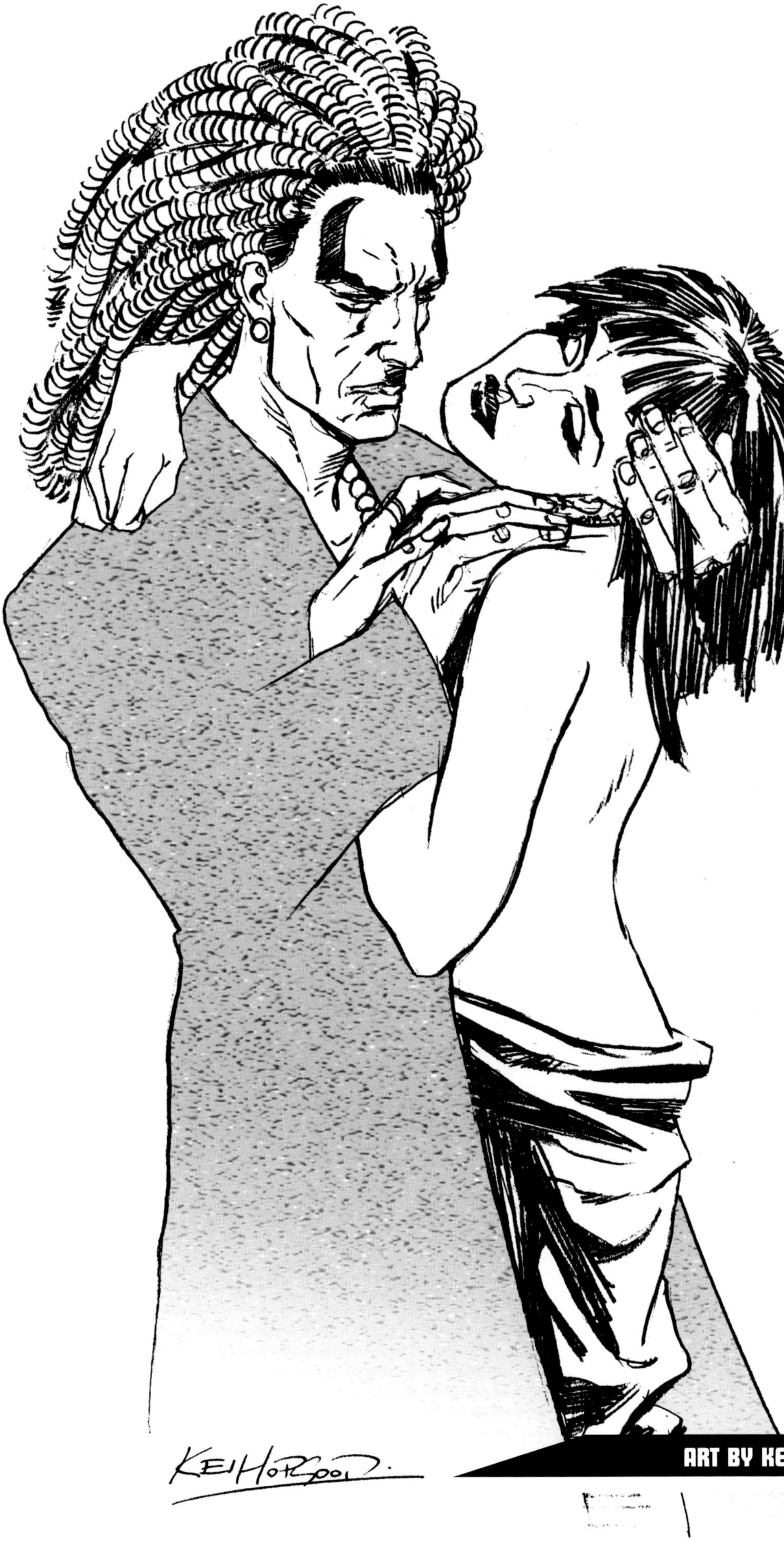
KEV HOPGOOD.

ART BY KEV HOPGOOD

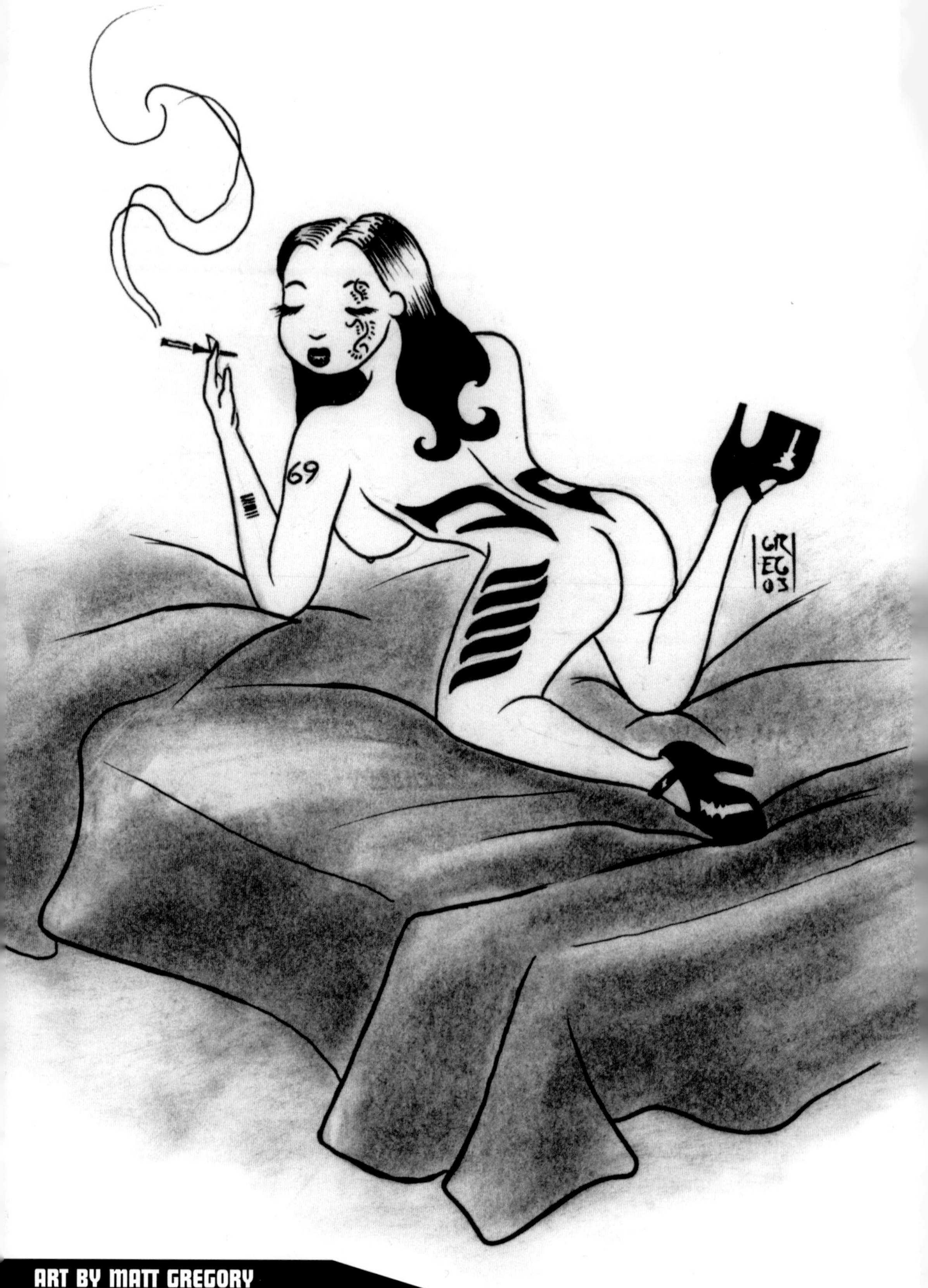
69
GREG 03

ART BY MATT GREGORY

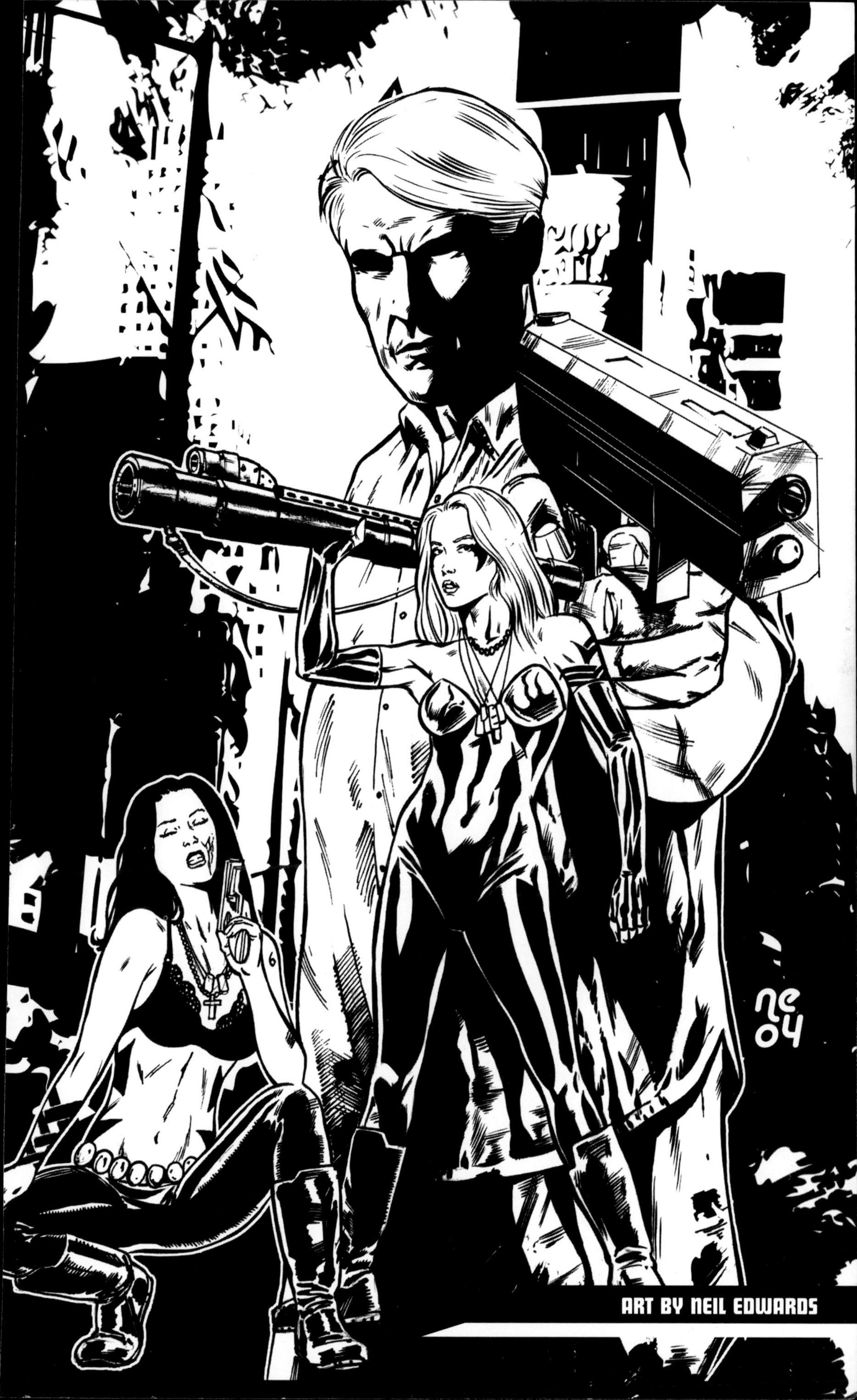
ne
04

ART BY NEIL EDWARDS

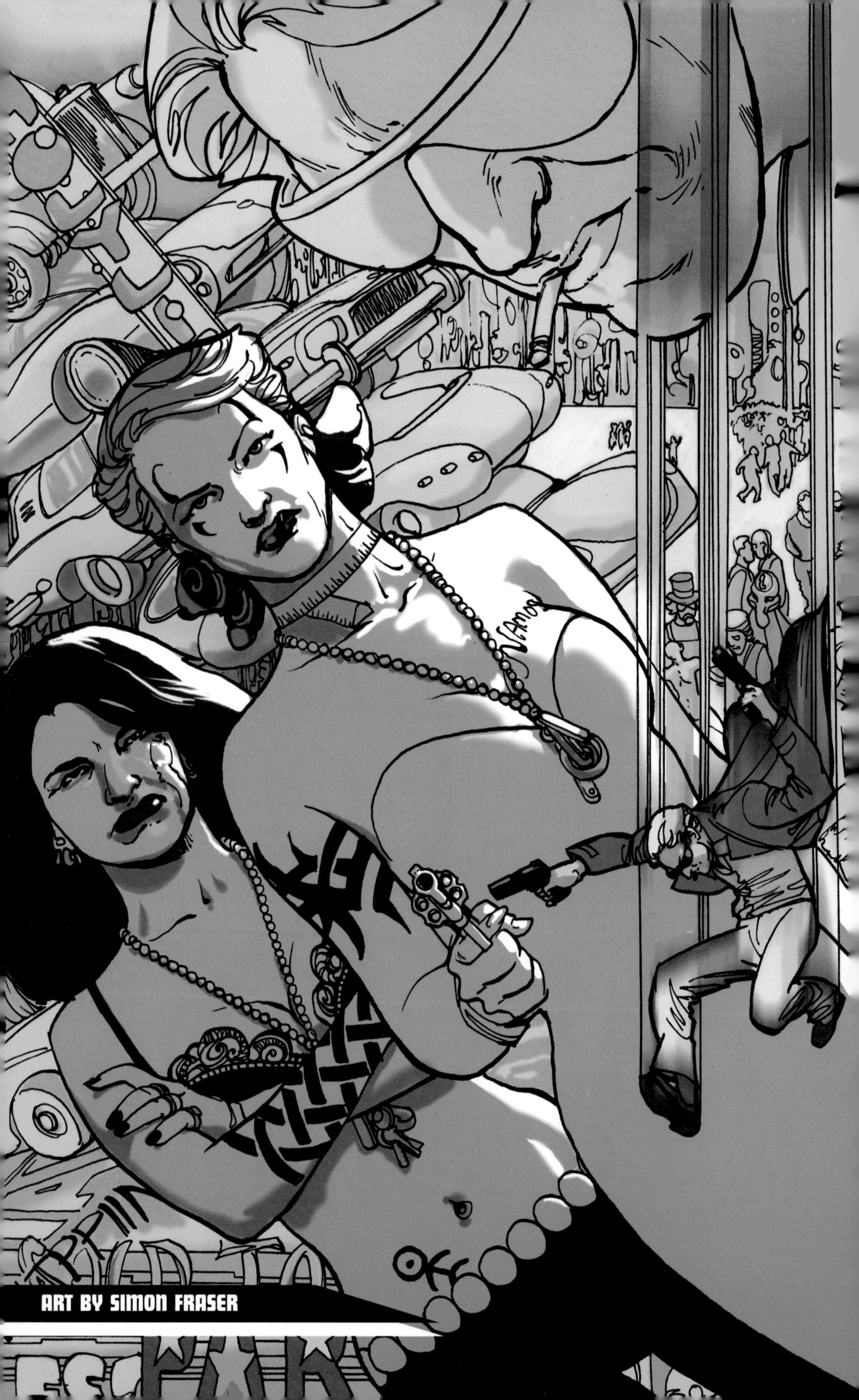

ART BY SIMON FRASER

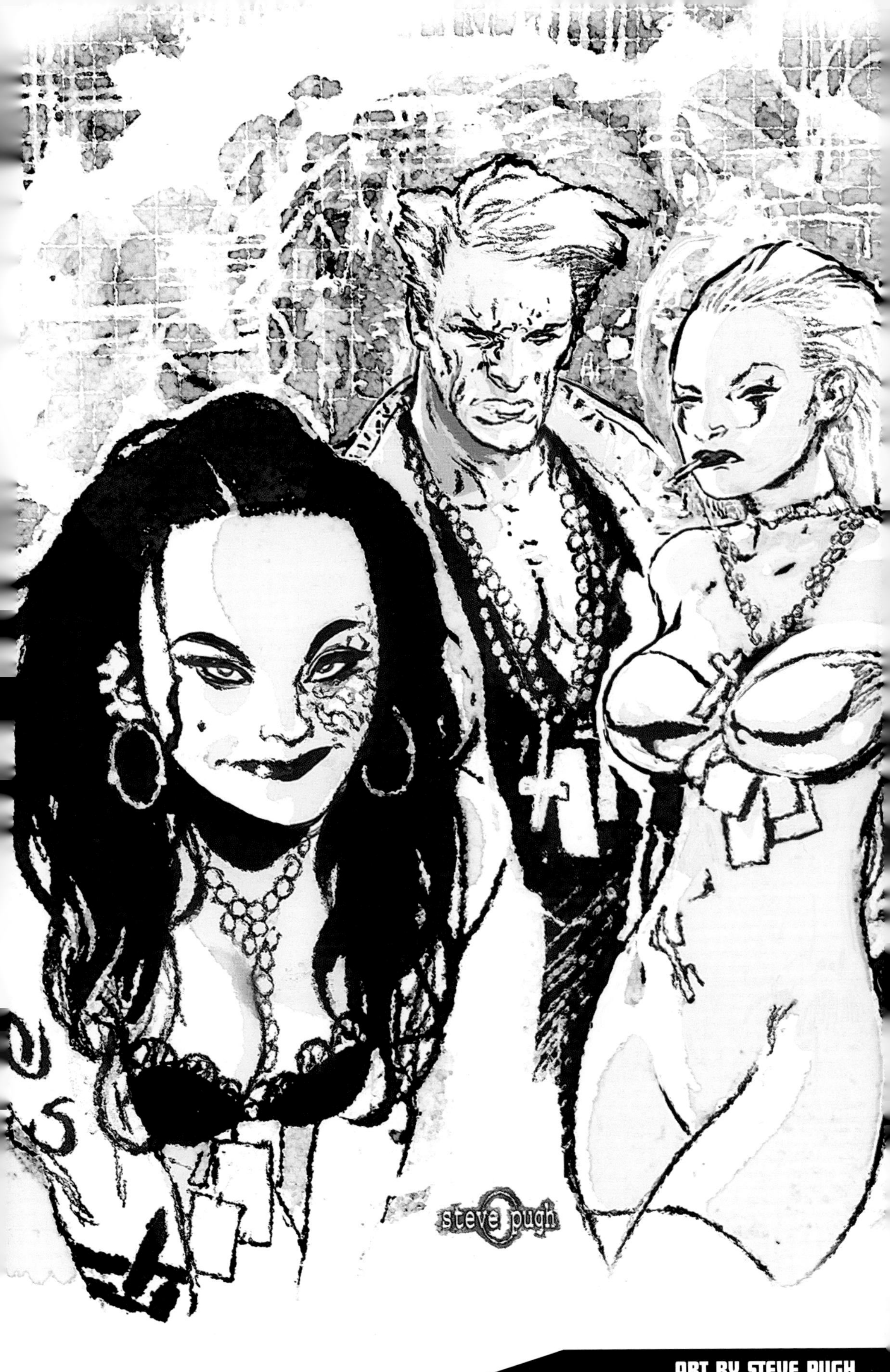
steve pugh

ART BY STEVE PUGH

image®
COMICS

BACKLIST

IMAGECOMICS.COM

MORE GREAT TITLES FROM IMAGE

A DISTANT SOIL VOL I
THE GATHERING
ISBN: 1-887259-51-2
STAR07382

AGE OF BRONZE VOL I
A THOUSAND SHIPS
ISBN: 1-58240-200-0
STAR13458

AVIGON
ISBN: 1-58240-182-9
STAR11946

BLACK FOREST
ISBN: 1-58240-350-3
JAN041286

BLUNTMAN AND CHRONIC
ISBN: 1-58240-208-6
STAR13070

BULLETPROOF MONK
ISBN: 1-58240-244-2
STAR16331

BUNKER, THE
ISBN: 1-58240-296-5
STAR18864

CHASING DOGMA
ISBN: 1-58240-206-X
STAR13071

CLERKS
THE COMIC BOOKS
ISBN: 1-58240-209-4
STAR13071

DIORAMAS, A LOVE STORY
ISBN: 1-58240-359-7
FEB041312

DAWN VOL II
RETURN OF THE GODDESS
ISBN: 1-58240-242-6
STAR15771

DELICATE CREATURES
ISBN: 1-58240-225-6
STAR14906

GOLDFISH
THE DEFINITIVE COLLECTION
ISBN: 1-58240-195-0
STAR13576

GRRL SCOUTS, VOL.1
ISBN: 1-58240-316-3
STAR19476

GRRL SCOUTS, VOL. 2:
WORK SUCKS
ISBN: 1-58240-343-0
DEC031320

HEAVEN LLC.
ISBN: 1-58240-351-1
JAN041297

JINX
THE DEFINITIVE COLLECTION
ISBN: 1-58240-179-9
STAR13039

KABUKI, VOL I
CIRCLE OF BLOOD
ISBN: 1-88727-9-806
STAR12480

KANE, VOL. 1:
WELCOME TO NEW EDEN
ISBN: 1-58240-340-6
NOV031264

LAZARUS CHURCHYARD
THE FINAL CUT
ISBN: 1-58240-180-2
STAR12720

LEAVE IT TO CHANCE, VOL I:
SHAMAN'S RAIN
ISBN: 1-58240-253-1
STAR16641

LIBERTY MEADOWS, VOL I:
EDEN
ISBN: 1-58240-260-4
STAR16143

MAGE
THE HERO DEFINED, VOL I
ISBN: 1-58240-012-1
STAR08160

NOWHERESVILLE
ISBN: 1-58240-241-8
STAR15904

PARLIAMENT OF JUSTICE
ISBN: 1-58240-
STAR19476

POWERS, VOL I:
WHO KILLED RETRO GIRL?
ISBN: 1-58240-223-X
STAR12482

PvP: THE DORK AGES
ISBN: 1-58240-345-7
DEC031330

SHANGRI-LA
ISBN: 1-58240-352-X
NOV031270

TORSO
THE DEFINITIVE COLLECTION
ISBN: 1-58240-174-8
STAR12688

WHISKEY DICKEL
INTERNATIONAL COWGIRL
ISBN: 1-58240-318-X
STAR19501

ZORRO
THE COMPLETE ALEX TOTH
ISBN: 1-58240-090-3
STAR14527

For The Comic
Shop Near You
Carrying Comics
And Collections
From Image
Comics, Please
Call Toll Free
1-888-Comic Book.

image comics presents

CITY OF SILENCE ™

image ®

writer
warren ellis

artist
gary erskine

colorist
d'israeli

separator
laura depuy

letterer
annie parkhouse

original
commissioning editor
marie javins

production editor
michael heisler

logo
nancy ogami

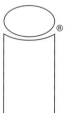

for image comics
erik larsen
publisher
todd mcfarlane
president
marc silvestri
ceo
jim valentino
vice-president

eric stephenson
managing editor
brett evans
production manager
cindie espinoza
controller
b. clay moore
public relations
& marketing
coordinator

allen hui
web developer
jon malin
production assistant
tim hegarty
booktrade/
international rights